Conflict Management in Libraries

Syed Mohd Abbas

Ess Ess Publications

4837/24, Ansari Road, Darya Ganj,
New Delhi-110002
Tel. : 23260807, 41563444
Fax : 011-41563334
E-mail: info@essessreference.com
www.essessreference.com

Ess Ess Publications
4837/24, Ansari Road,
Darya Ganj,
New Delhi-110 002.

Tel.: 23260807, 41563444
Fax: 41563334
E-mail: info@essessreference.com
www.essessreference.com

Rs.875/-

First Published - 2009

ISBN: 978-81-7000-554-4

Published By Ess Ess Publications and printed at Salasar Imaging Systems

Cover Design by Patch Creative Unit

PRINTED IN INDIA

Dedicated to

My Parents

S. Hasan Akhter Zaidi

&

S. Iqbal Fatima Zaidi

of

Nowgawan Sadat (U.P.)

شفقتیں ماں باپ کی اتنی نہ ملتی گر ہمیں

زندگی ایک خواب تھی اور وہ بھی دیوانے کا خواب

Acknowledgements

First of all let me remember the Almighty God who ignited me to work for this professional cause.

I wish to express my deep sense of gratitude to Dr. S.R.**Gupta**, *Former Reader, Department of Library and Information Science, University of Delhi* for inspiring me to undertake this study.

I am grateful to Prof. J.L. Sardana, and Prof. (Mrs.) S.P. Singh *Former Heads*, and all other teachers of the Department of Library and Information Science, University of Delhi, who have always been source of encouragement.

My sincere thanks are due to Dr. Nasim Abidi, *Professor in Quantative Techniques*, J.P. Institute of Technology, Noida, who helped me in problem solving through his expertise in statistical analysis.

I put on record my since thanks to all the university librarians in Delhi, especially Prof. S. Ansari, Dr. Gyas Makhdumi of JMI, Dr. S. Majumdar, University of Delhi and Deputy Librarians Dr. S.C. Jindal, Mr. Salim Anwar and late Mrs. Usha Rani, of DULS for their professional help and support during this study.

My special thanks are due to my friends Dr. Tariq Ashraf, Deputy Librarian, University of Delhi for going through the manuscript and helping in the process of its publication and Dr. A.M. Saddiqui, Country Coordinator, NEDO for his moral support.

During my book, I could not fulfill my basic responsibilities towards my family members. I must express my sincere and heart-felt thanks to my two brothers, Er. Ali Abbas Zaidi and Er.

Husain Abbas Zaidi, two sisters Mrs. Mah-e-Jabeen and Mrs. Nasreen, two sons, Mustafa and Murtaza, my daughter Fatima, and my wife Qamar Zehra, who had encouraged me and kept me cheerful and in high spirits by sacrificing their personal comforts and conveniences.

I am also thankful to the authorities of the School of Open Learning, University of Delhi, Especially Prof. H.C. Pokhriyal, E.D., Dr. S.C. Garg, Former D.D., Dr. Dinesh Kumar Gupta, D.D. and Mr. madan Lal, Incharge, Library for taking interest in the progress of this book.

In the end, I would also like to thank to Mr. Sumit Sethi, Ess Ess Publications for bringing out this publication in a very short span of time and adding value to my research effort.

Syed Mohd Abbas

Preface

Conflict exits in every organization and libraries are no exception. The traditional theorists viewed that conflict is a disease, it should be eliminated. The philosphers of Human Relation advocated that conflict is logical & ineritable. The Interactions view that conflict is inevitable, in organization and if it is less, it must be stimulated or encourage upto optimum level. The present study on "Conflict Management in Libraries" is an attempt to understand conflict, its management and various styles for managing conflict applied by the library professionals in libraries. The aim of the study is to investigate about the styles of conflict management with regard to superiors, peers and subordinates, adopted by the library professionals. Conflict Management in Libraries is interdisciplinary in nature drawing from the disciplines of sociology, psychology, management, organizational behaviour and library and information science. It is hoped that, the study will be of help to the library professionals with valuable insights into their present conflict management strategies at their work place and improve such strategies, if necessary, in the light of lucrative objectives.

Question arises how to cope and deal with various types of conflict situations that occur regularly in the work place? The best managers are those who accept the challenges and manage the conflict accordingly because organizational conflict can rapidly escalate and sour an organization's culture, managing organizational conflict is important priority. Conflict must be effectively managed for an organization to achieve its goals.

The book contains six chapters.

CHAPTER 1 : provides conceptual meaning and definitions of conflict, distinct from competition, stages of conflict, conflict process, level of conflict, effects of conflict, its relationship with organizational outcome, philosophies, which are developed by learned scholars, from traditional view, who avoided conflict to inter - actionist view, which encouraged conflict as well as variety of antecedents, which are prone to conflict.

CHAPTER 2 : presents the meaning of conflict management, conflict resolution, difference between conflict resolution and conflict management, approaches to conflict management, as have been suggested by the organizational behaviourists. These approaches have been discussed thoroughly.

CHAPTER 3 : The body of conflict is multidisciplinary. Therefore, a massive search for literature was conducted, such as, the literature related to conflict, its theories, interpersonal conflict, approaches of conflict management, empirical studies of styles of conflict management available, as primary and secondary sources of information, etc.

CHAPTER 4 : provides the analysis and interpretation of data on conflict issue and causes of interpersonal conflict. It contains analysis of data and responses regarding conflict issues and causes of interpersonal conflict are analysed.

CHAPTER 5 : provides the analysis and interpretation of data on styles of conflict management. This chapter analyses styles of conflict management with the superiors, peers and subordinates adopted by the library professionals.

CHAPTER 6 : concludes the study by summarizing the findings with regard to issue, causes and styles of managing conflict.

The above chapters are followed by an ellaborate Author and Subject Index and an Comprehensive Bibliography.

Needless to say, that study is aimed to be a poineering one which draws heavily on earlier such studies undertaken by thinkers in the area of behavioural studies, investigates and integerates with the contemporary situations pertaining to management of conflict in Library Systems.

Contents

1

Organizational Conflict : Conceptual Framework

Man lives on the earth and forms society. When we live in a society, interaction among the society members is essential. When we interact with each other, some issues emerge and every person has different views. Every person has his/her likes and dislikes, ideas and habits, flaws, needs and personality. Therefore, such differences can lead to conflict, and a person can not keep happy to all members of the society. Conflict exists in every human interaction, wherever people live, work, learn, or play together, there is conflict[1] Conflict is pervasive - on and off the job[2]. It is an inescapable feature of social life, and has been subject of extensive research.[3] As Newman and Warren[4] have pointed out "Life is not a grand harmony, Conflict exists". A total absence of conflict would be an unbelievable statement of facts.[5]. Here is a situation : Mr. Zaidi and Mrs. Zaidi are the husband and wife. Both are collaborative towards important issues which come up between them. They like each other and try to resolve issues for mutual satisfaction. However, on one particular night Doordarshan was telecasting a cricket match on channel I and at the same time a movie on the another channel of Mrs. Zaidi favourite. Although they like to collaborate, each regretfully perceived a conflict because the preferred programme was important to each.

In day to day life conflict occurs in different shapes like

mothers in Nizamuddin East want their kids to play in parks, but parks offer little scope to do so. The children are not allowed or encouraged to play in any of the parks.[6] A businessman may be faced with the choice of hiring a lazy relative or an efficient stranger for an important position.[7] A student of B.L.I.Sc., who appears in the examinations, says that "I have conflict in my mind whether to attempt question No. 4 or No. 8". It seems that he is in a dilemma and does not come out at decision. It denotes his state of mind. People may say that there are conflicting reports coming from war front, conflicting views on Shakespeare's biography. There is a lot of conflict between Ram and his father. There are some interests of conflict between two brothers over property. There is ethnic conflict in Nigeria. There is caste conflict in Bihar. There is conflict between Palestine and Israel. There is a border conflict between two countries. There is conflict between United States of America and Iraq on disarmament. There is conflict between Indian and American cultures. With regard to Post Cold War World, Narasimha Rao[8] is of the view that conflict had now to be logically, between Western and Non-Western cultures since the cultural dimension had played an important part in empire-building. There is conflicting version of war, in which American commanders have given sharply differing account of war, sometime creating the impression that two different wars are being fought.[9] That is, there may always exist a difference of opinion between two persons or groups. Each party develops strategies to meet the challenge of the other and get polarized into warring factions. One may say, *'they are in conflict'*,

Organizations, by definition, require people to work together and communicate with one another,[10] are social units formed to seek specific goals. To achieve these goals a formal organizational structure is formed, where people from different age groups, sex, educational background, attitude, religion, culture work together in different capacities as managers, subordinates, workers and co-workers in various departments or units depending on each other for resources, work or information. Conflict is likely to occur between departments, managers-subordinates, subordinates-workers, and workers. Such conflict occurs because of competitive but incompatible goals and differences in attitudes towards methods of operation. Conflict are normal and natural consequences of human interaction on organizational setting[11]. Conflict varies from person to persons, situation to situation, place to place and institution to institution[12].

1.1. CONFLICT DEFINED

For many years scholars have devoted considerable time and effort to the study of conflict. They have given their version and analysed different aspects about the conflict. Some such views are given in brief as follows.

Coser : Struggle over values or claim to status, power and scarce resources in which the aims of the conflicting parties are not only to gain the desired values but also to neutralize, injure, or eliminate their rivals. Such conflict may take place between individuals, between collectives or between collectives and individuals. Inter-group and intra-group conflicts are a perennial feature of social life[13].

According to Coser, conflict occurs between individuals, groups and between individuals and groups. It may occur due to factors such as status, power and scarce resources but there are some other potent factors which have not been mentioned. The definition seems to have been drawn in social context.

March and Simon : Conflict is breakdown in the standard mechanism of decision making so that an individual or group experiences difficulty in selecting an action alternatives[14].

When persons work in an organization, they take the decisions according to their status. Conflict occurs when an individual or group experiences a decision problem and does not select any alternative. Its scope is limited to the decision process.

Robbins : Conflict is a process in which an effort is purposely made by A to offset the efforts of B by some form of blocking that will result frustrating B in attaining his or her goals or frustrating his or her interest[15].

Robbins acknowledges perception, opposition, scarcity of resources and blockage. He also assumed conflict to be a determined action, which may exist at either latent or overt level. He did not mention some other antecedents of conflict.

Pondy : Conflict is described as (1) antecedent conditions (for example scarcity of resources, policy giving rise to conflictual behavior, (2) affective states (e.g., stress; hostility, anxiety, etc.) of the individual involved, (3) cognitive states of individuals (the perception of awareness of conflictual situations), and (4) conflictual behavior, ranging from passive resistance to overt aggression[16].

Pondy mentioned four stages of conflict (1) Latent, (2) Perceived, (3) Felt, (4) Manifest. He has not provided any criteria to distinguish from one stage to another stage. He treated conflict as a dynamic process in which there is a conflict 'aftermath' which can be either positive or negative for the organization depending on how conflict is resolved.

Schermerhorn, Jr. and others : Conflict occurs when parties disagree over substantive issues or when emotional antagonism creates friction between them[17].

Conflict occurs between the parties over substantive issues which create emotional antagonism while even a minor issue can cause conflict. Furthermore, they have included only emotional antagonism but all types of antagonism may create friction. The definition seems to be limited.

Rahim : Conflict is an 'interactive state' manifested in disagreement, differences or incompatibility, within individual or between individuals and groups[18].

Rahim holds the view that conflict occurs within individual, between individuals and groups. It perceives when parties are in disagreement, differences or compatibility. It is a very broad definition.

Thomas : Conflict is a process which begins when one party perceives that the other has frustrated or about to frustrate some concern of his[19]

Thomas considered conflict as a process which includes perception, emotion, behaviour and outcome of the two parties. The definition includes a wide variety of frustration, leaving some other variables which could have been included.

Chung and Megginson : Conflict is the struggle between incompatible or opposing needs, wishes, ideas, interest or people, it arises when individuals or groups encounter goals that both parties can not obtain satisfactorily[20]

Thus, conflict is an integral part of organizational life. It occurs because of disagreement or incompatibilities between, among and within individual, group and organization. It means that both the parties can not get goals up to their satisfaction level while in conflict situation one party met with goals and the other frustrates.

Hellriegel and others : Conflict refers to a process in which one party (person or group) perceives that its interests are being opposed or negatively affected by another party[21].

Accordingly, conflict is a process which includes party, perception, interests, opposition and negative outcome. It is not necessary that all conflicts have negative outcome, some have positive outcome also.

Likert and Likert : Conflict is viewed as the active striving for one's preferred outcome which, if attained, precludes the attainment by others of their own preferred outcome, thereby producing hostility[22].

Conflict occurs when one party's preferred outcome met by forcing his views over others. In this definition personality factors of an individual are involved. It seems to be in one direction where one party makes efforts to achieve without caring of the end result, which produces hostility.

Thompson : That behavior by organization members which is expanded in opposition to other members[23].

According to Thompson, conflict occurs when behaviour of organization members are in opposition to the other members. He emphasized on behavior but left other elements of the conflict.

Conflict has been used by different scholars in different sense. Sociologists focused on the type of conflict which occurs between social units. These social units may be individual, groups and organization. In behavioral sciences, the word 'conflict' has no clear referent. When used by psychologists, the word often denotes incompatible response tendencies, within an individual[24].

Kathman and Kathman : "We mean a situation exists where there are important unresolved differences or disagreements between individuals, groups or departments.[25]

Kathman and Kathman are of the view that conflict is unresolved differences or disagreements. It occurs between individuals groups or departments.

Some conflict has been characterized as interpersonal, while other conflict is described as intrapersonal with a typical definition. But Sandole and others[26] viewed that it occurs at all levels of socio-intra-psychic, intrapersonal, intra-group, inter-group intra-national and international. The views of Pareek[27] are similar, while Harriman[28] has opined that conflict refers to tension arising from incompatible unconscious wishes simultaneously operative.

1.2. CONFLICT : DISTINCT FROM COMPETITION

French[29] has discussed competition and conflict. Conflict in the organization consists of opposing behavior between two or more people or groups who have incompatible goals.

Competition, on the other hand, may involve common

goals and good deals of common interest, along with limited opposing behavior. An example may be given of two groups set up by management to develop a proto-type of some instrument with the winning group go ahead to manufacture and market the winning design. This kind of competition can have favourable outcomes, provided all the competitors have reasonable job security, all benefits from the gains that are made, and all are given recognition for their contribution.

Conflict is often contrasted with competition which emphasizes mutual striving or contest for the same objectives which cannot be shared, such as first place in race or market supremacy. Competition does not necessarily involve the destruction of a rival and can be friendly, gentlemanly or lady like softly and in accordance with mutually agreed rules of conduct competition may generate positive emotion such as exhilaration, whereas conflict always produces the negative emotion of anger, resentment and fear. The victors in friendly and legitimate competition are accepted with grace by the vanquished and there is generally an opportunity at some future time to turn the tables. In conflict the vanquished may feel a desire for revenge, to a degree reflecting the legitimacy of the methods used to gain victory. The competition is usually productive, while conflict is often counter productive. When competition and conflict within an organization are mismanaged or excessive, there are predictable negative consequences[30].

1.3. STAGES OF CONFLICT

According to Pondy[31] five stages of a conflict episode are identified.

1.3.1. Latent Conflict

Conflict begins when the conditions for it exists[32]. It is also called a phase of anticipation of conflict. The competition of scare resources, communication barriers, divergent sub-unit goals, role ambiguity are the antecedent conditions from which conflict can develop. When a change occurs latent conflict arises.

Conflict might be caused by a budget cut, a change in organization direction, a change in personal goal, the assignment of a new product to an already overloaded workforce, or an expected occurrence (such as salary increase) that does not happen[33].

1.3.2. Perceived Conflict

It is a phase of conscious but unexpressed differences. Conflict may some time be perceived when no condition of latent conflict exists, and latent conflict conditions may be present in a relationship without any of the participants perceiving the conflict[34]. Due to the parties misunderstanding each others true position, conflict occurs. Such conflict can be resolved by improving the communication between the parties. This is a stage where members become aware of a problem.

1.3.3. Felt Conflict

There is an important distinction between perceiving conflict and feeling conflict. 'A' may be aware that he is in serious disagreement of 'B ' over some policy. But this may not make A tense or anxious and it may have no effect on A's affection towards B. The personalization of conflict is the mechanism which causes many people concerned with dysfunction of conflict. There are two explanations for the personalization of conflict. First, the inconsistent demands of efficient organization and individual growth create anxieties within the individual. Anxieties may also result from identity crises or from extra organization pressure. Individuals need to vent these anxieties in order to maintain equilibrium. Secondly, conflict becomes personalized when whole personality of the individual is involved in the relationship. Hostile feelings are most common in the intimate relations that characterize institution like monastries and residential colleges[35].

1.3.4. Manifest Conflict

Manifest conflict is the phase of recognition or

acknowledgement of a conflict. It is a stage for open confrontation. It takes the form of conflictual behaviour, including open aggression, sabotage, apathy, withdrawal, disobedience to rules, etc. One may find that there are many stories and myths in organizations about board room fights in which managers actually come to blows as managers seek to promote their own concern at the expense of others. When Lee Lacocca was at Ford Motor Company, for example, and Henry Ford II decided to bring in the head of the General Motors as the New Ford CEO, Lacocca engineered the downfall of the new CEO within one year in order to promote his own rise to the top. Eventually Lacocca lost the battle. Henry Ford-II forced lacocca out because he feared that Lacocca would usurp his power[36]. At this stage conflict must be resolved or used constructively in order for effective organizational performance to continue.

1.3.5. Conflict Aftermath

The fifth stage of conflict is the situation after it has been resolved or suppressed[37]. It may have either positive or negative repercussion for the organization depending on how the conflict is resolved. If all the participants are satisfied and conflict is resolved genuinely there may be chances of more cooperation. On the other hand, if the conflict is merely suppressed but not resolved, the latent condition may be aggravated and explode in more serious form until they are rectified or until the relationship dissolves this legacy of conflict episode. The stage is called 'Conflict Aftermath' [38].

1.4. CONFLICT PROCESS

Different scholars are of the view that conflict develops as a process. Their different views on the process of conflict are given below.

1.4.1. Pondy On Conflict Process

According to Pondy[39], the process of conflict involves from latent to conflict aftermath which includes, felt, perceived and manifest in which conflicting parties can go through many different ways, and they can go through more than once. It is a dynamic, rather than static, concept. He considered conflict as a dynamic process, as shown in Figure 1.4.1.

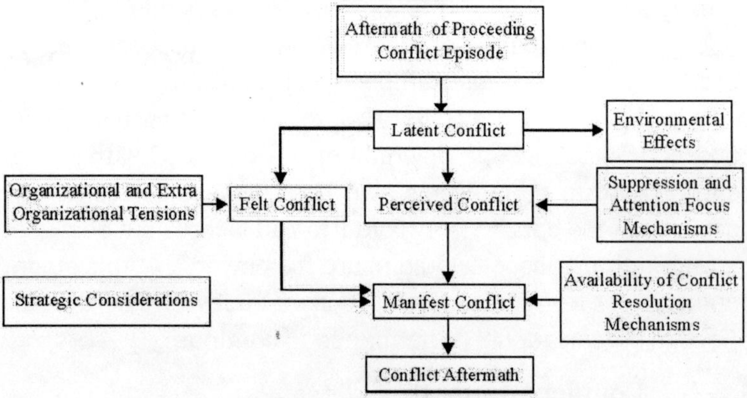

Fig. 1.4.1 : Dynamic Process of Conflict Episode

***Source*: PONDY (Louis R.)[40]**

1.4.2. Schmidt & Kochan On Conflict Process

Schmidt and Kochan[41] provide a framework for the process of conflict as shown in Figure 3.4.2. They are of the view that perceived goal incompatibility and perceived opportunity for interference immediately determine conflict. These variables are perceived from the vantage point of interdependent decision making units. Perceived incompatibility of goals result from particular motivational forces in a specific situation. Both the extent to which resources are shared and the degree to which the unit activities are interdependent determined any one's unit's perceived opportunity for interference. They consider conflict as a overtly behaviour outcome of this process.

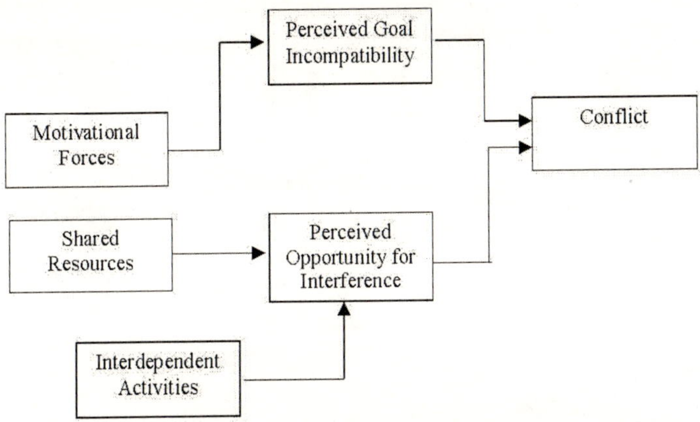

Fig. 1.4.2: Overtly Behaviour Outcome of Conflict Process

***Source*: SCHMIDT (Stuart M.) and KOCHAN (Thomas A)[42]**

1.4.3. Robbins On Conflict Process

Robbins[43] considered nature of conflict process hich is given in Figure 1.4.3 in which he has stated five stages of conflict process. (a) potential opposition or incompatibility, (b) cognition and personalization, (c) intention, (d) behaviour, (e) outcome. The first stage in the conflict process in the presence of conditions that create opportunities for conflict to arise. The potential for opposing or incompatibility becomes actualized in the second stage. The third stage in intention in which decisions to act in a given way in a conflict episode. When most people think of conflict situation, they tend to focus on stage fourth. The action reaction interplay between the conflicting parties result in consequences. It can be negative or positive.

1.4.4. Thomas Model of Dyadic Conflict

Thomas[45] depicts five main events within an episode, namely, (a) frustration, (b) conceptualization, (c) behaviour, (d) other's reaction, and (e) outcome as also shown in Figure 1.4.4.

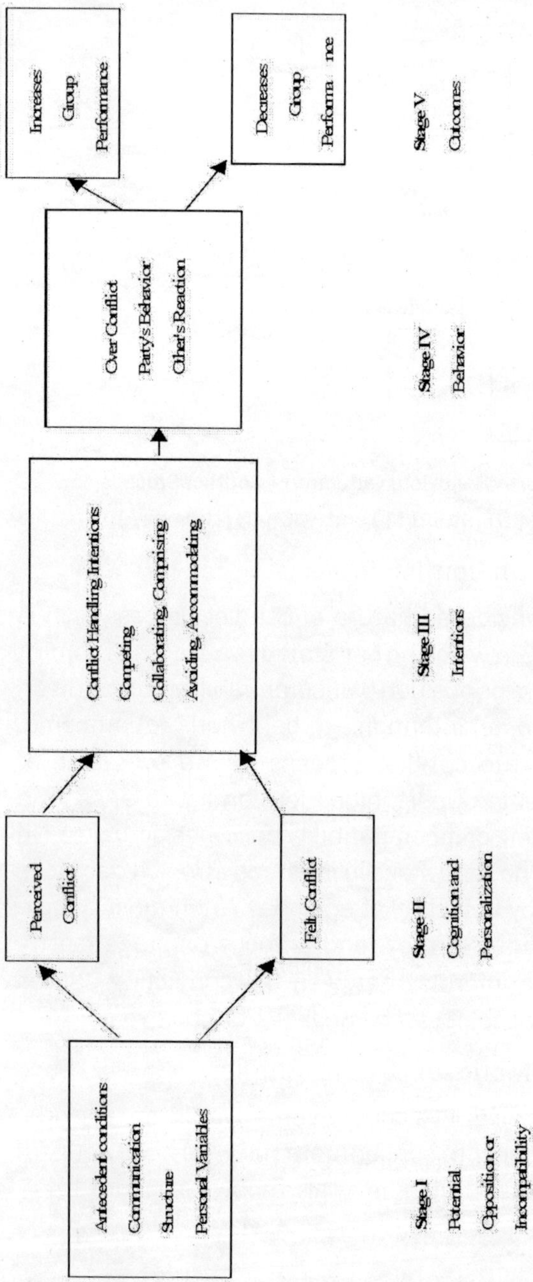

Fig. 1.4.3 : Robbins On Conflict Process

Source : ROBBINS (Stephen P)[44]

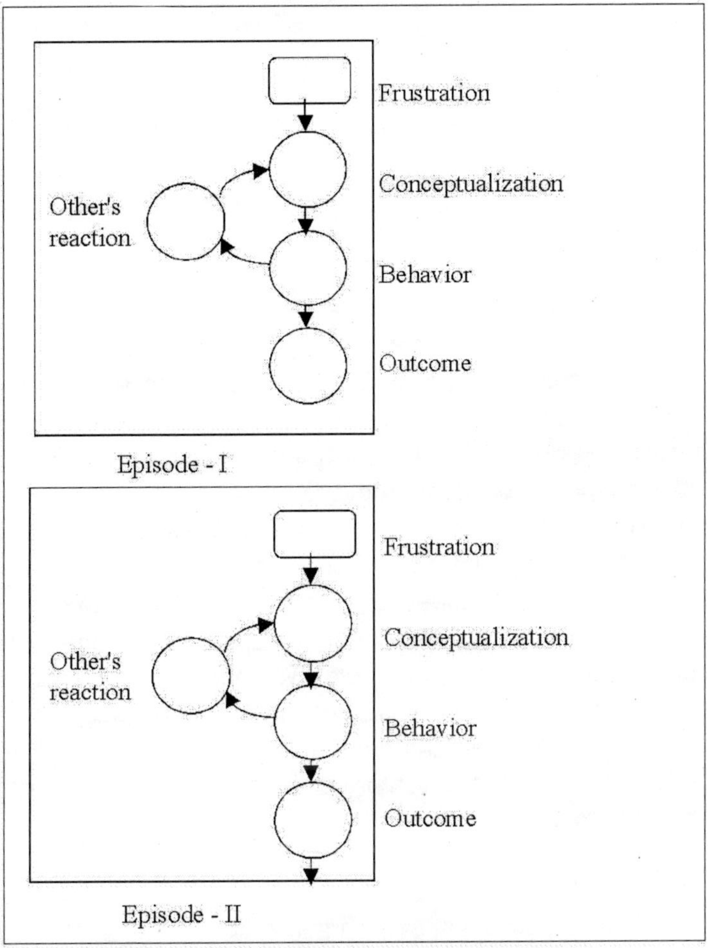

Fig. 1.4.4: Process Model of Dyadic Conflict Episodes

Source **: THOMAS (Kenneth)[46]**

Thomas developed this process model of dyadic conflict to establish that when one party experiences frustration or is about to frustrate, and this frustration deals with consciously; in such situations, the party conceptualizes the conflict. But, at this point, party is little aware about the conflict. The party then engages in behaviour with the other party to cope with the situation. The other party reacts to this behaviour. During the course of interaction, the conflicting issues which are conceptualized by each party may change according to his behaviour. When interaction ends, some outcome occurs. It may be joint agreement, domination by one party, joint avoidance of some issues and unresolved disagreement etc. This outcome has consequences for both parties. If the goals of the two parties continue to be frustrated, this will provide another interchange in the future.

1.4.5. Observations

Pondy[47] identified and examined the event within a conflict episode. He considered conflict as dynamic process. However Schmidt and Kochan[48] viewed conflict as an overt behavioural outcome. Robbins[49] also identified conflict as an episode. Thomas[50] developed a processes model of dyadic conflict episode, in which he gave five main events. But, Pondy's[51] episode starts from latent conflict or antecedents, while Schmidt and Kochan's[52] episode starts from motivational forces and shared resources. In view of Robbins[53] it starts from antecedent conditions and personal variables. While focus of the Thomas[54] episode is on frustration. It is agreed by all that result of previous event or episode lays the ground for future episode. All have concluded that conflict is a process but their application differ from one to another.

1.5. LEVELS OF CONFLICT

Conflict occurs in every organization. It may occur in the individual, between two individuals and groups. The management must understand, what are the levels of conflict and take decisions, whether to resolve or stimulate it. Newstrom and Davis[55] have classified three levels of conflict, explained in brief as follows.

1.5.1. Intrapersonal Conflict

Intrapersonal conflict occurs within an individual and usually involves some form of goals, cognitive, or affective conflict. It is internal to person and probably the most difficult type to analysis. An individual is caught in the web of his own making. He faces conflict within himself. A number of puzzling questions come in his mind whether to do or not to do. Basically intrapersonal conflict can be related to two things, conflict arising due to divergent goals and conflict arising out of multiple roles to be played daily. For example, a reference librarian in a university library may be advised and required to be polite to the users by the librarian who may also complain that he is spending too much time with the users.

1.5.2. Interpersonal Conflict

Interpersonal conflict occurs when two or more individuals perceive that their attitudes, behavior, or preferred goals are in opposition[56]. Two boys fighting for one cinema ticket, two men vying for one woman, two managers competing for the same promotion, two executives maneuvering for a large share of corporate capital, such examples of conflict between individuals are legion and quite familiar. It means that conflict between two or more individual is called interpersonal conflict. It may be due to manifest, rational or hidden factor or it inmates from personal factor. In a university library, incharge of circulation section may put the blame for low turn out of users on technical section in-charge not meeting his time schedule for books and the latter may start disliking the circulation section incharge as an incompetent person. Another example may be, when there are three equally deserving assistant librarians they all are up for promotion, but only one of them can be promoted because of budget and positional constraints.

Many intrapersonal and interpersonal conflicts are based on some type of role conflict and goal conflict which are described in breif as fallows :

1.5.2.1. Role Conflict

Role conflict arises from the simultaneous occurrence of two (or more) set of pressures such that compliance with one would make more difficult compliance than with the other[57]. It exists when expectation of a job is mutually different or opposite or individual cannot meet one expectation without rejecting the others. In a library, the work of the individual library administrator is seen as an array of roles which that person plays in the particular organization to which he or she belongs[58]. Therefore, role conflict is the result of divergent role expectations.

1.5.2.2. *Goal Conflict*

Goal Conflict occurs when a goal that an individual is attempting to achieve has both positive and negative features or when two or more competing goals exist. Lewin[59] identified three fundamental types of conflict, namely,

1.5.2.2.1. *Approach - Approach Conflict*

An individual must choose between two or more alternatives, each of which is expected to have a positive outcome. Such as, a choice between adding some new computers in the library network or adding some new data bases.

1.5.2.2.2. *Avoidance Conflict*

An individual must choose between two or more alternatives, each of which is expected to have a negative outcome (a choice between lesser of two evils) such as budget constraints force reduction of either the materials acquisition budget or the budget for staff position[60]

1.5.2.2.3. *Approach - Avoidance Conflict*

An individual attempts to achieve a goal that has both positive and negative outcome. One may get an excellent job like director of library, in a country where one is not willing to go.

1.5.3. Intergroup Conflict

Such conflict occurs between groups or task groups departments, sections in a organization, and is called inter-group conflict. It is highly visible and frequent. Conflict is also produced by differences in the way, the units are ranked along various dimensions of organizational status, namely, direction of initiation of action, prestige, power and knowledge[61]. Selecting an appropriate area for joint decision making is itself a decision on which organizational conflict is quite possible. For example, if pressure for joint decision making is essentially unilateral, we would anticipate resistance to it with resulting conflict[62]. Under the extreme conditions, relationship with each other that are characterized by distrust, rigidity, and focus only on self interest and a failure to listen to others etc.

1.6. - EFFECTS OF CONFLICT

All the conflicts are not bad. There are some conflicts which encourage new ideas, and enhance the creativity of the organization, and some conflicts which are not healthy for the organization, provide little or no impetus for change and innovation. These conflicts are described in brief as follows.

1.6.1. Functional Conflict

There are some conflicts which support the goals of the group and improve the organizational performance. These are called functional conflicts. The main purpose is to benefit the organization. In addition functional conflict can improve working relationship. When two parties work together they may feel that they have accomplished some thing together. By releasing tension and solving problems in working together, moral improvement becomes necessary[63]. Without conflict, goals would not be achieved and problems would not get solved[64]. Because, it tends to encourage creativity among individuals, the positive form of conflict can translate into increased productivity[65]. The outcome of functional conflict can take the form of increased motivation, commitment, high quality work and personal satisfaction[66]. It can also be of some value to an institution or enterprise. Franklin Roosevelt felt that conflict was necessary for effective policy making[67]. It means that functional conflict will improve productivity of the organization.

1.6.2. Dysfunctional Conflict

There are some conflicts which hinder organizational performance. These are called dysfunctional conflict. It threatens organizational interests. A key to recognizing a dysfunctional conflict is that its origin is often emotional or behavioural. Disagreements that involved personalized anger and resentment direct at specific individual rather than specific ideas are dysfunctional. The outcome of dysfunctional conflict may manifest themselves in employee turnover, sabotage, low quality work, absenteeism and stress.

Dysfunctional conflict can have serious consequences for the organizations ability to achieve its goal; however, functional conflict can be thought of in terms of organizational innovation, creating and adaptation[68]. We could therefore argue that dysfunctional conflict should be resolved and functional conflict stimulated. The managers must look out at the issue, diagnose it, and treatment need to be given accordingly.

1.7. CONLFICT & ORGANIZATIONAL OUTCOME

There is a close relationship between conflict and organizational outcome as also shown in Figure 1.7 and Table 1.7. Organizational outcome is low when conflict is extremely high or extremely low like point A and C. While moderate or optimal level conflict contributes to high outcome like point B. When the level of conflict is low the outcome suffers because of arousal or stimulation. Workers find the environment too comfortable and then become complacent. When they are not challenged and confronted, they fail to reach for environmental changes. On the other hand when level of conflict is extremely high like on point C. outcome suffers because of inadequate coordination and cooperation. Thus, the organization is in a state of chaos because of disruption due to critical activities. Most of the time, the individuals spend in defending themselves or attacking on others, rather than in accomplishing productive works.

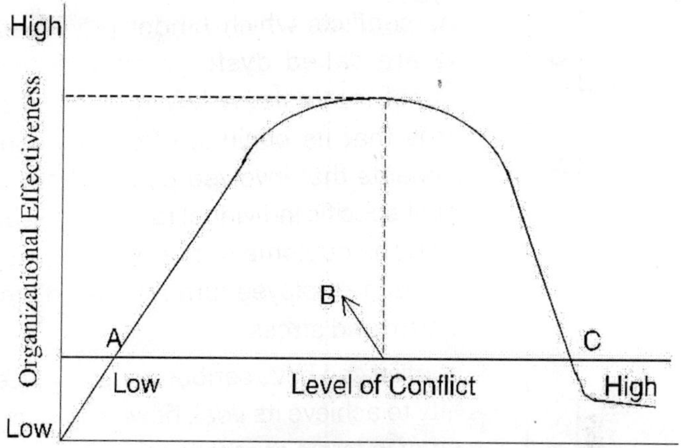

Fig. 1.7 : Conflict and Organizational Outcome

Source : ROBBINS (Stephen P)[69]

1.8. PHILOSOPHY OF CONFLICT

The development of conflict thought, as professed by academics, has gone into three distinct stages. Robbins[71] has labeled these stages as three philosophical views given in brief as follows.

1.8.1. Traditional View

Conflict was much before studied by the sociologists, anthropologists and psychologists. It was in 1930s, when organizational behaviorists started studying conflict. In this process traditional view was formed in 1930s. It covers the period 1930s to 1940s. The thinkers of this School of thought recognized conflict as a disease. They found it harmful and, hence, it should be avoided immediately. The conflict was identified with such terms as, violence, destruction, and irrationality in order to reinforce its negative connotation[72]. The opinion was that it disrupts the smooth functioning of organizational process, creates chaos and disorder. Mayo[73], Fox[74] have found conflict as damaging organizational growth. The perception of traditionalist toward conflict, found it an

Table 1.7 : Conflict and Organizational Effectiveness

Situation	*Level of Conflict*	*Type of Conflict*	*Organization Internal Characteristics*	*Organizational Effectiveness Outcome*
A	Low or None	Dysfunctional	Apathetic Stagnant Non-responsive to Change Lack of New Ideas	Low
B	Optimal	Functional	Viable Self-critical Innovative	High
C	High	Dysfunctional	Disruptive Chaotic Uncooperative	Low

Source : ROBBINS (Stephen P)[70]

organizational abnormality and it should be eliminated.

1.8.2. Human Relation View

The philosophical view of this school dominated conflict theory from the 1940s to 1970s. The traditional view was replaced by this view. According to this view, conflict was inevitable and prescribed acceptance of conflict. They also advocated conflict as even desirable in specific organizational and environmental conditions. The philosopher of this school advised the managers to learn to live with it.

1.8.3. Interactionist View

Robbins[75] argued there is a need of third philosophy - The interactionist, the emerging view is called interactionist view. Where as the human relation approach accepted conflict, the philosopher of this approach advocated to encourage conflict. The philosophy of this view is that conflict is inevitable in organizations and if it is less, it must be stimulated or encouraged upto optimum level. The optimum level of conflict should maintain so that innovation and creativity develop.

1.8.4. Observations

The three philosophical views on conflict have been compared and shown in Table 1.8.4.

Table 1.8.4 makes clear that conflict is inevitable in organizations. The traditional view advocated conflict as an abnormality, while Human Relation's philosophers are in the view that conflict is logical inevitable. The interactionist view advocated conflict is inevitable and it's optimum level absolutely necessary for the health of organization. If we look into these philosophies, it seems clear that the traditional philosophy is still the most prevalent in organization[76]. Managers are concerned to eliminate or suppress all conflicts. In reality, however, most organizations attempt to eliminate all types of conflict. The interactionist philosophy also does not favour of excessive level of conflict. There should be an optimum level of

Table 1.8.4 : Description of Philosophical Views on Conflict

S.N.	*Conflict*	*Traditional View*	*Human Relation View*	*Inter-actionist View*
1.	Period	1930s to 1940s	Late 1940s -1970s	1970s onwards
2.	Presence	Avoided	Accepted	Encouraged
3.	Outcome	Malfunctioning	Potential to be a Positive Force	Positive Force argue some Conflict is Absolutely Necessary
4.	Task of Management	To Eliminate the Conflict	To Resolve the Conflict	To Manage the Level of Conflict
5.	Philosophers	Barnard(1938) Mayo (1945) Fox (1972) Argyris (1964) Likert (1961)	Thompson (1961) Thompson (1967) Cyert & March (1963) Zaleznik (1970)	Robbins (1974, 1978) Katz (1974) Schmidt (1974) Pareek (1982)

conflict for the effectiveness of the organization.

1.9. CAUSES OF CONFLICT

There are certain conditions which are prone to the conflict. These conditions may be visible or latent. Therefore, it is important to know the potential causes of conflict. Knowing these causes, will help to understand conflict better. Various scholars have given different causes of conflict. Some such causes of conflict are being explained in brief as follows.

1.9.1. Competition Over Scarce Resources

Any time multiple parties must share resources, there is potential for conflict. This potential is enhanced when shared resources become scarce. Every organization has limited resources. Conflict often arises when there is a division or distribution of space, equipments or personnel. If one party receives more power, high status, better work assignments or more material resource, the remaining party often gets less. Dysfunctional conflict results from the win-lose competition over the resources. One major source of conflict in organizations, is competition of scarce resources and those too subjective budgetary allocations and/or supplies of inputs, viz., people and support service etc[77]. Competition, the pursuit of these limited resources by the individuals or departments whose successful performance requires these resources, is the common feature of large libraries[78]. In a processing section of university library, there are two sets of D.D.C. (Dewey Decimal Classification) for five working professionals. If these two sets are given to two professionals of the same section. The other professionals may develop conflict.

1.9.2. Jurisdiction Ambiguity

Individuals or groups are sometime uncertain as to who is responsible for performing various duties in an organization. When this occurs, each party disclaim responsibility, and conflict can develop over the issue. There is an unclear line of responsibility for a problem, workers avoid dealing with the problem. In a university library when a user makes use of a telephone with a problem and his call transfers through several staff members and sections. This situation illustrates jurisdiction ambiguity. Another example might be the responsibility of selection of reference materials. In many large libraries selection is assigned to subject specialists or area bibliographers. But, reference staff also needs such reference materials, then with whom does the responsibility lie[79]. Thus, ambiguity of responsibility and jurisdiction may develop the conflict.

1.9.3. Perceptions

Differences in perceptions can also lead to conflict. Different background, experience, education and training may result into individuals' different perceptions of similar realties, the result being an increase in the likelihood of interpersonal conflict. Conflict can be caused by differences in perceptions, beliefs, value systems, and general way of looking at life and world[80].

1.9.4. Personal Differences

In a library, interpersonal differences arise due to age, social status, educational background, race, ethnicity, length of service, salary level, etc. Such differences can cause or increase friction in the organization. It is a well known fact that authoritarian and dogmatic personalities tend to provoke conflict, whether such persons are in management positions or not; but when such persons hold responsible administrative positions, the consequences for the level of conflict in the library can be serious [81].

1.9.5. Differences In Value

Employees and organizations have some different value systems that creates conflicts[82]. Librarians, as human beings, have different personal and professional deals, belief systems, and cultural orientations. It is obvious that in a close working environment differences in religious, political, social or economic values can contribute to conflic[83]. Conflict arises when staff members try to apply their values and expectations to others. It may develop over the work ethos. For example, senior employees may take pride of their never missing a day of work, and may undermine those irresponsible employees who see the benefit of taking an occasional '*mental health*' day. In yet another case, the supervisor may think that you have the potential to be head of the technical services, and he may not understand your preference for cataloguing work. One may expect a meeting to start on time, and may become upset when others always come late[84].

1.9.6. Communication Barriers

When a message is distorted and delivered in the same form it may lead to conflict. Another communication barrier is value judgment, wherein a listener may assign his own worth to a message before it is received. Suppose a team member is a chronic complainer. When this individual enters the librarian's office, the librarian is likely to devalue the message before it is even delivered. In other situation, groups exchange information overt and covert differences between what was actually said, understood and implied can increase the likelihood the conflict between groups[85]. Conflict may arise when staff are separated from each other physically or by time. For example, the night-shift supervisors may not get important notice of change in policy if they do not attend the day time staff meeting[86]. Sometime, one communicates poorly, and conflict emerges because others mis- understand[87]. Due to such problems in communication, conflict may develop.

1.9.7. Interdependence

In most of the organizations, individuals, groups or units work together, and must depend on others for performance of their own jobs. They receive inputs from others and cannot proceed without it. When input is delayed or delivered in incomplete or unsatisfactory form strong conflict may result. For example, there is a high demand of books in the circulation section of a university library. But these books will be delivered through acquisition and processing sections of the library. If acquisition and processing section deliver the books very late or unsatisfactorily, it may perceive to conflict because departments are interdependent, the points where they must work together can become fresh point of conflict[88].

1.9.8. Goal Differences

In an organization when individuals or work groups have different goals, these goals may be incompatible and, hence, may lead to conflict. When one party's goal achievement is perceived as threatening to another's, the resulting conflict, likely to engender win-lose competition[89]. Conflict also arises from people having different view points, specially divergent goals and belief etc[90]. Differences of goals in individual and group levels cause conflict.

1.9.9. Performance Appraisal

Performance appraisal can be a major cause of individual conflict within an organization. No employee wants that his or her doing poor job, is put on record. Even when the employee and management approach the appraisal in a rational manner, a situation of conflict exists. On the other hand, supervisors unwillingly favour subordinates in the sense that they rate them good even when their work are not satisfactory otherwise they will be subject to threat by the subordinates. This particular situation develops conflicts among supervisors and subordinates and co-workers who perform comparatively well on their duties. The performance appraisal process is as likely to cause conflict in libraries as in any other type of organization[91]. Conflict occurs due to performance appraisal process.

1.9.10. Differences In Expertise

When jobs are highly specialized, employees become

expert at certain tasks[92]. For example one university library has one specialists for databases, one for software and another for cataloguing. Highly specialized job can lead to conflict because other employees know little about the tasks they are performing.

1.9.11. Distrust

One's ability to trust each other has great impact on one's working life. When a person works in an organization, he is supposed to have trust on other colleagues. The more strongly people suspect that another party is out to get them, and likely to act without their own best interest in mind, the more likely they are to have a relationship with that party riddled with conflict[93]. Distrust may also build up due to misunderstanding among the employees.

1.9.12. Technological Changes

We live in an era is a era of technology, where information technology plays an important role in the libraries. Introduction of technology in the library has the potential to cause conflict in many ways[94]. It may divide staff into those who are comfortable with the technology and those who are not. The attempt of some libraries to preserve traditional organizational structures and existing job descriptions while other demonstrate eagerness to adopt to new needs and such circumstances generate conflict at every level within the library[95].

In addition to above mentioned 12 causes of conflict, two more causes, which are potent to conflict in the libraries, need special mention here, as follows.

1.9.13. Participation In Professional Meetings

In libraries, participation in professional meetings such as group discussions, workshops, seminars and conferences is one of the causes of interpersonal conflict. Because, the supervisors either themselves attend or they permit their on favourites to participate in such meetings. There is not laid down any rationale or criteria for selecting employees for this purpose.

Conflict arises among others who are refrained from the benefits of such participation.

1.9.14. Vacant Posts

In many libraries, especially in university libraries in India, a sizeable number of posts of university librarian, deputy librarians, assistant librarians and documentation officers etc. lie vacant for long periods, but, posts of professional assistants and semi professional assistant are filled up, becasue these are promotional posts. According to an estimate, about sixteen assistant librarians (professional juniors) and three deputy librarians (professional seniors) posts are kept vacant in Delhi University Library System alone, It creates frustration among the employees. Professional juniors and professional seniors are having dual or triple charges of the sections even in some cases professional assistants are officiating to the posts of professional juniors and professional seniors. Having the dual or triple charge, they can not concentrate on all the sections. All the subordinates want their supervisor's attention and concentration toward their sections only. Being over loaded they can not give desirable time and attention to all the sections. This develops conflict among subordinates and supervisors both.

1.10. Conclusion

In the analysis of 'organizational conflict', the contribution of different scholars have been put together in the preceding paragraphs. Various fundamental issues related to organizational conflict are discussed. Conflict and its definition given by the psychologists, social scientists and organizational behaviourists have been interpreted and it is inferred that conflict is ever present in organization, however, its sources may differ from person to person and organization to organization. Conflict may lead to innovation and change, and the absence of conflict may lead to stagnation and chaos in the organization. Changing view from traditional approach, who considered conflict as a antithesis of cooperation, human relation approach, who accepted conflict in the organization, the scholars of Interactionist approach are of the view that conflict is inevitable and it is for betterment of the organization have been addressed. The level of conflict and conflict as a process are also given. The conditions which are potent for conflict are discussed thoroughly. It is hoped that this analysis will be helpful to the to the library professionals and they can understand conflict better. They will have a pragmatic view and take decision for the development and betterment of individual, group and organizational creativity.

REFERENCES

1. STIMAC (Michele). Strategies for resolving conflict : Their functional and dysfunctional sides. *Personnel*. 59; 1982; 54.
2. KING (Dennis). Three cheers for conflicts. *Personnel*. 58, 1; 1981; 13.
3. COSIER (Richard A) and RUBLE (Thomas L). Research on conflict handling behavior : An experimental approach. *Academy of Management Journal*. 24, 4; 1981; 816
4. NEWMAN (W H) and WARREN (E K). Process of management. 1979. Prentice Hall; New Delhi. p 174.
5. PRASAD (Lallan) and BANNERJEE (A M). Management of human resources. 1990. Sterling; New Delhi. p 56.
6. MAMGAIN (Asheesh). Conflict : Peace or play! Mothers in Nizamuddin East want their kids to play, but parks offer little scope to do so. *Hindustan Times*, HT South Delhi Live. 17 Oct., 2002; 1, 5-6.
7. MURRAY (Edward J). Conflict : Psychological aspect. *In* SILLS (David L), *Ed*. International encyclopedia of social sciences. V 3. 1968. Macmillan & Free Press; New York. p 220.
8. NARSIMAH RAO (P V) . Post-cold war world. *Hindu*. 22 Mar., 2004; 10, 3-7.
9. BORDER (John M) and SCHMITT (Eric). Conflicting versions of war. *Hindustan Times*. 30 Mar., 2003; 21, 1-3.
10. NEWSTROM (John W) and DAVIS (Keith). Organizational behavior: Human behaviour at work. Ed 10. 2001. Tata McGraw Hill; New Delhi. p 312.
11. DERR (C Brooklyn). Managing organizational conflict : Collaboration, bargaining, and power approaches. *California Management Review*. 21, 2; 1978; 76.

12. BHATTA (Bhim Dev). Conflict management. *Prashasan*. 19, 2; 1988; 15.

13. COSER (Lewis A). Conflict : Social aspect. *In* SILLS (DL), *Ed.* International encyclopedia of social sciences. V3. 1968. Crowell and Macmillan; New York. p 232.

14. MARCH (James G) and SIMON (Herbert A). Organization. 1958. John Wiley; New York. p 112.

15. ROBBINS (Stephen P). Essentials of organization behavior. Ed 5. 2001. Prentice Hall of India; New Delhi. p 169.

16. PONDY (Louis R). Organizational conflict : Concepts and models. *Administrative Science Quarterly*. 12, 2; 1967; 298.

17. SCHERMERHORN, Jr. (John R) and others. Organizational behavior. Ed 7. 2000. John Wiley; Singapore. p 374.

18. RAHIM (M Afzalur). Strategy for managing conflict in complex organizations. *Human Relations*. 38, 1; 1985; 81.

19. THOMAS (Kenneth W). Conflict and conflict management. *In* DUNNETTE (M D), *Ed*. Handbook of Industrial and organizational psychology. 1976. Rand McNally; Chicago. p 891.

20. CHUNG (Kae H) and MEGGINSON (Leon C). *Organizational behavior*. 1981. Harper & Row; New York. p 252.

21. HELLRIEGEL (Don) and others. Organizational behavior. Ed 9. 2000. South-Western; Mason. p 294.

22. LIKERT (R) and LIKERT (J. Gibson). New ways of managing conflict. 1976. McGraw Hill; New York. p 7.

23. THOMPSON (J D). Organizations in action. 1967. McGraw Hill; New York. p 54-55.

24. THOMAS (Kenneth W). Conflict and conflict management; p 890.

25. KATHMAN (Jane McGurn) and KATHMAN (Michael D). Conflict management in libraries. *In* Allen (Kent), *Ed*. Encyclopedia of library and information science. V 51. 1993. Marcel Dekker; New York. p 190.

26. SANDOLE (D J D). Conflict management and problem solving : Interpersonal to international application. 1987. Francis Pinter; London. p 17.

27. PAREEK (Udai). Managing conflict and collaboration. 1982. Oxford and IBH Publishing; New Delhi.

28. HARRIMAN (PL), *Ed*. Handbook of psychological terms. 1965. Asam; Totawa. p 27.

29. FRENCH (Wendell L). Human resource management. 1997. All India Publishers & Distributors; Chennai. p 119.

30. FRENCH (Wendell L). Human resource management; p 119.

31. PONDY (Louis R). Organizational conflict; p 300.

32. ANDERSON (Alan H) and KYPRIANOU (Anna). Result oriented organizational behaviour. 1998. Beacon Books; New Delhi. p128

33. COOK (Curties W) and HUNSAKER (Phillips L). Management and organizational behavior. Ed 3. 2001. McGraw Hill; New York. p 375.

34. PONDY (Louis R). Organizational conflict; p 301.

35. PONDY (Louis R). Organizational conflict; 302.

36. JONES (Gareth R). Organizational theory : Text and cases. 2000. Addison Wesley; New York. p 559.

37. ANDERSON and KYPRIANOU. Result oriented organizational behaviour; p129.

38. PONDY (Louis R). Organizational conflict; p 305.

39. PONDY (Louis R). Organizational conflict; p 306.

40. PONDY (Louis R). Organizational conflict; p 306.

41. SCHMIDT (Stuart M) and KOCHAN (Thomas A). Conflict : Towards conceptual clarity. *Administrative Science Quarterly*. 17, 3; 1972; 363.

42. SCHMIDT and KOCHAN. Conflict; p 363

43. ROBBINS (Stephen P). Organizational behavior. Ed 9. 2001. Prentice Hall of India; New Delhi. p 385.

44. ROBBINS (Stephen P). Organizational behavior; p 386.

45. THOMAS (Kenneth W). Conflict and conflict management; p 894.

46. THOMAS (Kenneth W). Conflict and conflict management; p 895.

47. PONDY (Louis R). Organizational conflict; p 296-320.

48. SCHMIDT and KOCHAN. Conflict; p 363

49. ROBBINS (Stephen P). Organizational behavior; p 382-411.

50. THOMAS (Kenneth W). Conflict and conflict management; p 889-935.

51. PONDY (Louis R). Organizational conflict; p 296-320.

52. SCHMIDT and KOCHAN. Conflict; p 359-68.

53. ROBBINS (Stephen P). Organizational behavior; p 382-411.

54. THOMAS (Kenneth W). Conflict and conflict management; p 889-935.

55. NEWSTROM and DAVIS. Organizational behavior: p 313.

56. HELLRIEGEL (Don) and others. Organizational behavior; p 299

57. KAHN (R L) and others. Occupational stress : Studies in role conflict and ambiguity. 1964. John Wiley; New York. p 19.

58. LEE (Susan A). Conflict and ambiguity in the role of the academic library

director. *College & Research Libraries*. 38, 5; 1977; 397.

59. LEWIN (Kurt). Dynamic theory of personality : Selected papers. 1935. McGraw Hill; New York. p 87.
60. PETTAS (William) and GILLILAND (Steven L). Conflict in the large academic library : Friend or foe? *Journal of Academic Librarianship*. 18, 1; 1992; 25.
61. WALTON (Richard E) and DUTTON (John M). Management of interdepartmental conflict : A model and review. *Administrative Science Quarterly*. 14, 1; 1969; 74.
62. MARCH and SIMON. Organization; p 123.
63. TJOSVOLD (D). Conflict positive organization. 1991. Addison Wesley; Massachusetts. p 4.
64. STIMAC (Michele). Strategies for resolving conflict; p 54 .
65. TJOSVOLD (D). Making conflict productive. *Personnel Administrator*. 29, 6; 1984; 121-30.
66. ANDERSON and KYPRIANOU. Result oriented; p125.
67. ALI (Syed Hashim). Conflict management. *University News*. 25, 43; 1987; 2.
68. STRICKLAND (Bonne), *Ed*. Gale encyclopedia of psychology. Ed 2. V2. 2000. Gale Group; New York. p 148.
69. ROBBINS (Stephen P). Organization theory: Structure, design and applications. Ed. 3. 2001. Prentice-Hall of India, New Delhi; p 415.
70. ROBBINS (Stephen P). Organization theory; p 415 .
71. ROBBINS (Stephen P). Organization theory; p 384
72. ROBBINS (Stephen P). Essentials of organizational behavior. Ed 5. 2001. Prentice Hall of India; New Delhi. p 169.
73. McGREGOR (D M). Professional manager. 1967. McGraw Hill; New York.
74. FOX (A). Coming to terms with conflict. *Personnel Management*. 14, 1; 1972; 20-23.
75. ROBBINS (Stephen P). Conflict management and conflict resolution are not synonymous terms. *California Management Review*. 21, 2; 1978; 69.
76. ROBBINS (Stephen P). Conflict management; p 68.
77. MISHRA (Prashant) and DHAR (Upinder). Liveraging functional conflict. *Indian Journal of Industrial Relations*. 38, 1; 2002; 115
78. PETTAS and GILLILAND. Conflict in the large; p 25.
79. PETTAS and GILLILAND. Conflict in the large; p 26.

80. CONROY (Barbara) and SCHINDLER-JONES (Barbara). Improving communication in the library. 1986. Oryx; Phoenix. p 95.

81. PETTAS and GILLILAND. Conflict in the large; p 25

82. FLIPPO (Edwin). Personnel management. 1988. McGraw Hill; New York. p 479.

83. PETTAS and GILLILAND. Conflict in the large; p 25

84. KATHMAN (Jane McGurn) and KATHMAN (Michael D). Conflict management in the academic library. *Journal of Academic Librarianship*. 16, 3; 1990; 146.

85. FERRARO (Vincent L) and ADAMS (Sheila A). Interdepartmental conflict : Practical ways to prevent and reduce it. *Personnel*. 61, 4; 1984; 13.

86. KATHMAN and KATHMAN. Conflict management; p 147.

87. STONER (James A) and others. Management. 1999. Prentice Hall of India; New Delhi. p 539.

88. KATHMAN and KATHMAN. Conflict management; p 146.

89. COOK and HUNSAKER. Management and; p 377.

90. SUMAN (H C). Anatomy of conflict and its management. *Prashasnika*. 35, 1; 1998; 15.

91. FISHER (W) and KOUE (Glen). Conflict management. *Library Administration and Management*. 5, 3; 1991; 149.

92. GREENBERG (Jerald) and BARON (Robert A). Behaviour in organizations : Understanding & managing the human side of work. Ed 5. 2000. Prentice Hall of India; New Delhi. p 438.

93. GREENBERG and BARON. Behaviour in organizations. p 433

94. FISHER and KOUE. Conflict management; p 146.

95. PETTAS and GILLILAND. Conflict in the large; p 26.

2

Conflict Management : Approaches and Modes

Conflict exists in every organization. Its intensity may be low or high. In both the cases the effectiveness of the organization suffers. Managers spend a lot of time dealing with conflict of various forms. Thomas and Schmidt[1] found that managers spend 20 percent of their time in dealing with conflict, middle level managers spend 25 percent of their time dealing with conflict between supervisors and subordinates. They also found that at low-level managers, e.g., first line supervisors spend even more time on handling conflict. It means that one fourth or one-fifth days of a week were spent on conflict. Conflict in organizations is challenge for the managers. How to cope and deal with various types of conflict situations that occur regularly in the work place? The best managers are those who accept the challenges and manage the conflict accordingly because organizational conflict can rapidly escalate and sour an organization's culture, managing organizational conflict is important priority. Conflict must be effectively managed for an organization to achieve its goals. Tjosvold[2] argues that well managed conflict adds to an organization's innovation and productivity. When human resource managers take the right approach, conflict between employees become opportunities to improve the work environment[3].

2.1. MEANING OF CONFLICT MANAGEMENT

'*Conflict management*' means different things to different people. In the face of generation of conflict in the American society, the terms 'conflict' and 'management' separately and together, have become catchwords for various forms of social protest and social control[4]. In the view of Chesler, and others[5] there are two key issues for managing conflict, namely, 'Management by Whom' and 'Management of What'.

'*Management by Whom*' means, a group of persons, on the top of the organization, taking decisions. Although, conflict is handled at all the levels of organization, but top management serves as the final arbiter for many of these issues. '*Management of What*' means group of persons on top management and society tends to place a high value on maintaining the orderly conduct of affairs. Rahim[6] argues that process of managing conflict involves diagnosis intervention, conflict handling interpersonal styles and conflict effectiveness. By diagnosis, he meant to identify the nature and sources of conflict. Some time it may not be what appears on the surface. Without a proper diagnosis, if an intervention is made, there may be chances for solving a wrong problem. When there is too low or too high conflict and organizational members are not handling conflict effectively, an intervention may be needed. In all cases intervention is not necessary, and it depends on the situation, as also shown in Figure 2.1.

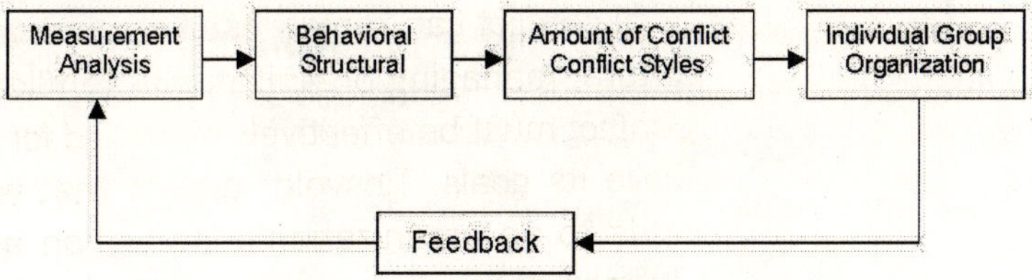

Fig. 2.1: A Model for Managing Organizational Conflicts

***Source* : RAHIM (M Afzalur)[7]**

Rahim further argues that behavioural and structural are

the two approaches of intervention. Rahim and Bonoma state that effectiveness of the organization may be improved by structural changes, such as, values, culture, attitudes, norms etc. and it is designed to learn interpersonal conflict handling styles according to the situation. Hellriegel and others state that 'conflict management consist of diagnostic process interpersonal styles, negotiation strategies and other interventions that are designed to avoid unnecessary conflict and reduce or resolve excessive conflict'. It means that this definition is very much similar to the definition given by Rahim in which he had argued that conflict management is a process, which includes diagnosis, intervention, interpersonal handling styles and effectiveness while in the definition of Hellrigel and others diagnosis, intervention and interpersonal handling styles are common. Later, they also included negotiation. It was not included in earlier definition.

Robbins[8] developed that conflict management is like a coin, which has two parts; one part is resolution of conflict, and he had warned that we should not forget the other part of the coin, which is conflict stimulation. He further stated that for the survival of the organizations there is a need of functional conflict. If there will be a situation where conflict level is low, managers should stimulate the conflict. Conflict can be stimulated by the techniques which are explained as follows.

2.1.1. Stimulating Techniques

Robbins[9] considers that stimulation techniques are primitive relative with the resolving techniques and suggested into three categories, namely,

(i) Manipulate communication channel

- Deviate message from traditional channel
- Repress information
- Transmit too much information
- Transmit ambiguous or threatening information

(ii) Alter the organization structure (redefine jobs, after task, reform units or activities)

- Increase a unit's size
- Increase specialization and standardization
- Add, delete or transfer organizational members.
- Increase inter-dependency between units.

(iii) Alter personal behavior factors

- Change personality characteristics of leader
- Create role conflict
- Develop role incongruence

Brown[10] argues that little conflict may be problematic as too much in some situations and also suggested that conflict management can require intervention to reduce conflict, if there is too much or too little intervention to promote conflict. It means that Brown's views on conflict management are similar with the views of Robbins.

Goel and Shalini Rajneesh[11] define conflict management as "to develop the techniques that may help in stimulating the conflict, when it is at a very low level and resolve conflict, when it has reached a very high proportion". They also mentioned stimulating conflict and resolving conflict. Conflict should be stimulated up to the optimum level.

Early investigators of conflict management Deutsch[12] (1973) and Thomas[13] (1976) came to the conclusion that conflict is dysfunctional in organization, needs some regulation or resolution while Schmidt and Kochan[14] (1972) focused on causes and resolution of conflict. The modern thinkers of the conflict and its management, such as, Robbins, Brown, Goel and Shalini Rajneesh recognized that too little conflict may be as problematic as too much in some situations. Too little conflict may stagnate the efficiency of the organization. In their view, stimulating conflict up to acceptable or optimal level is desirable.

It is true that conflict management is like a coin, having

two parts resolution and stimulation. The views of Robbins, Brown and Goel and Shalini on the conflict management have adopted almost same pattern, and the concluding definition of conflict management may be given as follows.

"Conflict management is a process where techniques are applied to encourage conflict if it is too low and resolve conflict if it is too high".

If one is to avoid the potentially disruptive effects of conflict, one must know when to resolve it and when to stimulate it. When a harmful conflict situation exists, the manager needs to work for conflict resolution. When an organization is stagnant and no innovative activities occur, the manager requires to learn and to apply stimulation techniques. It depends on the situation when to engage resolving/stimulating strategies.

2.1.2. Conflict Resolution

Conflict resolution is reduction or de-escalation of conflict among the conflicting parties, who may be international, intra national, inter state, inter organization, intra organization, inter personal and inter group. According to Encyclopaedia of Psychology[15] "Any reduction in the severity of social conflict is referred to as conflict resolution". It means reducing the intensity of conflict, It is a broad definition. Another definition, which is mentioned in the Gale Encyclopaedia of Psychology[16] is, "The process of defusing antagonism and searching agreement between conflicting parties, especially through some form of negotiation. Also, the study and practice of solving interpersonal and inter group conflict". According to this definition conflict resolution is a process, where parties reach an agreement through negotiation for de-escalating the conflict. The weightage is given to the negotiation while resolution may take place through other techniques. Boulding[17] and Thomas[18] define resolution in abstract term as 'a behaviour aimed at resolving perceived incompatibilities'. Tinsley[19] has mentioned the same definition in his article. It seems that definition is overtly broad.

Conflict should be resolved before being problematic, because, conflict among groups in an organization can create myriad problems. Human resources management experts are frequently called upon to resolve such conflict[20] Conflict with supervisors, peers or subordinates is incredible in organizations, and the way it is resolved, can have for searching consequences.[21] But, conflict resolution depends on a particular situation.

2.2. CONFLICT RESOLUTION & CONFLICT MANAGEMENT

According to modern view of the organizational behaviourists, conflict in management is resolved and stimulated where it is needed. Rahim[22] argues that conflict resolution implies reduction or elimination of conflict, whereas the management of conflict does not necessarily imply reduction in the amount of conflict. He meant that conflict management does not only reduce the amount or intensity of conflict, but it may also stimulate conflict in the situation where there is low conflict. Robbins[23] develops that conflict management and conflict resolution are not synonymous. Boulding[24] and Robbins[25] are of the view that the differences between resolution and management of conflict are more than semantic. Overall, conflict management is broader while conflict resolution is narrower. Conflict management is a body having two parts, namely, conflict stimulation and conflict resolution.

Different scholars viewed Third-Party mediation for resolving conflict. Whitefield argued "using Third-Party intermediary is a tried and true method of conflict in Indonesia"[26] Cook and Hunsaker[27] are of the opinion that conflict parties may appeal to a boss or an advisor judge to work as a mediator in resolving their dispute. In the Self Transformation Series, it is suggested that when issues are difficult to resolve, call in a Third-Party to mediate. In such situations, Gupta[28] advocates in convincing terms that Library Management Consultant or

'Chartered Librarian', may play a vital role for resolving conflict.

In the 'Self As Mediator Seminar'[29] it was argued that powerful communication tool is self mediation for managing differences. Chatterjee[30] is of the opinion that conflict resolution begins at home. According to him "a qualitative transformation must, therefore begin from within, where the conflict originates. According to a Sufi saying, the peacemaker must first make peace with himself before trying to make peace in world. The Bhagwat Gita teaches self-restraint, fortitude, truthfulness and faith as essential attribute of character.

As we are moving in the 21st century, the global environment is changing rapidly and speedy changes occur upon work place. The key tasks, with respect to conflict, include managing its occurrence, deriving the benefits of conflict while minimizing its harmful effects and not eliminating it entirely. In this process of conflict management, the role of manager is much challenging. He accepts the challenges and will act according to situation. Das[31] advocates various approaches, which managers adopt, like role of policeman, role of advocate, role of an adjudicator, role of mediator and has suggested the need for managerial approach to resolve conflict. For effective leadership, the knowledge of working styles is essential so that the leader or the manager copes with the situation or accepts the challenges in managing the conflict.

2.3. BEHAVIOURAL STYLES

Conflict is an integral part of the organization. But negative or dysfunctional conflict is problematic for the organization. The first and foremost goal of the managers is to prevent negative or dysfunctional conflict from occurring, while encouraging healthy conflict. To avoid dysfunctional conflict certain scholars, such as, Blake and Mouton[32] (1964), Schmidt and Tannenbaum[33] (1960), Thomas[34] (1976), Hall[35] (1969), Filley[36] (1978), Derr[37] (1978), Rahim[38] (1983), Pareek[39] (1982), Likert and Likert[40] (1976), Blake and others[41] (1964), all have suggested certain approaches for dealing with conflict. These are the behavioural styles or mode of handling interpersonal conflict. A manager can choose and adopt one of these styles while dealing with interpersonal conflict in organization, discussed as follows.

2.3.1. Grid Approach to Managing Conflict

Blake and Mouton[42] (1964) presented a theoretical framework for managerial behaviour in two dimensions: (i) Concern for production, results, bottom line, profit and (ii) concern for people. These two dimensions are given in Figure 2.4.1 as nine points scale wherein 1 represents minimum concern, 5 represents intermediate or an average amount of concern, 9 is maximum concern. When manager confronts a situation in which work to be accomplished through people, there is a range of alternative ways for him to go about managing. To increase his managerial competence he needs to know them and to be able to select the best course of action for a particular situation, such as, Task (9,1), Country Club (1,9), Improvised (1,1), Depend Pendulum (5,5), and Team (9,9). Under each of these situations, they give the strategies for dealing with the conflict. They are: forcing, smoothing, withdrawing, compromise, confrontation or problem solving. Blake and Mouton's Conflict Management Style is given in Figure 2.3.1.

2.3.1.1. Forcing

A manager strives to be powerful, to control, and to dominate. He is driven to win and to prove himself capable of mastering all, submitting to nothing and no one. Primary emphasis is placed on the importance of will power. This can lead to an almost inflexible determination to come out on top.

In this, a manager places high value on making decisions on that yard-stick or doing things his own way because it is his way. In terms of conviction, he is ready to stand up for his own ideas, opinions, and attitudes and to press forcefully for their acceptance, even when others are resisting or pushing for their

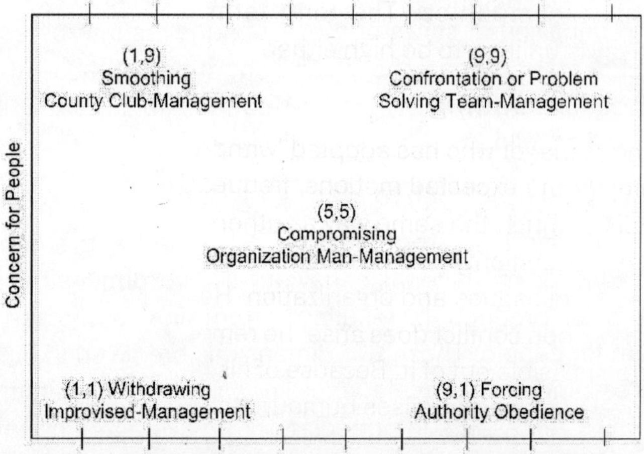

Fig. 2.3.1: Blake and Mouton's Conflict Management Style

***Source*: BLAKE (Robert R) and MOUTON (Jane S)[43]**

own against him. Webber[44] (1979) strongly favour and put it "The simplest conceivable resolution is the elimination of the other party, to force opponents to flee and give up the flight or stay them".

A high productivity may be achieved in short term but in the long term the output may be lowered because of hidden conflicts often repeat.

2.3.1.2. *Smoothing*

A manager believes in that the attitudes and feelings of his colleagues, peers, subordinates are of utmost importance. He accepts that they need to feel emotionally secure. He is likely to be excessively attentive to what supervisors, subordinates, peers and colleagues think. He remains secure, when surrounded by people who give sup ort and appreciation. His natural bent is to anticipate the desires and wishes of others and to do their bidding. He pleases all others. He initiates positive leadership and establishes harmony.

Smoothing is common in high project margin and quasi-monopolistic setting and unlikely to be formed in highly competitive companies. The long term and short term productivity is unlikely to be high either.

2.3.1.3. *Withdrawing*

The manager who has adopted 'withdrawing' orientation goes through the expected motions, frequently following rules of conduct in much the same way as others. He preserves his job and builds seniority but without making a contribution that benefits his colleagues and organization. He expects little and gives little. When conflict does arise, he remains neutral and to the degree possible out of it. Because of his neutrality, he really gets stirred up, if he expresses humour others may think point less.

Productivity may sink to the lowest level. If it is increased mandatory, employ more people or purchase more equipments. It incurs more expenses without solving the basic problem.

2.3.1.4. *Compromising*

A manager is likely to develop pleasant manners. His goal is to make many friends, even though not close ones. He is motivated by membership tends to be superficial in his own convictions. He is cautious to avoid self-exposure. Prevailing opinions are his opinion. What others reject, he rejects. Therefore, he is unlikely to have deep ideological commitment. Compromising involves, 'splitting the differences' exchanging concessions and seeking a quick middle ground solution. It may be used by the manager, in resolving conflict with his supervisors, peers, and subordinates. But the reservation and doubts that led to initial differences are likely to remain.

2.3.1.5. *Confrontation or Problem-Solving*

When a manager presumes an inherent contradiction between organizations' needs of production and the needs of the people, production may be achieved through integrating people involving their emotions and ideas in solving problems through teamwork. Confidence is demonstrated by boss and subordinates. It provides an understanding with goals and objectives and the basis for cooperation. When conflict arises, the managers adopts confrontation or problem solving techniques, and getting it on the table and resolved by the parties. Each party is responsible for his own activities as well as sharing responsibility for team effort.

2.3.2. Thomas Approach to Conflict Management

Blake and Mouton[45] (1964) made a significant contribution to the description of interpersonal conflict behaviours by introducing a five-category scheme for classifying interpersonal handling modes. Their scheme includes: (a) competing, (b) collaborating, (c) compromising, (d) avoiding, and (e) accommodating. Thomas[46] (1976) interpreted these five modes as reflections of two dimensions: (i) cooperation (attempting to satisfy the other person's concern) and (ii) assertiveness (attempt to satisfy one's own concern). As shown in Figure 2.3.2(a), he introduced joint outcome space as a format for representing the party's conceptualisation of alternatives, such as, A, D, B, E, C and their outcomes in terms of the degree of satisfaction of concerns. The horizontal and vertical axis, represent the degree to which the party perceives that other's concern and party's concern respectively would be satisfied by a given alternative. Point will be the alternative where the party's concerns reach near satisfaction. At point D both the parties concerns would be frustrated. At point A party satisfies his concern while other is frustrated. At point B one party satisfies its concern, but other party's concerns are frustrated. Point E is a point representing an alternative when both the parties satisfy up-to some level.

Further, Thomas model categorizes party orientation on the basis of the degree to which he would like to satisfy his own concern and the degree to which he would like to satisfy concern of other. He has given this in Figure 2.3.2(b) in which he uses 'joint outcome space' to plot 'five orientations', such as, (a) competitive, (b) collaborative, (c) avoidant, (d) accommodative, and (e) sharing together with their preferred outcomes.

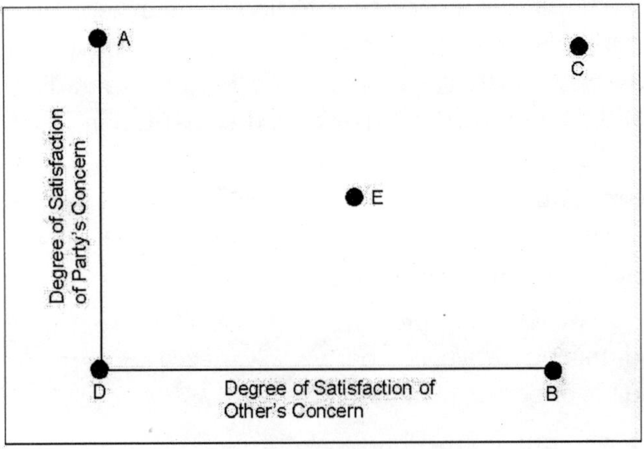

Fig. 2.3.2(a): Joint Outcome Space

Source **: THOMAS (Kenneth)[47]**

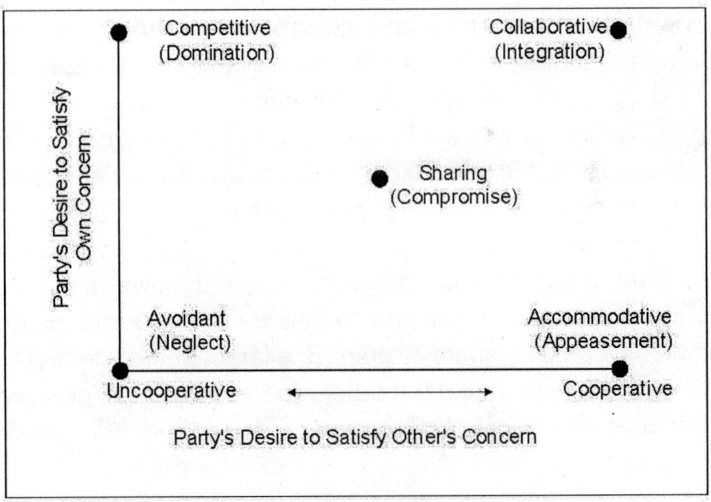

Fig. 2.3.2 (b): Five Conflict-Handling Orientations

Source **: THOMAS (Kenneth)[48]**

In the competitive orientation, party wins or satisfies own concern at the expense of the other party, namely to dominate. While in accommodative orientation party neglects his own concern to satisfy the concern of other's party.

Compromising is taking an intermediate position by both the parties. Each party tries to find some expedient, mutually acceptable solution which partially satisfies both parties. Party gives up some thing and keep some thing. Horse-trading in union management orientation reflects the orientation.

In collaborative orientation, one party attempts to work with the other party to find solutions that would be satisfying to both the parties. It represents a desire to fully satisfy the concerns of both the parties.

Avoidance approach is used when party is unassertive and uncooperative, i.e., party has very low concern for his own and his opponents' needs.

2.3.3. Filley Approach to Conflict Management

The problem-solving method of conflict management has been suggested by Filley[49] (1978). In contrast with the power-oriented method, he assumed problem-solving method for finding a solution to the conflict that will benefit both the parties. He did not assume a zero sum situation, since the gain of one party is not equal to the loss of the other; instead both parties may gain with the outcome. If a person and the other want the same apple, they may fight. The person wins, gets 100 percent of # apple as shown at point A in Figure 2.3.3 and other gets nothing. If person and other may decide to solve the dispute and split the apple, the person may try to move from point C, making a smaller share to point B, a larger share. But at point D, both the person and the other receive nearly 100 percent of the possible pay off. In this method, first identify the goals and values, which each party wants with the present preferred alternatives, and then, an exhaustive search for solutions that meet such combined goals.

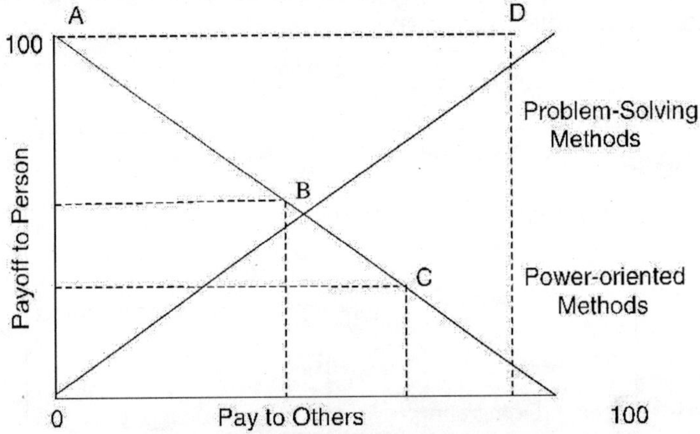

Fig. 2.3.3 : Methods of Conflict Resolution

Source :FILLEY (A C)[50]

Observation : The problem solving methods involve the application of facts and logic to solving problems that are created by conflictive situations. They evoke intellectual intensity rather than emotional intensity or power. Whenever a conflict is present, the perceptions, attitudes, feelings, situation, and process produce power-oriented relation between parties. Conflict management may alter these conditions, allowing the use of problem solving methods.

Filley also suggested certain conditions such as, perceptual, effective and situational, which might allow problem-solving methods of conflict resolution to replace power-oriented method.

2.3.4. Rahim's Style of Handling Conflict

Using a conceptualization similar to Blake and Mouton[51] (1964) and Thomas[52] (1976), Rahim[53] (1983) styles of handling conflict were differentiated on two basic dimensions : concern for self and for other. The first dimension explains the degree (high or low) to which a person attempts to satisfy his or her own concern. The second dimension explains the degree (high or low) to which a person wants to satisfy the concern of others[54].

Combination of the two dimensions, result in five specific styles of handling conflict as shown in Figure 2.3.4.

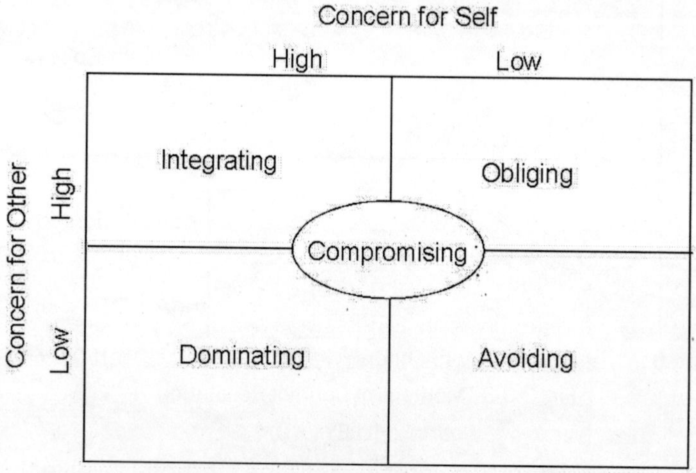

Fig. 2.3.4 : Rahim's Model for Handling Interpersonal Conflict

***Source* : RAHIM (M A)[55]**

2.3.4.1. *Integrating*

This style involves high concern for self as well as the other party involved in conflict. It is concerned with collaboration between parties (i.e., openness, exchange of information and termination of differences) to reach a solution acceptable to both parties. Lawrence and Lorsch[56] found the problem solving (integrating mode) to be more effective than other modes for attaining integration of the activities of different sub systems.

2.3.4.2. *Obliging*

This style involves low concern for self and high concern for the other party involved in conflict. An obliging person attempts to play down the differences and emphasizes commonalities to satisfy the concern of the other.

2.3.4.3. *Dominating*

This style involves high concern for self and low concern for the other party involved in conflict. It has been identified with a win-lose orientation or with forcing behaviour to win one's position.

2.3.4.4. Avoiding

This is associated with low concern for self as well as for the other party involved in conflict. It has been associated with withdrawal, passing-the -buck, side - stepping or "***see no evil, hear no evil, speak no evil*** " situation.

2.3.4.5. Compromising

This style involves moderate concern for self as well as the other party involved in conflict. It is associated with give and take or sharing whereby both parties give up something to make a mutually acceptable decision.

2.3.5. Derr's Modes Of Conflict Management

Derr[57] (1978) has given three conflict management modes as shown in Table 2.3.5. These are (a) collaboration, (b) bargaining, and (c) power play. In collaboration, people should surface their differences (get them out in the open) and then work on the problems until they have attained mutually satisfactory solutions.

* Shared information (open)
* Required consensus
* Collaborative ethics
* Power party assumed
* Theory and method explicit
* Voluntary organizational sup ort
* Win-win

* Shared information strategic
* Requires agreements
* Open collaborative between negotiations

* Theory and method in explicit
* Adversary ethic (initially)
* Self interest assumed
* Forced organizational sup ort
* Compromise, win lose

* Adversary ethic
* Self interest assumed
* No organizational sup ort
* Strategic use of information
* Win lose
* Power oriented ethic
* Recognize power inequalities
* Theory and method initiative

Fig. 2.3.5 : Relationship among strategies

Source **: DERR (C Brooklyn)[58]**

In bargaining, while neither party may emerge completely satisfied and one party may be clearly dissatisfied under the modes, both will at least come to terms openly how best to resolve the most immediate issues. Bargaining can be a more or less elaborate mode of conflict management depending on the situation from interpersonal trading to collective negotiation.

In contrast to collaboration, power-play will be dominant conflict management strategy for those who seek autonomy. Power play is a secretive mode that could work in the best interest of those whose covert objective is autonomy and whose desired impression is that of being committed.

Collaboration may be best employed when work relationships, must become interdependent. Bargaining seems to work best to establish power parity as a means of distributing scarce resources and as somewhat efficient option for achieving a formal agreement to a common dispute, while power play is an important way to cope with conflicts for the autonomous.

2.3.6. Schmidt & Tennenbaum Approach To Managing Conflict

Schmidt and Tennenbaum[59] (1960) have suggested four approaches which may be used by a manager at different times to deal with the conflicts, explained as follows.

2.3.6.1. Avoidance of Differences

A manager can avoid the occurrence of many differences among his subordinates. This approach may work well in certain situations only. The manager who uses this approach, continuously runs the risk of total loss of creativity of staff.

2.3.6.2. Repression of Differences

The manager, using this approach, keeps the differences under cover. He is aware that certain differences exist among number of groups, but would not allow open expression of these differences.

2.3.6.3. Confrontation Or Sharpening Differences

When a manager is aware that differences exist among the members of the group, he may try to create an arena in which conflicting parties may fight it out.

2.3.6.4. Mediation Or Transformation Of Conflict

The persons involved in the conflict can bring to bear on the problem a greater variety of insights. If the differences are seen as enriching, the individuals involved are likely to come up with a better solution because many problems can be seen clearly only if the individuals who see different aspects can come together and pool their information.

2.3.7. Hall's Two Dimensional Model

Hall's[60] (1969) conflict handling styles are based on two dimension model. He has developed an instrument in which he has divided conflict into four aspects. On the whole the instrument contains 12 items, three each among four categories like, (a) personal view of conflict, (b) interpersonal conflict, (c) conflict in task groups, and (d) relation between groups. In his study, the respondents were asked one of the five alternatives provided against each item. These alternatives are the five styles of handling conflict, which shows different degree of concern for two dimensions, personal goals and relationships. He has given five styles of conflict management, namely, (a) 9,9 (High concern for both personal goals, and relationship), (b) 5,5 (moderate concern for both personal goals and relationship), (c) 1,9 (low concern for personal goals and high concern for relationship), (d) 9,1 (high concern for personal goals and low concern for relationship), and (e) 1,1 (low concern for both personal goal and relationship).

2.3.8. Pareek's Approach-Avoidance Modes

Paree[61] assumed that conflict may mainly depend upon the perception of out-group (the other group, contrasted with our group) in Figure 2.3.8. He suggested that perception should, perhaps, be used as a basic in understanding the mode of conflict management. Perception of the out group has two dimensions. It may be perceived as always opposed to the interests of in-group and as being belligerent (conflict is seen as inevitable). Similarly, the out-group may be perceived as unreasonable resulting in lack of hope for any solution or as open to reason with resultant hope of a solution to the problem. He further advocated that general orientation of a group may be avoidance orientation or approach orientation. Avoidance is characterized by a tendency to deny, rationalized or avoid the problem, to displace anger or aggression or to use emotional appeal. Avoidance approach is significant and determines the effectiveness of managerial behaviour. It is based on fear and its outcome is dysfunctional. Approach orientation is characterized by making effort to find a solution to the problem by one's own efforts or with the help of others. It is based on the hope and its outcome is functional. The active and passive mode suggested by Blake and others[62] is close to this. The combination of two types of perceptions of out-groups with avoidance approach dimensions has given eight modes, namely, (i) resignation, (ii) withdrawal, (iii) appeasement, (iv) diffusion, (v) confrontation, (vi) arbitration, (vii) compromise, and (viii) negotiation.

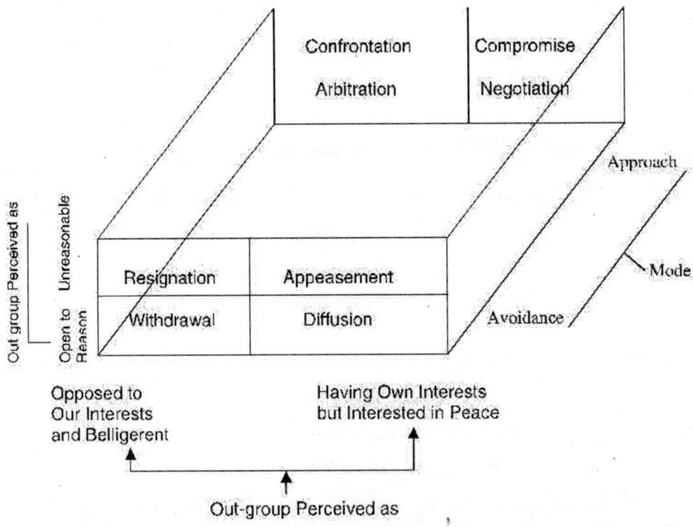

Fig. 2.3.8 : Approach – Avoidance Styles of Conflict Management

Source **: PAREEK (Udai)[63]**

2.3.9. Likert & Likert's Model For Managing Conflict

Likert and Likert[64] (1976) integrated the basic principles used by the highest producing managers with a general organizational system called system 4, as also shown in Figure 2.3.9.

Figure 2.3.9 shows a schematic location of system (little differentiation of function, excessive span of control, confusion of functionalization and motivational forces used (involving people in decision-making, recognition of achievements, providing opportunity for self-actualisation, etc.).

The Y Axis shows the extent to which the basic concepts

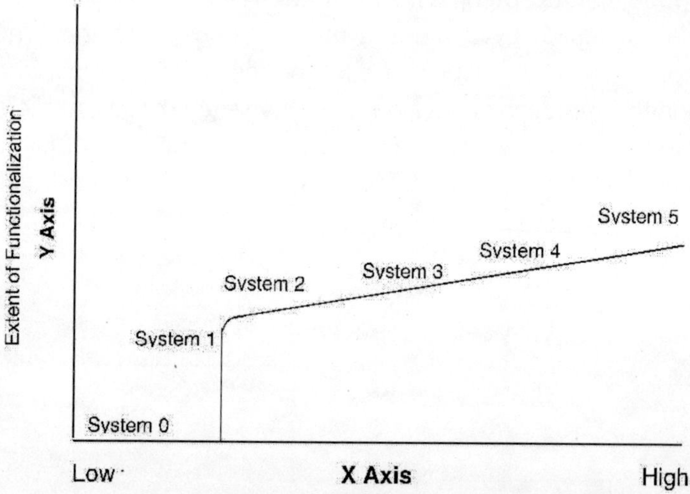

Fig. 2.3.9 : Likert & Likert System for Motive Source Used

Source **: LIKERT (Rensis) and LIKERT (Jane Gibson)[65]**

of functionalization are applied through appropriate structure; the X axis shows the extent to which major motive sources are used in ways that reinforce rather than conflict with one another. The manner in which an organization copes with conflict is governed by the operative characteristics of its interaction influence network and the management system upon which its interaction influence network is based. The more an organization moves towards system 4, less will be the intensity and harmful effects of conflict. It is clear that the participatory style of management helps in handling the conflict in organizations.

2.3.10. Blake, Shepard And Mouton Mode

Blake and others[66] (1964) assumed that there are three attitudinal sets (for basic assumption) that people can have towards inter-group conflict, namely, (a) conflict is inevitable, agreement is impossible, (b) conflict is not inevitable, yet agreement is impossible, and (c) although there is conflict, agreement is possible. These attitudinal sets will lead to predictable behaviour depending upon the way the people involved see the "stakes". If people think that conflict is inevitable, agreement is impossible then they will tend to let fate decide the conflict. When the stakes are moderate, they will permit a third party judgement to decide the conflict. Finally, when stakes are high, they will actively engage in a win–loose confrontation or power struggle, as shown in Figure 2.3.10.

Active ↑	Conflict Inevitable, Agreement Impossible	Conflict not inevitable yet agreement not possible	Although There is Conflict, Agreement is Possible	High Stakes ↑
	Win-Loose Power Struggle	Withdrawal	Problem Solving	Moderate Stakes
	Third Party Intervention	Isolation	Splitting the Difference (Compromise, Bargaining, Mediation etc.)	↓
↓ Passive	Fate	Indifference or ignorance	Peaceful Co-Existence (Smoothing Over)	Low Stakes

Fig. 2.3.10 : Basic Attitudes Towards Conflict and Stakes Increases/ Decreases.

***Source*: CHHABRA and SURI[67]**

Figure 2.3.10 shows that if people think that conflict is not inevitable, yet if it occurs, agreement is impossible, they will be passive and indifferent if the stakes are low. When the stakes are moderate, they will isolate themselves from such a conflict situation. But when the stakes are high and then find actively involved, they will eventually withdraw.

If the people think that although there is a conflict, agreement is possible, they will be passive and attempt to smooth over the situation when the stake are low. When the stakes are moderate, they will engage in bargaining or some form of negotiation. But if the stakes are high, they will actively engage in problem solving.

2.4. CONCLUSION

An attempt has been made in the preceding paragraphs to group the various approaches to conflict management, as given by the different scholars. After a thorough analysis, it has been made clear that Blake and Mouton[68] (1964) were the first thinkers to present a grid for classifying the modes for handling interpersonal conflict into five types. It has striking come back in the Conflict. Management literature, as studied by Kabnoff[69] (1987); Pruitt and Rubin[70] (1986); Schockley-Zalabak[71] (1988), Ven de Vliert and Prein[72] (1989). Most of the authors have treated managerial grid as a five category scheme for classifying behavioural styles or modes handling social conflict. Other authors like Rahim[73] (1983) and Thomas[74] (1976) labelled the two dimensions differently, but the basic assumption have remained similar. People are classified into five interpersonal handling styles with two dimensions.

Conflict management, conflict resolutions and their approaches have been explained and discussed in this Chapter. It is inferred from these approaches that in different cases, their number vary. While, most of the authors have suggested *five styles* of handling interpersonal conflict, their basic interpretations are similar, but their styles name have been changed like, 'domination, competing, forcing, collaboration, integration, confronting, problem solving, accommodating, smoothing, avoidance, withdrawing. One of the most common among the styles of conflict management is 'compromising'. Empirical researches were conducted by the researchers, namely, Burke[75] (1969), Jamieson and Thomas[76] (1974), Lawrence and Lorsch [77] (1967), Renwiek[78] (1975), [79](1975), Sharma and Samantra[80] (1994), Das[81] (1987), Sharma and Samantra[82](1995), Mathur and Saeed[83] (1980), Weider-Hatfield and Hatfield[84] (1996), Singh and Parthasarthy[85] (1985), Mishra and others[86] (1999), Wall Jr. and Callister[87] (1995), Samantra[88] (1999), Sayeed[89] (11990), Howat and London[90] (1980), Samantra[91] (2003), Bhowon[92](1999) and (1998)[93]. Howsoever, there is a need for more rigorous studies and research about 'conflict handling behaviour' to keep pace with the ever changing scenario of conflict in organizations, especially in Indian context.

REFERENCES

1. THOMAS (Kenneth W) and SCHMIDT (Warren H). Survey of managerial interest with respect to conflict. *Academy of Management Journal.* 19, 2; 1976; 315.
2. TJOSVOLD (Dean) and JOHNSON (David W). Productive conflict management perspective for organizations. 1983. Irvington Publishers; New York.
3. STAMATIS (D H). Conflict you've got to accentuate the positive. *Personnel.* 64, 12; 1987; 47
4. CHESLER (Mark A) and others. Power training: An alternative path to conflict management. *California Management Review.* 21, 2; 1978; 84.
5. CHESLER (Mark A) and others. Power training; p 86-87.
6. RAHIM (M Afzalur). Strategy for managing conflict in complex organizations. *Human Relations.* 38, 1; 1985; 81-89.
7. RAHIM (M Afzalur). Strategy for managing conflict; p 86.
8. ROBBINS (Stephen P). Conflict management and conflict resolution are not synonymous terms. *California Management Review.* 21, 2; 1978; 67.
9. ROBBINS (Stephen P). Conflict management; p 71.
10. BROWN (L D). Managing conflict at organizational interface. 1983. Addison – Wesley; Massachusetts.
11. GOEL (S L) and RAJNEESH (Shalini). Management techniques : Principles and practices. 2001. Deep & Deep; New Delhi. p 429.
12. DEUTSCH (M). Resolution of conflict. 1973. Yale University Press; Connecticut.
13. THOMAS (Kenneth W). Conflict and conflict management. *In* DUNNETTE (M D), *Ed.* Handbook of Industrial and organizational psychology. 1976. Rand McNally; Chicago. p 889-935.
14. SCHMIDT (Stuart M) and KOCHAN (Thomas A). Conflict: Towards conceptual clarity. *Administrative Science Quarterly.* 17, 3; 1972; 359-68.
15. KAZDIN (Alan E), *Ed.* Encyclopedia of psychology. V 2. 2000. American Psychological Association, Washington. p 261.
16. STRICKLAND (Bonne), *Ed.* Gale encyclopedia of psychology. Ed 2. V2. 2000. Gale Group; New York. p 148.
17. BOULDING (Kenneth). Conflict and defense. 1963. Harper & Row; New York.

18. THOMAS (Kenneth W). Conflict and conflict management; p 889-935.

19. TINSLEY (C). Models of conflict resolution in Japanese, German, and American cultures. *Journal of Applied Psychology*. 83, 2; 1998; 316.

20. FERRARO (Vincent L) and ADAMS (Sheila A). Interdepartmental conflict: Practical ways to prevent and reduce it. *Personnel*. 61, 4; 1984; 12.

21. PHILLIPS (Eleanor) and CHESTON (Ric). Conflict resolution : What works. *California Management Review*. 21, 4; 1979; 76.

22. RAHIM (M Afzalur). Strategy for managing conflict; p 81-89.

23. ROBBINS (Stephen P). Conflict management; p 67-75.

24. BOULDING (K B). Preface to special issue. *Journal of Conflict Management*. 12; 1968; 409-11.

25. ROBBINS (Stephen P). Conflict management; p 67-75.

26. http://www.expat.or.id/business/conflictresolution.html

27. COOK (Curties W) and HUNSAKER (Phillips L). Management and organizational behavior. Ed 3. 2001. McGraw Hill; New York. p 372-409.

28. GUPTA (S R). Discussion on 6/7/2007.

29. http://www.mediationworks.com/dmi/rsch/bibcr.htm

30. CHATTERJEE (M N). Conflict resolution begins at home. *Times of India*. 15 Jan., 2004; 16, 5-6.

31. DAS (S L). Conflict : Basis of collective and constructive functioning. *Indian Management*. 21, 12; 1982; 21.

32. BLAKE (Robert R) and MOUTON (Jane S). Managerial grid. 1964. Gulf Publishing; Houston.

33. SCHMIDT (W H) and TANNENBAUM (R). Management of differences. *Harvard Business Review*. 38, 6; 1960; 107-15.

34. THOMAS (Kenneth W). Conflict and conflict management; p 889-935.

35. HALL (J). Conflict management survey : A survey on one's characteristic reaction to and handling conflicts between himself and others. 1969. Telecometrics International; Taxas.

36. FILLEY (A C). Some normative issues in conflict management. *California Management Review*. 21, 2; 1978; 61-66.

37. DERR (C Brooklyn). Managing organizational conflict : Collaboration, bargaining, and power approaches. *California Management Review*. 21, 2; 1978; 76-83.

38. RAHIM (M A). Organizational conflict inventory i & ii : Professional manual. 1983. Consulting Psychologists Press; Palo Alto.

39. PAREEK (Udai). Managing conflict and collaboration.1982. Oxford and

IBH Publishing; New Delhi.

40. LIKERT (R) and LIKERT (J. Gibson). New ways of managing conflict. 1976. McGraw Hill; New York.
41. BLAKE (RR) and others. Managing inter-group conflict in industry. 1964. Gulf Publishing; Houston.
42. BLAKE (Robert R) and MOUTON (Jane S). Managerial grid. 1964. Gulf Publishing; Houston.
43. BLAKE (Robert R) and MOUTON (Jane S). New managerial grid. 1985. Jaico, Bombay. p 11.
44. WEBBER (Ross A). Management: Basic elements of managing organization. 1979. Richard D Irwin; New York. p 453.
45. BLAKE and MOUTON. Managerial grid.
46. THOMAS (Kenneth W). Conflict and conflict management; p 900.
47. THOMAS (Kenneth W). Conflict and conflict management; p 900.
48. THOMAS (Kenneth W). Conflict and conflict management; p 900.
49. FILLEY (A C). Some normative issues; p 61-66.
50. FILLEY (A C). Some normative issues; 62
51. BLAKE and MOUTON. Managerial grid.
52. THOMAS (Kenneth W). Conflict and conflict management; p 889-935.
53. RAHIM (M A). Measure of styles of handling interpersonal conflict. *Academy of Management Journal*. 26, 2; 1983; 365-76.
54. RAHIM (M A) and BONOMA (T V). Managing organizational conflict : A model for diagnosis and intervention. *Psychological Reports*. 44; 1979; 1323-44.
55. RAHIM (M A). Measure of styles; p 369.
56. LAWRENCE (P R) and LORSCH (J W). Organization and environment. 1967. Irwin – Dorsey; Burr Ridge.
57. DERR (C Brooklyn). Managing organizational conflict; p 76-83.
58. DERR (C Brooklyn). Managing organizational conflict; p 80.
59. SCHMIDT and TANNENBAUM. Management of differences; p 107-15.
60. HALL (J). Conflict management survey.
61. PAREEK (Udai). Managing conflict and collaboration.
62. BLAKE (RR) and others. Managing inter-group conflict in industry.
63. PAREEK (Udai). Managing conflict and collaboration; p 36.
64. LIKERT and LIKERT. New ways of managing conflict.
65. LIKERT and LIKERT. New ways of managing conflict; p 18.

66. BLAKE (RR) and others. Managing inter-group conflict in industry.

67. CHHABRA (TN) and SURI (RK). Management process and perspectives. 2000. Kitab Mahal, New Delhi. p 535.

68. BLAKE and MOUTON. Managerial grid.

69. KABANOFF (Boris). Predictive validity of the mode conflict instrument. *Journal of Applied Psychology*. 72, 1; 1987; 160-63.

70. PRUITT (DG) and RUBIN (J Z). Social conflict : Escalation, stalemate, settlement. 1986. Random House; New York.

71. SCHOCKLEY – ZOLABAK. Assessing the Hall's conflict management survey. *Management Communication Quarterly*. 1, 3; 1988; 302-20.

72. VAN de VLIERT (E) and PREIN (H CM). Difference in the meaning of forcing in the conflict management of actors and observers managing conflict: An interdisciplinary approach. 1989. Praeger; New York.

73. RAHIM (M A). Organizational conflict inventory i&ii.

74. THOMAS (Kenneth W). Conflict and conflict management; p 889-935.

75. BURKE (R J). Methods of resolving interpersonal conflict. *Personnel Administration*. 32, 1; 1969; 48-55.

76. JAMIESON (D W) and THOMAS (K W). Power and conflict in the student-teacher relationship. *Journal of Applied Behavioral Science*. 10; 1974; 321-26.

77. LAWRENCE and LORSCH. Organization and environment.

78. RENWICK (P A). Perception and management of superior-subordinate conflict. *Organizational Behavior and Human Performance*. 13, 3; 1975; 444-56.

79. RENWICK (P A). Impact of topic and source of disagreement on conflict management *Organizational Behavior and Human Performance*. 14, 3; 1975; 416-25.

80. SHARMA (R A) and SAMANTRA (R). Conflict Management in an Indian firm : A case study. *Decision*. 21, 4; 1994; 235-49.

81. DAS (G S). Conflict management styles of efficient branch managers : As perceived by others. *ASCI Journal of Management*. 17, 1; 1987; 31-38.

82. SHARMA (R A) and SAMANTRA (Rabinarayan). Conflict management in an Indian firm. *Indian Journal Industrial Relations*. 30, 4; 1995; 439-53.

83. MATHUR (H B) and SAYEED (Omer Bin). Application of conflict management strategic as perceived by the manager for himself and for his superior: Comparison. *Indian Journal of Social Work*. 41, 2-3; 1980; 163-68.

84. WEIDER-HATFIELD (Deborah) and HATFIELD (John D). Supervisors' conflict management strategies and subordinate outcomes. *Management Communication Quarterly*. 10, 2; 1996; 189-208.

85. SINGH (P) and PARTHASARTHY (Kokila). Conflict management strategy: A scenario of avoidance. *Abhigyan*. 3, 2; 1985; 57-84.

86. MISHRA (Prashant) and others. Re - strategising the management of conflict: An empirical study. *Indian Journal Industrial Relations*. 35, 2; 1999; 160-74.

87. WALL Jr. (J A) and CALLISTER (R R). Conflict and its management. *Journal of Management*. 21, 3; 1995; 515-58.

88. SAMANTRA (Rabindrayan). Conflict management strategies and their impact on organizational effectiveness in Indian industry. 1999. Ph.D. Thesis; Supervisor: R. A. Sharma, University of Delhi. (unpublished).

89. SAYEED (Omer Bin). Conflict management styles : Relationship with leadership styles and moderating effect of esteem for co-worker. *Indian Journal of Industrial Relations*. 26, 1; 1990; 28-52.

90. HOWATT (Gary) and LONDON (Manuel). Attribution of conflict management strategies in superior-subordinate dyad. *Journal of Applied Psychology*. 65, 2; 1980; 172-75.

91. SAMANTRA (Rabinarayan). Management of superior-subordinates conflict: An exploration. *Indian Journal of Industrial Relations*. 38, 4; 2003; 444-59.

92. BHOWON (Uma). Perceived organizational climate and interpersonal handling strategies. *Indian Journal of Industrial Relations*. 35, 1; 1999; 43-51.

93. BHOWON (Uma). Perceived power and interpersonal handling strategies. *Indian Journal of Industrial Relations*. 34, 2; 1998; 183-92.

3

Conflict Management : A Historical Perspective

It has been observed that the organizational behaviourists have presented a number of methods to deal with 'conflict'. One, therefore, needs to know about the views of the theorists on conflict. The conflict has been studied over the years by sociologists, anthropologists, economists, political scientists, and psychologists[1]. A brief historical overview is described below:

3.1. CONFLICT: ITS ASPECTS

With a purpose to understand more comprehensively, the views given by the scholars in different fields of conflict, have been recapitulated here. It includes conflict in its different aspects, its consequences, interpersonal conflict, factors causing interpersonal conflict, and remedies for minimising the conflict in management of libraries.

3.1.1. Sociological Aspect

In the Nineteenth century social thinkers paid much attention to the social conflict. But a difference of opinion emerged in their views. Mayo[2] (1945) and his school define social conflicts as a social disease, and promotion of equilibrium or a state of collaboration define as a social health. Warner and Low[3] (1947) consider conflict in negative connotation. Parsons[4]

(1951) views that social conflict is primarily disruptive, disassociating and dysfunctional consequences. Beals and Siegel[5] (1966) used the term conflict as a "breach in normally expected behavior". On the other hand, some sociologists considered conflicts were fundamental and constructive part of social life. Weber[6] (1904-17) considered conflict a major social phenomenon. He insisted, "Conflict can not be excluded from social life ... peace is nothing more than a change in the form of the conflict or in the antagonists or in the objects of the conflict, or finally in the chance of selection". Simmel[7] (1908) insisted, "conflict is a form of socialization and that: a certain amount of disorder, inner divergence and outer controversy, is originally tied up with the very elements that ultimately hold, the group together".

Cooley[8] (1918) has affirmed that more one thinks of it, the more he will find that the conflict and cooperation are not separable, but the two essential phases of one process which always involves some thing of both. Ross[9] (1920) goes even further, "in a way open opposition preserves society.... In any voluntary association the corking up of protest and opposition of the rest...whereby dominant element is likely to lead splitting of the group". Cooley[10] (1918) regarded conflict as a part of social change and progress, when he says, "Conflict of some sort is the life of society and progress emerges from a struggle in which individual, class or institution seek to realize its own idea of good". Park[11] (1941) considers conflict among the few basic forums of human interaction. "Only where there is a conflict in behavior conscious and self conscious only there are conditions for rational conduct". Further he is of the opinion that conflict is not only mechanism through which self-consciousness is achieved but it is in fact constitutive of any organized society. Again he points out that "conflict tends to bring about an integration and super ordination and subordination of conflict group".

Churchill[12] (1928) while giving an account of World War I, opined that conflict makes group members more conscious of their group bonds and increase their participation. Coser[13] (1956) documented how conflict plays a role in preserving society as much as conscious does. He also shows how conflict may serve to bring some isolated individuals into active role for change. Fink[14] (1968) was of the view which focused on conceptual disarray and commented, "...the existing diversity of empirical and theoretical approaches to the study of social conflict has produced a state of conceptual and terminological confusion, which impedes both comparison between distinct classes of conflict phenomena and process of theoretical integration."

Dahrendorf[15] (1959) used the term conflict for contests, competitions, disputes, and tensions as well as for manifest clashes between social focus. All reactions between sets of individuals that involve an incompatible differences of objective, i.e., in the most general form, a desire on the part of both contestants to obtain what is available only to one, or only in part are in these sense, reason of social conflict. Levine[16] (1961) working on anthropology and conflict, distinguishes five forms of conflict indicating behaviour: physical aggression, public verbal dispute, covert verbal aggression, breach of expectation and avoidance. All of these forms may be found within the same culture.

3.1.2. Psychological Aspect

In psychological aspect conflict refers to a situation in which a person is motivated to engage in two or more mutually exclusive activities[17]. Freud[18] (1893-95) used the first psychological concept. He worked on hysterical neurosis and explained hysterical symptoms as the consequence of conflict between incompatible ideas. In his subsequent development of psychoanalytic theory, Freud placed a great deal of emphasis on a conflict between sexual and self-preservative instincts. Lewin[19] (1935) made a comprehensive analysis of personality in terms of field theory. He distinguished three types of conflict : (1) where a person - between two goals of positive valence; (2) where a person faces a goal with both positive and negative valence; and (3) where a person is between two goals of negative valence. These types of conflict have become known as approach-approach, approach-avoidance, and avoidance-avoidance respectively.

Miller[20] (1944) concentrated on approach-avoidance conflict on the assumption that this type was of the most significant in psycho-pathology and social behaviour. He established a theoretical model of conflict on the bases of carefully controlled laboratory experiments with animal subjects and then to extent these principles to complex human behaviour. Dollard and Miller[21] (1950) have made extensive use of conflict model. These theories have reinterpreted many of psychoanalytic observations on psycho-sexual development in terms of conflicts learned in childhood. Punitive parental training methods can establish conflict in the areas of weaning, cleanliness, sexual, sexual behaviour and aggression.

In the early twentieth century, Freud[22] (1920) underscored the pernicious effects of emotional conflicts on behaviour and personality, and his principle that conflicts occur especially at the unconscious level, are the well spring of neurosis had been widely accepted. Pavlov[23] (1927) supported experimentally to Freud[24] (1920) finding that dogs which were required to learn difficult discriminations, often developed an "experimental neurosis" marked by persisting abnormal behaviour. Rapoport[25] (1960) views that "conflict...is a theme that has occupied the thinking of man more than any other, save only God and love."

3.1.3. Organizational Aspect

Conflict is a central issue and its research has implications for understanding society and organizations. The study of conflict in organizations has evolved significantly over recent decades. Much research in 1960s focus on growing functional specialization in organizations and conflict inherent in the performance of organizational task carried out by diverse sub units[26]. Thomas[27] (1976) regarded conflict as a popular topic. Organizational conflict and its related topic studied by the scholars, such as, Lammers[28] (1969) "Strike and mutinies", Jehan[29] (1995) "Benefit and determine of intragroup conflict", Palen[30] (1969) "Organizational collapse", Frederickson[31] (1969) "Conflict in the public domain", Assael[32] (1969) "Economic conflict between organizations", Peterson and others[33] (1995), "Role conflict ambiguity and overload", Kahn and others[34] (1964) "Role conflict and ambiguity", Walton and others[35] (1969) "Interdepartmental conflict", Coverman[36] (1989) "Role overload, role conflict and stress", Warren[37] (1969), "Non conformity of subordinates", Rahim[38] (1983) "Measurement of organizational conflict", Corwin[39] (1969) "Routine staff conflict".

Suman[40] (1998) argues that in industrial terminology, the term 'conflict' usually refers to the divergent interests of management and labour. Follett[41] (1951) considers conflict as the result/appearance of difference, difference of opinions of interests. Chesler and others[42] (1978) assumed that conflict is in natural existence in any multiparty heterogeneous system. It is an inherent social condition derived from the fact that persons, parties and social group, and collectivities differ from one another on a variety of value, goals and material resources, in addition they are interdependent and must interact with regard to these differences. Derr[43] (1978) considers conflicts are normal and natural consequences of human interaction in organizational setting. Louis[44] (1977) present an initial model of how individual conceptualize conflict, identifying steps in the process by which individual conceptualizes conflict and highlighting the role of significant personal/development factor in this process. The model was developed to fill a significant gap in existing theory of conflicting behaviour.

Assael[45] (1969) argues that conflict between business organizations may have constructive consequences. He distinguishes between constructive and destructive conflict by drawing five premises about intergroup conflict from sociology and applying them to manufacturer and dealer relation. In the studies of Ridgeway[46] (1957), Berg[47] (1963) and Asseal[48] (1968), the potential for conflict is high in systems of selective and exclusive distribution, since they are characterized by high level of functional interdependence between manufacturers and dealers. Thomas[49] (1976) stated that conflict begins with a feeling of frustration by one or both parties over, in its or their ability to reach one or more goals. This prompts the frustrated party to conceptualize a subjective mental picture of the relationship, which subsequently affects the behaviour of that frustrated party. Zaleznik[50] (1970) argued that conflict is endemic, inevitable, and necessary to organizational life and always involves some testing of power situation.

Ferraro and Adams[51] (1984) argue that conflict arises because today's complex organizations with their high degree of occupational specialization, variety of employees with diverse backgrounds, and constantly changing environments not only put incredible pressure on the organization to adapt, but also present a difficult challenge to those who must work with one another. March and Simon[52] (1958) are of the view that conflict is break down in standard mechanism of decision making. Walton[53] (1966) stated that conflict is opposition process in any of several forms competition, status, rivalry, bargaining, sabotage, verbal abuse, etc.

Coser[54] (1956) considers conflict as antagonistic struggle especially cites the need to distinguish between the existence of incompatible goals and actual conflict. Robbins[55] (1974) notes, conflict is not seen as natural in many parts of American society; it is seen as distasteful unnecessary and even dangerous. Kolb and Bartunek[56] (1992) are of the view that conflict can be a disagreement, the pressure of tension, or some other difficulty within or between two or more parties. Conflict can be public or private, formal or informal, or be approached -

rationally or irrationally. Pondy[57] (1969) compared seven empirical studies of conflict within and between organizations- a distinction is made between frictional conflict within a stable organization structure and strategic conflict aimed at changing the organization structure. He also discussed importance of attitudes as cause and effect of conflict.

Sheppard[58] (1992) has argued that much of the confusion of present conflict theory can be understood in terms of the different levels of analysis and perspective associated with those levels. Kanter[59] (1977) stated that difference in culture is poorly understood and it is difficult to control conflict escalation, especially when they are closely related with the power differences. Corwin[60] (1969) identified relationship of indices of organizational conflict and several measures of each five organizational variables: structural differences, participation in authority system, regulating procedures, heterogeneity and stability of personnel and interpersonal structure. The data collected from 28 public schools. It was found that size, specialization, hierarchy, complexity staff additions were related to organization conflicts, participation in the authority and cohesiveness of peer, group relations seems to be conductive variable facilitating conflict, while experiences, and close supervision seemed to be integrative variables. However it was also found that the same variables were correlated with conflict in different ways, depending upon the bureaucratic and professional context and the type of conflict involved. Martins and others[61] (2002) studied and examined moderate effects of individual differences and sources of support on the negative relationship between work-family conflict and career satisfaction. Findings clearly suggest that work family conflict is an important factor that must be taken into account in such models.

De Long and Seemann[62] (2000) argue that it is the ability of leaders to identify potential conflicts and to help their organizations work through them will be an essential element of success. Pondy[63] (1967) identified three types of conflict among the sub units of formal organizations: bargaining conflict among the parties to an interest group relationship; bureaucratic conflict between the parties to a superior-subordinate relationship; and system conflict among the parties to a lateral or working relationship. In each of these three cases, conflict is treated as a series of episodes, each episode including stage of latency, feeling, perceptions, manifestation and aftermath. Schmidt and Kochan[64] (1972) distinguish conflict from competition in the intra organizational context and present a behavioural conceptualization of the process of conflict. It is proposed that goal incompatibility, perceived opportunity for interference and interdependent activities among organizational sub units increase the potential for conflict. This conceptual scheme is then applied to a situation involving city government officials engaged in bargaining with a city employee union.

Pinkley[65] (1990) in a multi dimensional scaling analysis of disputants interpretations of conflict, discovered that people differentiate between task and relationship conflict. Wall and Nolan[66] (1986) differentiated between relationship focused people conflicts and conflicts about the substantive content of the task.

Corwin[67] (1969) found teachers age and conflict to be negative related. Paul and Schooler[68] (1978) stated that conflict to be related to faculty members, rank tenure status, and committee membership. But Rahim[69] (1979) considers organizational conflict is a subset of social conflict which is susceptible to rigorous analysis.

Sheppard[70] argued that research on conflict in organizations has been portrayed as analogous to a schizophrenic having several personalities, each one largely unaware of the existence of the others. At least 3 levels of analysis exist in conflict research: 1. macro (institutions), 2. intermediate (relationships), and 3. individual (dispute episodes). Unfortunately, field of study and individual research efforts have tended to be trapped within a single level. Different researchers are operating with quite distinct assumptions about the nature of the institutional level. The benefits of integrating the various views of conflict in organizations would include: 1. the development of a formal means of evaluating the generalization of any conflict model or study, 2. the enhancement of the relevance of conflict research to practicing managers and policy-makers, and 3. the acquisition of important knowledge, even if efforts to develop an integrated model fail.

Litterer[71] (1966) argued that generally, conflict in organizations is condemned. This article examines some of the functions which conflict can fill and also some of its roots. It is shown that the roots of conflict are embedded in some of the basic characteristics of organizations, and hence it is to some degree inescapable. It is also shown that conflict can have useful effects in organizations. Essentially, the article shows that conflict is a controllable element in organizations, and can, therefore, be adjusted to minimize its dysfunctional and maximize its functional characteristics.

3.1.4. Consequences of Conflict

In every day life, conflict has negative connotation. In fact conflict in organizational environment operates like a proverbial 'double edge sword' depending upon the situation and conditions. Conflict has negative as well as positive effects. Majority of management scientists treat conflict positive and state that conflict is healthy ingredient of the organizational life. Assael[72] (1969), Evan[73] (1965), Hall and William[74] (1966), Janis[75] (1972), Pelz[76] (1967) noted positive consequences. Robbins[77] (1974),[78] (1978) goes even to the extent prescribing conflict as a dose for organizational growth and survivals Katz[79] (1974), Maier[80] (1963), McGregor[81] (1967), Deutsch[82] (1973), Rizzo and others[83] (1970), Tedesch and others[84] (1973), Schmidt[85] (1974), King[86] (1981) and Pareek[87] (1982) concluded, conflict produces better ideas and new alternatives. Baron[88] (1991), Tjosvold[89] (1983)and Van de Vliert and De Dreu[90] (1994) infer that conflict is beneficial and provide changes in organizational environment. Thomas, Jamieson and Moore[91] (1978) agreed that conflict is inevitable in organizations and it can have important positive consequences. Positive views on conflict were reinforced by the researchers, such as, Chanin[92] (1980), Mason[93] (1969), Mitroff and Mason[94] (1981).

Mayo[95] (1945) and Fox[96] (1972) consider conflict is a negative phenomenon. Argyris[97] (1964) and Likert[98] (1961) are of the view that conflict is an undesirable, detrimental, inherently destructive and unacceptable. Marek[99] (1966) inferred that conflict is a threat to cooperation. Litterer[100] (1966) concluded that these classical views on conflict as a undesirable, detrimental to the organization is similar to the views or other on the handling of tension within people. Rahim[101] (1979) observed that healthy organization seek to increase intra organizational conflict. The classical organization theorists did not see to appreciate different impact that conflict can have in organization. Now, the consensus emerged among the organization theorists, is that a moderate amount of conflict is necessary for attaining an optimum organizational effectiveness.

3.1.5. Interpersonal Conflict

Stimac[102] (1982) viewed that interpersonal conflict is ubiquitous and pervasive. He states that not conflict in general that we should try to avoid, because constructive conflict is the essence of problem solving. Boulding[103] (1963) argues, conflict as perceived incompatibilities or perceptions by the parties involved that they hold discrepant views or have interpersonal incompatibilities. Guetz Kow and Gyr[104] (1954) distinguished between conflict based on the substance on the task that the group is performing and the conflict based on interpersonal relation. Dalton[105] (1959) records actual conflict that occurred between line and staff personnel one of his major conclusion was that line managers often view staff advice as a threat. Kahn[106] (1964) viewed that both supervisors and professional employees are subject to special forms of tensions because of anomalies.

Ford and Johnson[107] (1998) consider conflict are common place in formal organizations, for example managers and subordinates often disagree over issues such as performances reviews, salary increases, work assignment and resources allocations. Gouldner[108] (1959) stated that pressures from superiors for efficiency and technical competence may be inconsistent with the professional value for technical procedure, and executives in complex organizations typically are less qualified than some of their own subordinates to judge the specialists below them. Preim and Price[109] (1991) who characterized two type of conflict as cognitive, task related conflict and social and emotional conflicts arising from interpersonal disagreements not directly related to the task.

Kolb and Putnam[110] (1992) consider that conflict may be said to exist when there are real or perceived differences that arise in specific organizational circumstances and that engender emotion as a consequence. In the early strands of organization theory, the management of conflict - whether by force or consensus - is central to the smooth, integrated functioning of organizations. While there are strong pulls toward the integration of these strands, a contrasting perspective highlights the disintegrative tendencies of conflict in organizations based on differences in occupations, gender, ethnicity, and culture. By taking a disputing perspective, it is possible to uncover the other faces of conflict processes in organizations. A disputing perspective bridges the public and private domains, and it therefore provides a basis for examining the links between bipolar opposites or the different faces of conflict in organizations. Unlike the public arena, private disputes occur as covert or hidden conflict, often fused with other activities.

Tjosvold and Poon[111] (1990) argued that the conflicts over scarce resources intensify competition and conflict but can be useful for an effective distribution of resources. A total of 59 managers with budget responsibilities from both expanding and retrenching organizations were interviewed on specific budget conflicts. Consistent with the power perspective, these conflicts could be productive. Open-minded discussion of opposing views contributed to making these conflicts useful for productivity, relationship development, and unity. In contrast with organizational power theorizing, cooperative goals, not competition shaped the productive management of conflicts over scarce resources.

Martocchio and Judge[112] (1995) provided a within-subjects assessment of the factors associated with absence disciplinary decisions for both supervisors and subordinates. In addition, this study examined discrepancies in disciplinary decisions between supervisors and their subordinates based on differences in psychological and demographic attributes. A sample of non-academic employees from 19 intact triads (one supervisor: two subordinates) at a large Midwest university responded to hypothetical scenario describing factors that might contribute to the absence of disciplinary decisions. The results demonstrated that both supervisors and subordinates generally place similar weights on factors that are relevant to disciplinary decisions. Perhaps more importantly; a number of psychological and demographic differences between supervisors and subordinates related positively to discrepancies in disciplinary decisions.

3.1.6. Causes/Sources of Conflict

An attempt has been made to give the account of cause of conflict through the views of different scholars. Ferraro and Adams[113] (1984) specified three major sources of interdepartmental conflict that occurs as a by product when the organization tries to meet its own particular corporate challenges. These three sources are communication differences, structural difference and personal differences. Walton and Dutton[114] (1969) presented a model describing nine major types of antecedents: mutual dependence, asymmetries, rewards, organizational differentiation, role dissatisfaction, ambiguities, common resources, communication obstacles, and personal skill and trait.

Thomas and Schmidt[115] (1976) emphasized upon the sources of conflict that all the three levels of management expressed most interest in misunderstanding, or communication failure. Personality clashes and value differences are also rated highly interesting. Phillips and Cheston[116] (1979) state conflict usually arise from problems in communication or personal relationship, or are inherent in the organizational structure. Conflict may include elements or more than one of these causes. Derr[117] (1978) argues that conflict may occur for multiple reasons: for example, internal stress coming from the person and overlapping into the work place, incompatible expectations among workers and work group, differences over task procedure, value, orientation and desired outcome, increasing interdependencies and work load, and external pressure and crises. Suman[118] (1998) argues that conflict do arise from both core issues value based and motivational. In every conflict, there is interplay between these two kinds of issues. Emotional conflict can be caused by people deep rooted personal feelings about one another, while core issues are most often at the best of conflict can be caused by disagreement over goals.

Stimac[119] (1982) describes that conflict has multiple sources, may arise in predictable circumstances or unexpected situations. Some sources of conflict are: differing ideas, conflicting perceptions, conflicting values, aggressive behaviour that hurts, and personality clashes. Blackwell Encyclopedic Dictionary[120] (1997) expressed that the sources of conflict are legion; the most explicit attention is often paid to resources, task and power, differences in less visible cultural factors may some time produce the most explosive result. Greenberg and Baron[121] (2000) have divided causes into two major groups, such as, (a) factors relating to organizational structure such as competition over scarce resources, ambiguity over jurisdiction, interdependence, reward system and power differentials between organizational members. (b) Factors relating to interpersonal relations such as grudges, faulty attributions, faulty communications and distrusts.

Nelson and Quick[122] (2003) have stated causes in two parts. The first part is causes of conflict related to the organization's structure include specialization, interdependence, common resources, goal differences, authority relationship, status inconsistencies and jurisdiction ambiguities. The second part of causes of conflict that arise from individual differences include skills and abilities, personalities, perceptions, value and ethics, emotion, communication barrier and cultural differences. Singh[123] (2001) views that interpersonal conflict arises from a variety of source such as organizational change, personality clashes, different set of value, threat to status, contrasting perceptions. Whetten and Cameron[124] (1991) propose four sources of interpersonal conflict; personal differences, information deficiency, role incompatibility and environmental stress.

Likert and Likert[125] (1976) analyzed some general causes of conflict created by the modern society, which are behaviourally oriented. These include unrealized expectations and complexity of social organization systems. The widening gap between 'haves' and 'have-nots' causes considerable conflict between the two because unprivileged believe that they are not given the same opportunities as the privileged. Thus the expectations of the underprivileged are unrealized and this causes frustration and conflict. Cook and Hunsaker[126] (2001) present primary causes of conflict considered into five categories: goal incompatibility, structural design, role expectations, degenerative climate and personal differences. Newstrom and Davis[127] (2001) are of the view that interpersonal conflict arises out of variety of sources such as organizational change, personality clashes, different sets of values, threat to status and contrasting perceptions. De Long and Seemann[128] (2000) identified four sources of conflict such as struggle for control of specific resources, ideological conflict, major integration of different units required and conflict over control of 'knowledge management franchise'.

Nair[129] (1990) studied and identified the four major sources of conflict in the higher education system, such as,

a. Ambiguity in role and responsibility due to the absence of clear organizational objectives.

b. Lack of resources or inadequate resources in relation to competing demands.

c. Limitations associated with the implementation of scalar principle.

d. Leadership style of head of institutions.

3.1.7. Conflict in Management of Libraries

A survey of library literature has revealed that like other organizations, conflict is present in libraries also. Bundy[130] (1966) has published a seminal article. His was the first published effort wherein he analysed the inter-group and interpersonal conflict in libraries. This analysis shows that existing organizational relationship in libraries let 'means' become 'ends'. Strong forces towards conformity hamper desirable growth and change. The restructuring of libraries is proposed along the professional lines, rather than semiprofessional organizations. Principal changes to be made are in existing processing service relationship and administrative professional relationship.

Ranganathan and Bhattacharya[131] (1969), [132](1970), [133] 1969) stated in the articles about the conflict of authorship : Corporate body Vs Corporate body, Person Vs Corporate body and Person Vs Person. Goil[134] (1967) states conflict between objectives and contents: need for enlargement and readjustment of the scheme of papers for Master of Library Science.

Allaway[135] (1998) has stated that a recently appointed

librarian at Holborn Library (London Borough of Camden), in London, describes the unsuccessful strike called by the trade union, Unison, over parallel reviews of staffing structure and library services and fears over the effects of the former on library staff.

Foerstel[136] (1994) noted that contribution to an issue devoted in part to censorship. As homosexual life acquired a higher profile in US society, there will be more books on the subject and increased conflict over library access to such books. Complainants should be encouraged to recommend titles they want to read for purchase by the library rather than insisting on withdrawal of materials, which they do not consider suitable for others to read. This would ensure satisfaction of the broadest range of individual reading needs while assuming and demonstrating a broad tolerance for everyone's reading tastes.

Pettas and Gilliland[137] (1992) have stated that conflicts of various kinds have always existed in academic libraries. They are a normal concomitant of the bureaucratic nature of the organizational structure of libraries and universities. Looks at the views of some of the seminal contributors to the development of conflict theory and then describes the broad range of library conflicts, the value and dangers of these conflicts, and same of the techniques available for lowering or raising the level of conflict.

Hudson[138] (1999) stated that in recent years, staff members in many libraries have struggled to adjust to an accelerating rate of change. Researchers and observers have noted increasing levels of stress and conflict in the workplace, probably related to rapid pace of change. In view of the transformation that is taking place in libraries and library service, it has become essential that library managers assist staff in coping with the resultant stress and conflict. To manage change effectively, it is important to differentiate between 'change' and 'transition', and to be aware of the process staff members are experiencing. Developing an inclusive decision making style, fostering positive employee attitudes towards change, and utilizing effective communication skills can help make change a more positive experience.

Janssen[139] (1999) discusses that in December 1998 the library committee of Hoevelaken Public Library in the Netherlands resigned en masse in protest at the town council's budget cuts to the library service. Mrs De Boer, outgoing chair of the library committee, explains that the recent budget cuts were the latest in a series of cutbacks in the library service. She hopes the committee's resignation will strengthen the position of the incoming library committee. Tonny Van Dinther, Head of Hoevelaken Public Library, explains that lack of communication between the two parties was the major factor.

Rayward[140] (1983) discusses the conflicts in librarianship between practicing librarians and library educators. Maintains that library educators have not succeeded in forming true academies within the universities and until they eschew the limitations of vocational and technical training they will not produce indisputable learned, professional graduates.

Eggleton[141] (1979) describes that the American Management Association reports that the typical manager spends about 20% of his time involved in, or as manager of conflict. Defines 'conflict' and reviewed management literature on the subject. Describes a problem solving model, and reviews library literature on conflict, suggesting implications for libraries.

Lee[142] (1977) reported that for the academic library director there is a multitude of expectations derived from diverse and often conflicting individuals and groups with whom this individual is concerned. Using the framework of role theory, describes and analyses the role of the library director, influencing factors are viewed in terms of the director's perceptions, with particular attention to the presence of conflict and ambiguity. Director's perceptions regarding sources of role, definition, relations with immediate superiors and perceptions of role-related expectations within the academic community are discussed.

3.2. CONFLICT MANAGEMENT

In the views of classical theorists, conflict was regarded as a disease and they were in view that it should be eliminated from the organization. Litterer[143] (1966) is also of the view that conflict in the organization may be problematic, which requires change.

The focus of organization behaviourists has been shifted from elimination to managing conflict. In this process, the researchers presented theories for handling interpersonal conflict.. Follett[144] (1951) found three main methods dealing with conflict – domination, compromise and integration as well as the other secondary ways, such as, avoidance and suppression. Blake and Mouton[145] (1964) were the first to present a grid in classifying techniques of handling interpersonal conflict with five techniques, namely, *forcing, withdrawing, smoothing, compromise, and confrontation*. Thomas[146] (1976) suggested five modes, namely, competing, collaborating, compromising, avoiding and accommodating. Filley[147] (1978) assumes problem-solving method for handling conflict. Rahim[148] (1983) proposed the modes of handling interpersonal conflict – integrating, obliging, dominating, avoiding and compromising. Derr[149] (1978) is of the view that there are three modes of conflict management – collaboration, bargaining and power play from which one can draw to formulate a situational theory. Schmidt and Tannenbaum[150] (1960) suggested four approaches for conflict management – avoidance of difference, confrontation and mediation.

Pareek[151] (1982) found resignation, withdrawal, appeasement, diffusion, confrontation, arbitration, compromise and negotiation modes for dealing with conflict. Likert and Likert[152] (1976) extended the concept of participatory management i.e., System 4 interaction influence network to the area of conflict management. Blake and others[153] (1964) suggested that there are three basic assumption for conflict management (a) conflicts are inevitable and agreement is not possible, (b) conflicts are not inevitable, and yet agreement is impossible and (c) although there may be conflict, agreement is possible.

Mathur and Sayeed[154] (1983) examined the conceptual focus of conflict management literature and supported the assumption that if conflict is managed properly it may be functional and useful to the organization in general and group goals in particular. To manage interpersonal conflicts strategies opted in a given situation and time frame assume great importance and can be linked to three potentially important background factors, such as conflict perception, interaction, orientation and willingness to attempt a strategy. Based on these factors and the variety of strategies, one can opt for any strategy in the interpersonal situation, from the proposed model of conflict management strategies. In view of the model, it is possible to explore proclivity for a given type of strategy while taking into account other personal, organizational and group parameters.

Cosier and Ruble[155] (1981) examined conflict handling behaviour which is based on a two dimensional model that identifies five modes for managing conflict. This study was conducted which illustrated the potential benefits of the methodology. The availability of five choices did result in some behaviours that would have been 'hidden' in two choice experimental games.

Van de Vliert and Kabanoff[156] (1990) used the theory of managerial grid, a model of interrelations among styles of management as the criterion for validating the two best known self-report measurers of conflict management styles. They re-analysed six studies that used those measures and found that both appeared to be moderately valid. However, the measures failed to reflect the underlying theory in a few respects, which suggested specific area for improving them.

Kabanoff[157] (1987) studies sixty three members of an MBA (Master of Business Administration) class who completed the MODE instrument, which measure preference for five conflict modes competing, collaborating, avoiding, compromising, and accommodating. In addition to a member of personality measures, one year later, people were rated on their observed use of these five conflict modes over the year. Little association was found between MODE scores and rated conflict behaviors, but several of the personality measures were correlated with the ratings.

Ohlendorf[158] (2001) argued that Conflict in project management is not necessarily unfavorable when properly managed. Several advantages have been identified such as increasing personal growth and morale, enhancing communication, and producing better project outcomes. However, conflict can be the decline of an organization if it is not effectively managed. The challenge for organizational leaders and project managers is to try to maintain the right balance and intensity of conflict in project management. By utilizing project management principles, understanding the dynamics of conflict, and learning approaches to conflict resolution, managers will be able to establish an environment in which creativity and innovation is encouraged and project goals are accomplished.

Rahim and Magner[159] (1995) confirmatory factor analyses of data (from 5 samples, n = 484 full time employed management students; n = 550 public administrators; n -214 university administrators, n = 250 bank employees in Bangladesh; and n = 578 managers and employee) Rahim organizational inventory – II were performed. The result provided support for the convergent and discriminate validities of subscales measuring the 5 styles of handling interpersonal conflict (integrating, obliging, dominating, avoiding, and compromising) and general support for the invariance of the five factor model across referent roles (i.e., superiors, subordinate, and peers), organizational levels (top, middle, lower and non- management) and 4 of the 5 samples.

Chesler and others[160] (1978) assumed that conflict is related to power and the difference of power between managers and subordinates allow managers to control organization directly and indirectly. In their view training in the procedures required for gaining and using power is an essential pre-requisite for effective conflict management.

Rahim[161] (1979) conducts a laboratory study with organization design for managing the intra-organizational conflict.

Stimac[162] (1982) defines the interpersonal conflict and is of the view that conflict can be resolved if the appropriate strategy is used when the effectual manager or the astute employee locks horn with another individual, an understanding of the complexity of the situation and a knowledge of the strategies available can help effect such resolution while Jones and Melcher[163] (1982) suggested that the personality profile of the individuals play a significant role in the choice of the mode of resolving conflict.

Thomas and others[164] (1978) studied the four articles and found that some of the most striking differences among the articles involved the criteria used to define the effectiveness of different conflict handling modes. They compiled variables, as components of the 'goodness' (*constructiveness, functionality, effectiveness*) or 'badness' of a conflict outcome. It is apparent, for example, that Filley[165] (1978) and Robbins[166] (1978), in their articles, are relatively unconcerned with changes in the power positions of individuals, while Chesler and others[167] (1978) are relatively unconcerned with the quality of decision making in the larger organization.

Phillips and Cheston[168] (1979) suggested popular

strategies for resolving conflict with superiors, peers and subordinates are tough guy approach and problem solver approach. The tough guy is assertive, decisive, and skilled at using power to force others to accept his solution. The problem solver is objective, egalitarian, and skilled at creating a climate in which parties to the conflict can arrive jointly at a solution. These approaches were most frequently used; the managers also used compromise and avoidance. They also suggested that organizations which used a single method of conflict resolution should probably re-assess their practices.

Ferraro and Adams[169] (1984) are of the view that conflict management is complex and some time hard too achieve, a greater understanding of the behavioural skills associated with it can have a bottom line impact on organizational productivity and performance. This fact leads to three important implications for management, such as,

a. There is no one best conflict resolution technique that mangers can use in every situation.

b. Managers should understand that some conflict that affects organizational performance needs their immediate intervention to resolve potentially dangerous issues.

c. Managers should recognize that organizational development (OD) programmes can train and educate both managers and subordinate in using such fruitful resolution techniques are collaboration, and these can lead to a more cooperative productive atmosphere over the long run.

Thomas and Schmidt[170] (1976) conducted a survey, which was sponsored by American Management Association. The study sought to (a) determine the general importance of conflict management as perceived by the mangers, (b) categorize their interest in conflict, and (c) identify special interests at different levels of managers. The result clearly suggests that managers from middle to top levels have lively and growing interest in learning more about the prevention and management of conflict.

Mishra and Dhar[171] (2002) viewed that conflict is a double edged, dealing effectively with conflict required understanding, introspection, reaching out to others and effective management of feelings. They further viewed for positive management of conflict.

Varma[172] (2000) describes interpersonal conflict and its importance. He argued that for managing conflict at work, managers should understand the attitudinal approach that not all persons are difficult; many are persons with difficulty. This realization, in itself, can go a long way to orient you in a right manner, and influence the others into moving ultimately to a collaborative attitude towards you. If you can cushion all this with a sense of humor, conflicts do gets diffused.

Lawrence and Lorsch[173] (1967) study the six plastic firms and examined the effectiveness of various styles for handling conflicts and found that each of these techniques was used in organizations to handle conflict. The distinction was that the high performing organization used confrontation techniques for more frequently than did lower performing organizations. Organizations with average performance used more smoothing techniques than did either high or low performer. They could not find any clear pattern with the use of forcing.

Kathman and Kathman[174] (1990) viewed that conflict clearly arises in libraries as well as other organizations. This paper explores conflict management and its application for the academic library. Five responses to conflict–using are the power of one's position, avoiding, accommodating, compromising and collaborating or problem solving.

Fisher and Koue[175] (1991) argue that the key to a low conflict environment is good communications. If members of an organization communicate well, there will be an atmosphere of trust and understanding. In dealing with conflict they suggested avoiding, accommodating, and forcing methods should be avoided, if possible. The compromising and collaborating methods involve more work, but they will give long lasting result. A third party should preferably be involved whenever possible.

Kathman and Kathman[176] (1993) suggested that there are two steps in conflict management. The first step in managing conflict is to recognize that conflict can have destructive and constructive consequences. The second step is to understand the sources of conflict. They further suggested that dealing with conflict in to utilize the power of one's position, avoiding, accommodating, compromising and the preferred approach-problem solving.

Singh and Sengupta[177] (1998) suggested that there is a need to resolve conflict in a constructive way in order to increase group cohesiveness and embeddedness. The finding further suggests that the respondents seem to believe strongly in teamwork and developing the work force in order to managing conflict and enhance productivity.

Greenberg and Baron[178] (2000) favour the managing conflict by minimizing its harmful effects and not eliminating entirely. They suggest bargaining or negotiation is the most common procedure for resolving organizational conflict. Third party intervention such as mediation and arbitration can also prove helpful in resolving conflict.

Hellriegel and others[179] (2000) suggest five interpersonal conflict handling styles avoiding, forcing, accommodating, collaboration and compromising. An individual may have a natural preference for one or two of these styles but is likely to use all of them over time when dealing with various interpersonal situations. They also argue that negotiation is important process in conflict management.

Nelson and Quick[180] (2002) viewed that there are five styles of managing conflict, avoiding, accommodating competing, compromising and confronting.

Kreitner and Kinicki[181] (2000) are in favour of stimulating functional conflict and suggest alternative styles handling dysfunctional conflict, as based on Rahim[182] (1983) model, which includes integrating (problem solving), obliging (smoothing), dominating (forcing), avoiding and compromising.

Cook and Hunsaker[183] (2001) suggested five conflict management styles orientation competing, accommodating, avoiding, collaborating and compromising. They also favour negotiation or bargaining for managing conflict.

Newstrom and Davis[184] (2000) identified at least four clearly different strategies: avoiding, smoothing, forcing, confronting (and a combination, called compromising)

Kilmann and Thomas[185] (1977) describe the rationale and development of a new measure of five interpersonal handling modes (competing, collaborating, compromising, avoiding and accommodating) which attempts to control for the social desirability response bias. The instrument is entitled: Management of Difference Exercise, or MODE instrument. The result of this study indicate that the new instrument significantly reduces the social desirability bias for over all population in comparison to three other conflict behaviour instruments, although all four instruments may still be susceptible to some individual tendencies in this response bias. This study also investigated other aspects of sustentative validity and structural validity. Lastly, this paper presented emerging evidence on external validity. This, while encouraging, suggests the need for continuing research effort to investigate this aspect of validity for the new MODE instrument.

Rahim[186] (1985) argues that management of organizational conflict involves diagnosis of and intervention in conflict at intrapersonal, interpersonal and intergroup levels. A diagnosis should indicate whether there is need for intervention and the type of intervention needed. In general, an intervention is designed to attain and maintain a moderate amount of conflict a various levels and to enable the organization members to learn the styles of handling interpersonal conflict so that the individual, group and over all effectiveness is enhanced.

Meyer and others[187] (1997) conducted study to identify dimensions of outcome criteria commonly used in the evaluation of managerial intervention in conflicts among subordinates. Undergraduate students in organizational psychology rated the likelihood that each of 24 outcomes would result from the use of 6 intervention strategies. A principal components analysis revealed 3 bipolar factors: system versus individual goal attainment, subordinate satisfaction versus efficiency, and smoothing versus permanence. The various strategies were perceived to be differentially effective in attaining the outcome categories. Implications of the findings for the development of a normative model of conflict management are discussed.

Two studies were conducted to investigate whether individuals use the two dimensions in understanding another's conflict-handling behaviour. In Study-I, 150 subjects were engaged in negotiation task. Each subject rated another's use of five conflict-handling modes and described the person on a semantic differential. A factor analysis of the semantic differential yielded an evaluative factor and a dynamism factor. Next, ratings of the other's conflict-handling modes were collapsed into indices of cooperation and assertiveness. The index of cooperation was correlated with the evaluative factor but not with the dynamism factor. In contrast, the index of assertiveness was correlated with the dynamism factor but not the evaluative factor. In Study-II, 65 subjects completed semantic differentials in response to hypothetical conflict-handling behavior of another. A factor analysis again identified evaluative and dynamism factors. The mean ratings of the evaluative and dynamism factors for the five conflict-handling modes were consistent with the expectations based on the two-dimensional model. Thus, these studies, using different designs, yielded rather consistent results supporting the two dimensional model.

Sessa[188] (1996) conducted a study on antecedents and consequences of conflict in teams. It looks at the influence of perspective taking on types of conflict and the influence of conflict on affect. Teams using perspective taking were hypothesized to perceive conflict as task oriented, as opposed to people oriented. Although both types of conflict were hypothesized to lead arousal within the team, people-oriented conflict is expected to lead to a more negative team tone. To test hypotheses on perspective taking, 15 medical teams participated in a perspective-taking training program, while 15 teams served as a control group. Perspective taking was also measured using self-report scales. Conflict and affect were measured using observation and self-report. Although the training program Fwd no impact on perceived conflict, teams with higher perspective taking (using self-report measures) were likely to perceive conflict as task oriented and less likely to perceive it as people oriented. Hypotheses on the impact of conflict on affect were supported. This study suggests that conflict and negative affect do not necessarily go hand in hand, and that perspective taking is one mechanism, which the teams can use to manage conflict.

Renwick[189] (1977) examined the impact of an employee's sex on the management of superior-subordinate conflict and how behavior during such interaction af-fected perceptions of the constructive use of disagreement and performance on the job. Male (n = 55) and female (n = 40) management personnel described how they dealt with differences and disagreements involving their immediate supervisor and how he/she responded to such conflict. Significant differences emerged between the perceptions of males and females reporting to males concerning the behavior of their supervisors. Preliminary analyses suggested that the sex of a supervisor was unrelated to female subordinates' perceptions of conflict management. No differences were observed between the likelihood with which male and females subordinates would use various methods to deal with disagreement. The manner in which the subordinate dealt with conflict was significantly related to perceptions of the constructive use of disagreement in the female sample but not in the male sample. None of the five methods of managing conflict examined in the study were related to supervisor evaluations of either the subordinate's performance or effort on the job.

Howat and London[190] (1980) examined the extent to which measures of conflict management and interpersonal relations are attributed to individuals who perceive conflict. Data were collected from one supervisor and one subordinate in 113 park and recreation agencies. The results support the conclusion that perceived conflict frequency is associated 'with attributions of conflict. Supervisors and sub-ordinates who perceived higher conflict frequency tended to be seen by each other as using force, a strategy indicative of conflict intention. Super-visors who perceived higher "conflict frequency" were viewed by their sub-ordinates as likely to withdraw from conflict, whereas subordinates who perceived higher conflict frequency were viewed by their supervisors as likely to avoid confrontation and compromise. Perceptions of conflict frequency were negatively correlated with ratings of the favorability of interpersonal relations. The need for further investigations of the relationships between the occurrence of conflict and conflict attributions is discussed.

Bhowon[191] (1998) examined the relationship of targets (superiors/ subordinates) perceived bases of power and respondents' interpersonal conflict handling strategies. Data were gathered from 225 middle and lower level managers through a questionnaire. Factor analysis constrained to five styles of which integrating and 'dominating' were the most and least preferred less for handling conflict with both superiors and subordinates. Information, connection and personal bases of power (expert and referent) predicted the use of 'integrating' and 'obliging' with subordinates, whereas organizational reward, coercion, and legitimate connection, and personal power contributed to 'avoiding', 'integrating' and 'obliging' styles with superiors.

Hartwick and Barki[192] (1999) argued that conflict and conflict resolution are important to an understanding of the information system development (ISD) process. The present paper explores conflict management behaviors and relates their use to the satisfactory resolution of conflicts in ISD. Project-level scores representing users' and analysts' typical modes of behavior were developed for 116 ISD projects. Analysis of these behaviors indicated remarkable similarities in user and analyst actions. Both engaged in high levels of integrative problem-solving behaviors and low levels of avoiding behaviors, with levels of compromising, asserting and avoiding actions in between. Users and analysts also had similar reactions to the use of these different styles. Problem-solving was found to be the most effective behavioral style for engendering satisfaction, both for oneself and for the other party in a conflict situation. Avoiding and asserting were each found to be dysfunctional.

Volkema and Bergmann[193] (1995) examined the relationships between the assertiveness and cooperativeness dimensions of conflict styles, as determined by the Thomas-Kilmann Conflict MODE In-strument, and the specific behaviors, as identified through a situational conflict questionnaire, used by American Business School students in a recent interpersonal conflict. The results suggest that preferences for assertiveness are reflected in both strategic and tactical use of behaviors, whereas cooperativeness is associated with last -choice behaviors-.

Sayeed[194] (1990) explores meaning and construct identity of the Conflict Management Strategies as viewed by the managers In a superior-sub-ordinate context covering a wide variety of conflict situations or topics besides identifying Indian manager's preferences of various strategies. Attempt has also been made to cross validate the main 'study consisting of eleven sub-samples against study the sample of which was drawn from a group of managers representing a wide array of organizational setups.

Samantra[195] (2003) attempted to explore certain basic issues relating to superior-subordinate conflict and its management in the organisational setting. Statistical analysis of 'perceptual' data obtained from 72 managers of an aluminum-manufacturing organisation operating in the public sector, indicated that matters relating to the technical and operative aspects of the job emerged as important issues of superior-subordinate conflict whereas individual differences between managers were viewed as the significant sources of such conflict. In general, it was observed that managers' conflict resolution behaviour was characterized by an immense utilization of problem-solving, smoothing and compromising modes together with the relative absence of withdrawing and forcing behaviours. It is noteworthy, however, that there. Were some significant differences between the superiors and their subordinates with respect to their utilization of various conflict management strategies.

Bhowon[196] (1999) aimed at identifying the styles of handling interpersonal conflict and the impact of perceived organizational climate on the respondents' use of these styles with their superiors and subordinates. Altogether 225 male executives representing six manufacturing concerns participated in the study. Factor analysis results of the conflict handling styles scale constrained to five factors namely, integrating, avoiding, compromising, obliging, and dominating. Integrating and dominating, were the most and least preferred styles for handling conflict with both targets. Power and independence oriented climates predicted the use of avoiding and integrating, style in both contexts whereas achievement and independence climates determined the use of integrating, avoiding, and dominating styles only with superiors.

Morris and others[197] (1998) have observed that a problem

in joint ventures be-tween U.S. and Asian firms is that cultural differences impede the smooth resolution of conflicts between managers. In a survey of young managers in the U.S., China, Philippines, and India we find support for two hypotheses about cultural differences in con-flict style and the cultural values that account for these differences: Chinese, managers rely more on an avoiding style because of their relatively high value on conformity and tradition. U.S. managers rely more on a competing style because of their relatively high value on individual achievement.

Parthasarathy and Singh[198] (1984) concluded that managers value the style of collaboration very high while dealing with the colleagues of their own department. In managing conflict with other organizational groups – superiors, subordinates, colleague of other departments and the union leaders – they however, prefer to follow the strategies of avoidance and compromise.

Renwick[199] (1975) concluded a field survey of employee responses to a variety of topics and sources of inter-personal conflict was conducted in two manufacturing firms. Observations of sig-nificant Topic X Method and Source X Method interactions indicated that conflict management was to some extent dependent upon the specific nature of the disagreement. Correlational evidence suggested that behavioral predispositions also played a major role in shaping reactions to conflict. Results were interpreted and discussed in terms of response hierarchies and within the context of organiza-tional climate.

Bhatta[200] (1988) identified the problem of conflict and suggested some of the prescription in order to prevent conflict. All these tools could be applied by every management. Considering the time, place and situation and nature of problem a given tool could be applied. How to use these tools, when and to who should be concerned of middle and top level management?

Chan[201] (1989) studies conflict and conflict management styles between R&D project managers and technical staff, competing and avoiding styles resulted in more frequent conflict and lower performance whereas the collaboration style resulted in less frequent conflict and better performance.

Barker and others[202] (1988) studied the project managers and found that managers, who used a combination of competing and avoiding styles, were seen as ineffective by the engineers who worked on their project teams.

Kozan[203] (1989) argues that cultural differences also influence use of different styles of conflict management. This study compared Turkish and Jordanian managers with United State managers. All three groups preferred the collaborating style. Turkish manager also reported frequent use of competing style, whereas Jordanian and U.S. managers reported that it was one of their least used styles.

Chanin and Schneer[204] (1984) investigated potential predispositions to interpersonal handling behaviour. The design of the study represents advancement over previous research as both males and females were studied in a control context of conflict introduced via a business simulation game. Jungian personality dimensions and conflict handling modes were assessed a significant relationship was found between subject decision making preference (thinking –feeling) and their choice of conflict handling behaviour. Some sex differences in the conflict handling behaviour were also found. The finding of this study has implications for conflict management, personnel section, and placement of individuals in organization.

Mills and others[205] (1985) studied 199 project management personnel took the Myers-Briggs Type indicator and the Thomas – Kilmann conflict mode instrument. Result supported the earlier research of Thomas and Kilmann[206] (1975) with two extension. Extraversion of the sample was not associated with cooperation, and it correlated with both the distributive and integrative dimensions of conflict handling.

Burke[207] (1969) attempted to analyse conflict management method in superior and subordinate context and found that the superiors not only perceived confrontation to be the most effective strategy, but also described it as the most frequently used method for dealing with superior and subordinate conflict. In this study the manager were asked to think of a time when they felt especially good or bad about the way an interpersonal conflict in which they were also involved was resolved. The description of the conflicts as provided by them was separated in terms of effective resolution (felt especially good) and ineffective resolution (felt especially bad).

London and Howat[208] (1978) studied the relationship between three measures of employee commitment (commitment to the organization, profession and community) and the use of five strategies of conflict management in the context of interpersonal conflict between the supervisors and subordinates. The study revealed that 'confronting was positively related to subordinates organizational commitment while supervisors, professional and organizational commitment were negatively related to their use of forcing. Commitment to the community was negatively related to the withdrawing for the total sample.

Renwick[209] (1975a) using the same methods of resolving conflicts, as were identified by Blake and Mouton[210] (1964), found that the superiors relied more on confrontation were more likely to use 'compromise', 'confrontation', and forcing in that order. In this study, respondent dyad of superiors and subordinates were asked to indicate how likely it is that they will use various ways of dealing with differences and disagreement between them.

Burke[211] (1970) investigated five methods of resolving conflict in the context of superior and subordinate in two major areas, one is making constructive use of differences and disagreement, and second is planning job target and evaluating accomplishments. It was found that 'withdrawal', 'forcing' and 'compromise' were consistently negatively related while 'confrontation' was positively related to these two areas. The use of 'smoothing' was however, inconsistently related to these areas.

Rahim and Buntzman[212] (1988) inferred that supervisors showed that a reward power base was positively correlated with integrating and avoiding style of handling conflict with subordinates, legitimate power was positively correlated with dominating style; expert power was positively correlated with integrating and dominating styles but negatively correlated with avoiding styles and referent power was positively correlated with integrating, obliging and compromising styles but negatively correlated with dominating style. Legitimate power was positively correlated with satisfaction with supervision. Integrating style was positively correlated with attitudinal and behavioural compliance satisfaction with supervision; obliging style was positively correlated with attitudinal compliance; and compromising style was inversely related to behavioural compliance.

Mishra and others[213] (1999) argued that in today's dynamic and competitive world of business, quality and effectiveness of decision making is of utmost importance for an organization. But diversity in attitudes and approach of individuals towards problem solving gives rise to conflicts among employees in an organization though several efforts have been made to explore the conflict management strategies applied by working executives, these attempts have thrown up diverse results, their further increasing the complexities of conceptualization of strategies to handle conflict. As present environment is very demanding in terms of improved skills both an technical and interpersonal fronts, individuals too are expected to change according to the environment. In addition to this cultural and societal differences among individuals too impact the strategies applied to handle conflict. In this light the author has attempted to explore the conflict management strategies applied by executives working in different organizations in India and argues for a cultural specific scale to measure conflict handling strategies.

Mathur and Sayeed[214] (1980) hypothesized that the managers prefer to opt the same strategy in resolving the conflict as that of his immediate superior in the context of job related matters. Another factor, which was investigated was to determine whether the manager or his immediate superior has adopted any variation in conflict management strategies. For this purpose 86 executives were taken as a respondent to test the hypothesis. The study revealed that there was a moderate degree of dissimilarity between the manager's own practices and his perception about his immediate superior regarding application of conflict management strategies. It was also found that there was a variation in applying the strategies to resolve the conflict in case of both the manager and his immediate superior.

Sayeed[215] (1990) attempted to examine conflict handling strategies, leadership behaviour and leadership styles (relationship and task motivated styles) in a common formulation. It was found that conflict management strategies represented two conflict management styles, viz., reciprocal problem solving style and authoritative system supported style, which tend to be related selectively with five leadership dimensions. Reciprocal problem solving style significantly related with participative, nurturant and task oriented leadership behaviour, while authoritative conflict management style had significantly relationships with authoritarian and bureaucratic leadership behaviour. The low esteem of co-worker (task motivated leadership style) had a strong relationship with the application of force as a conflict management strategy, besides revealing some moderating influences of esteem for co-worker between leadership behaviour and conflict management strategies.

Sharma and Samantra[216] (1994) analysed relative efficacy of conflict management styles in terms of their impact on various dimensions of organizational effectiveness: (a) productivity, (b) adaptability and (c) flexibility. The result revealed that confrontation or problem solving was most significantly associated with organizational effectiveness, followed by smoothing. The compromising and withdrawing styles were also positively related to effectiveness, but their effects seem to be relatively insignificant. It was also noted that forcing style emerged as ineffective.

Sharma and Samantra[217] (1995) analysed and provided several valuable insights into the dynamics of conflict (superior –subordinate) management in the industrial settings. The conflict management techniques of the mangers are characterized by a predominant use of smoothing, accommodating, confrontation and compromising modes together with occasional or infrequent use of forcing or withdrawing. Thus, the managers tend to emphasize upon harmonious and compatible relations with their subordinates through which workable solutions to conflicts might be developed and implemented in the organizational setting.

Samantra[218] (1999) in the first phase investigated in an aluminum-manufacturing organization operating in the public sector to a certain basic issues as well as underlying sources of superior-subordinate conflicts, managers utilization of various conflict management strategies. In the second phase of the study, he examined the conflict management behaviours of the two steel manufacturing organizations operating within the public sector, and found that:

a. Work standards to be accomplished by employees, amount of time spent by them on the job, planning of work activities, supervision, direction and control, utilization of equipment and facilities etc., emerged as major issues of conflicts arising between superiors and their subordinates at the work situation.

b. It was observed that differences in knowledge or expertise, differences in basic values, belief or opinions, and personality differences are cited as the significant causes of conflict.

c. The conflict resolution behaviours of managers within various industries is characterized by an immense utilization of problem solving, compromising and smoothing together with the relative absence of withdrawing and forcing behaviour.

d. The managers belonging to each of the hierarchical levels made a considerable greater use of problem solving, compromising and smoothing than the forcing and withdrawing modes.

e. The flexibility aspect of effectiveness emerged as the most significant one in each organization and it was followed by productivity and adaptability.

Weider-Hatfield and Hatfield[219] (1996) investigated the relationship between management strategies and subordinate outcome and reports the results of a study investigating between a manager's use of collaborating, forcing and accommodating and four types of reward (system, job, performance, and interpersonal) subordinate might experience at work. The result shows significant positive relationship between, or manager's collaborating strategies and subordinate's experiencing interpersonal area performance rewards and significant negative relationship between manager's forcing strategies and those with the same outcomes. No relationship was found between a manger's accommodating strategies and subordinates perceived rewards or between any of the strategies and system rewards.

Wall Jr. and Callister[220] (1995) in their study found that differences in approaches of the conflict management exist, such as,

a. Males tend to use the forcing approach as their dominate style; female use forcing less and often rely on range of other tactics.

b. Managers tend to use the forcing approach; their employees prefer avoiding, smoothing or compromising.

c. American managers tend to be competitive, Japanese mangers to use cooperative approach.

Singh and Parthasarthy[221] (1985) have studied systematically and comprehensively the managerial strategy of conflict resolutions. It examines the factors that affect the choice of conflict management strategies and also aim at identifying the most prevalent and practiced styles while dealing with superiors, subordinates, colleagues and union leaders. The findings of this study are :

a. The strategies of conflict management do not significantly vary while dealing with superiors, subordinates, colleagues and union leaders.

b. The choice of conflict management strategy across the managerial hierarchy, line and staff functions, and the corporate ownership present a scenario of significant similarity.

c. There is an absence of distinctive and dominant conflict management style, since no single style has been preferred by more than 55 percent of the respondents in any group. Such a finding demonstrates the prevalence of managerial stylelessness for managing conflicts.

d. The strategies of avoidance and compromising have been found to be the most operative strategies in more or less all the groups and categories of management.

e. The lower management group adopts preponderantly the strategies of collaboration in dealing with supervisors. However, while dealing with others this group also dominantly operates on the strategy of avoidance and compromise.

f. Managers value the style of collaboration very highly while dealing with the colleagues of their own department. In managing conflict with other organizational groups –

superiors-subordinates, colleagues of other departments and the union leaders- they however, prefer to follow the strategies of avoidance and compromise.

g. The strategies of competing and accommodation have emerged as the medium preferred strategies.

h. Adoption of target substitution, third party intervention and clique formation are found to be the least operative strategies.

Das[222] (1987) analysed the ways and styles of bank manager's adopt in managing interpersonal conflict, especially in relation to their superiors and subordinates. The author tries to examine: (a) the dominant conflict management styles used by branch managers vis-à-vis their superiors and subordinates; (b) whether the branch managers use different styles of managing conflict with superiors than with their subordinate; and (c) whether the managers who have been evaluated as efficient following one criterion use different styles of managing conflict than the manager who have been evaluated as efficient due to a different criterion. In this study he used five subscales: Integrating, obliging, dominating, avoiding, and compromising. He used Rahim's Organizational Conflict Inventory (ROCI) Rahim[223] (1983) for measuring styles of interpersonal conflict. He concluded that the managers use different styles to manage interpersonal conflict while dealing with their subordinates, almost pointing towards a set pattern. While dealing with their superiors, they follow no such patterns.

3.3. CONCLUSION

Literature on conflict, its stages, approaches and styles of conflict management has been reviewed in the preceding paragraphs. Based on the analysis of the available literature, certain inferences have been drawn. These are being given in brief, as follows.

The conflict problem has been studied over the years by

sociologists, anthropologists, economists, political scientists, and psychologists

In the early twentieth century, Freud underscored the pernicious effects of emotional conflicts on behaviour and personality, and his principle that conflicts, especially at the unconscious level, are the well spring of neurosis, had been widely accepted. Pavlov supported experimentally to Freud finding that dogs who were required to learn difficult discriminations often developed an "experimental neurosis" marked by persisting abnormal behaviour. Rapoport views that "conflict...is a theme that has occupied the thinking of man more than any other, save only God and love."

Conflict is a central issue and its research has implications for understanding society and organizations. The study of conflict in organizations has evolved significantly over recent decades. Much research in 1960s onwards focus on growing functional specialization in organizations and conflict inherent in the performance of organizational task carried out by diverse sub units.

Conflict is in natural existence in any multiparty heterogeneous system. It is an inherent social condition derived from the fact that persons, parties and collectivities differ from one another on a variety of value, goals and material resources, in addition they are interdependent and must interact with regard to these differences.

Conflict is endemic, inevitable, and necessary to organizational life and always involves some testing of power situation.

Conflict is opposition process in any of several forms competition, status, rivalry, bargaining, sabotage, verbal abuse, etc.

Conflict can be a disagreement, the pressure of tension, or some other difficulty within or between two or more parties. Conflict can be public or private, formal or informal, or be approached - rationally or irrationally.

There are three types of conflict among the sub units of formal organizations, namely, **bargaining conflict** among the parties to an interest group relationship; **bureaucratic conflict** between the parties to a superior-subordinate relationship; and **system conflict** among the parties to a lateral or working relationship. In each of these three cases, conflict is treated as a series of episodes, each episode including stage of latency, feeling, perceptions, manifestation and aftermath.

Research on conflict in organizations has been portrayed as analogous to a schizophrenic having several personalities, each one largely unaware of the existence of the others. At least 3 levels of analysis exist in conflict research, namely, (i) macro (institutions), (ii) intermediate (relationships), and (iii) individual (dispute episodes). Unfortunately, field of study and individual research efforts have tended to be trapped within a single level. Different researchers are operating with quite distinct assumptions about the nature of the institutional level. The benefits of integrating the various views of conflict in organizations would include: (a) development of a formal means of evaluating the generalization of any conflict model or study, (b) the enhancement of the relevance of conflict research to practicing managers and policy-makers, and (c) the acquisition of important knowledge, even if efforts to develop an integrated model fail.

Healthy organization seek to increase intra organizational conflict. The classical organization theorists did not see to appreciate different impact that conflict can have in organization. Now, the consensus emerged among the organization theorists, is that a moderate amount of conflict is necessary for attaining an optimum organizational effectiveness.

Conflict may be said to exist when there are real or perceived differences that arise in specific organizational circumstances and that engender emotion as a consequence.

In the early strands of organization theory, the management of conflict - whether by force or consensus - is central to the smooth, integrated functioning of organizations. While there are strong pulls toward the integration of these strands, a contrasting perspective highlights the disintegrative tendencies of conflict in organizations based on differences in occupations, gender, ethnicity, and culture. By taking a disputing perspective, it is possible to uncover the other faces of conflict processes in organizations. A disputing perspective bridges public and private domains, it provides a basis for examining the links between bipolar opposites or the different faces of conflict in organizations. Unlike the public arena, private disputes occur as covert or hidden conflict, often fused with other activities.

Three major sources of interdepartmental conflict occur as a by product when the organization tries to meet its own particular corporate challenges. These three sources are: *communication differences, structural difference* and *personal differences*

Blackwell Encyclopedic Dictionary explains that the sources of conflict are legion; the most explicit attention is often paid to resources, task and power, differences in less visible cultural factors may some time produce the most explosive result.

Some general causes of conflict created by the modern society which are behaviourally oriented. These include unrealized expectations and complexity of social organization systems. The widening gap between **'hayes'** and **'have-nots'** causes considerable conflict between the two because unprivileged believe that they are not given the same opportunities as the privileged. Thus the expectations of the underprivileged are unrealized and this causes frustration and conflict.

Primary causes of conflict have been considered into five categories, such as, (a) goal incompatibility, (b) structural design,

(c) role expectations, (d) degenerative climate, and (e) personal differences. Newstrom and Davis are of the view that interpersonal conflict arises variety of sources such as organizational change, personality clashes, different sets of values, threat to status and contrasting perceptions. De Long and Seemann identified four sources of conflict, such as, struggle for control of specific resources, ideological conflict, major integration of different units required, and conflict over control of 'knowledge management franchise'.

Four sources of conflict such as struggle for control of specific resources, ideological conflict, major integration of different units required and conflict over control of 'knowledge management franchise'.

In the existing organizational relationship in libraries, let '**means**' become '**ends**'. Strong forces towards conformity hamper desirable growth and change. A restructuring of libraries is proposed along the professional lines, rather than semiprofessional organizations. Principal changes to be made, are in existing processing service relationship and administrative professional relationship.

Staff members in libraries have struggled hard for adjusting to an accelerating rate of changes. In view of the transformation that is taking place in libraries and library services, it has become essential that library managers assist library staff in coping with the resultant stress and conflict. Developing an inclusive decision making style, fostering positive employee attitudes towards change, and utilizing effective communication skills can make change a more positive experioncc.

The conflicts in librarianship between practicing librarians and library educators. Maintains that library educators have not succeeded in forming true academies within the universities and until they eschew the limitations of vocational and technical training they will not produce indisputable learned, professional graduates.

Blake and Mouton were the first to present a grid in classifying techniques of handling interpersonal conflict with five techniques – forcing, withdrawing, smoothing, compromise and confrontation.

If conflict is managed properly it may be functional and useful to the organization in general and group goals in particular. To manage interpersonal conflicts strategies opted in a given situation and time frame assume great importance and can be linked to three potentially important background factors, such as conflict perception, interaction, orientation and willingness to attempt a strategy. Based on these factors and the variety of strategies, one can opt for any strategy in the interpersonal situation, from the proposed model of conflict management strategies. In view of the model, it is possible to explore proclivity for a given type of strategy while taking into account other personal, organizational and group parameters.

Popular strategies for resolving conflict with superiors, peers and subordinates are tough guy approach and problem solver approach. The tough guy is assertive, decisive, and skilled at using power to force others to accept his solution. The problem solver is objective, egalitarian, and skilled at creating a climate in which parties to the conflict can arrive jointly at a solution. These approaches were most frequently used; the managers also used compromise and avoidance. It has been suggested that organizations, which used a single method of conflict resolution, should probably re-assess their practices.

Conflict management is complex and some time hard too achieve, a greater understanding of the behavioural skills associated with it can have a bottom line impact on organizational productivity and performance. This fact leads to three important implications for management, such as,

a. There is no one best conflict resolution technique that mangers can use in every situation.

b. Managers should understand that some conflict that

affects organizational performance needs their immediate intervention to resolve potentially dangerous issues.

c. Managers should recognize that Organizational Development (OD) programmes can train and educate both managers and subordinate in using such fruitful resolution techniques are collaboration, and these can lead to a more cooperative productive atmosphere over the long run.

The key to a low conflict environment is good communication. If members of an organization communicate well, there will be an atmosphere of trust and understanding. In dealing with conflict, avoiding, accommodating, and forcing methods should be avoided, if possible. The compromising and collaborating methods involve more work, but they will give long lasting result. A third party should preferably be involved whenever possible.

The rationale and development of a new measure of five interpersonal handling modes (competing, collaborating, compromising, avoiding and accommodating), which attempts to control for the social desirability response bias. The instrument is entitled: Management of Difference Exercise, or MODE instrument. The result of this study indicate that the new instrument significantly reduce the social desirability bias for over all population in comparison to three other conflict behaviour instruments, although all four instruments may still be susceptible to some individual tendencies in this response bias. This study also investigated other aspects of sustentative validity and structural validity. Lastly, this paper presented emerging evidence on external validity. This, while encouraging, suggests the need for continuing research effort to investigate this aspect of validity for the new MODE instrument.

Management of organizational conflict involves diagnosis of and intervention in conflict at intrapersonal, interpersonal and intergroup levels. A diagnosis should indicate whether there is need for intervention and the type of intervention needed. In general, an intervention is designed to attain and maintain a moderate amount of conflict a various levels and to enable the organization members to learn the styles of handling interpersonal conflict so that the individual, group and over all effectiveness is enhanced.

The extent to which the measures of conflict management and interpersonal relations are attributed to individuals who perceive conflict. Data were collected from one supervisor and one subordinate in 113 park and recreation agencies. The results support the conclusion that perceived conflict frequency is associated 'with attributions of conflict. Supervisors and sub-ordinates who perceived higher conflict frequency tended to be seen by each other as using force, a strategy indicative of conflict intention. Super-visors who perceived higher "conflict frequency were viewed by their sub-ordinates as likely to withdraw from conflict, whereas subordinates who perceived higher conflict frequency were viewed by their supervisors as likely to avoid confrontation and compromise. Perceptions of conflict frequency were negatively correlated with ratings of the favourability of interpersonal relations. The need for further investigations of the relationships between the occurrence of conflict and conflict attributions is discussed.

The relationship of targets (superior/subordinates) perceived bases of power and respondents' interpersonal conflict handling strategies. Data were gathered from 225 middle and lower level managers through a questionnaire. Factor analysis constrained to five styles of which integrating and 'dominating' were the most and least preferred 'les for handling conflict with both superiors and subordinates. Information, connection and personal bases of power (expert and referent) predicted the use of 'integrating' and 'obliging' with subordinates, whereas organizational (reward, coercion, and legitimate), connection, and personal power contributed to 'avoiding', 'integrating' and 'obliging' styles with superiors.

In today's dynamic and competitive world of business, quality and effectiveness of decision making is of utmost importance for an organization. As present environment is very demanding in terms of improved skills both an technical and interpersonal fronts, individuals too are expected to change according to the environment. In addition to this cultural and societal differences among individuals too impact the strategies applied to handle conflict. To maintain the objectivity of a scientific study, the study may preferably be got done by an outside expert, similar to a 'Chartered Librarian'[224] or a 'Library Professional Management Consultant'[225]

Before concluding the topic 'conflict', reference may be made to the study conducted by Pairot Chalaragase[226] on the topic "Co-operation and Conflict among the Library Professionals in the University Libraries in Thailand". Pairot starts with the belief that 'if the worker is satisfied, he cooperates; and if the worker is dissatisfied, he enters into conflict'. Furthermore, while evaluating the Maslow's theory of 'Hierarchy of Needs' and his views on 'Need of Self Actualization', Pairot and his Research Guide Dr. S.R.Gupta, evolved the theory of '**Needlessness**" near to concept of '**Nirvana**' in Buddhist philosophy. The similarity observed is simple to understand, such as, '*the need, the satisfaction*, and *the Nirvana* are the occurrences in the state of mind of the human beings.

Abbas[227] (2008) concluded that there is a homogeneity in the methods of managing conflict with superiors, peers and subordinates in the behaviour of library professionals of DULS and JNUL. They prefer integerating method. In ZHL, obliging is preferred, while dealing with superiors, and integerating is being utilized with peers and subordinates.

The literature available has been reviewed in brief in the preceding paragraphs. Many studies of the conflict management were conducted in American industrial settings. Some such studies have also been conducted, almost on similar pattern, in India. Though there has been a felt need to examine styles of conflict resolution in university libraries, research institutions and their library systems, especially in India, hardly any in-depth study could be made available.

REFERENCES

1. SILLS (David L), *Ed.* International encyclopedia of social sciences. V 3. 1968. Macmillan & Free Press; New York. p 220.
2. MAYO (Elton). Social problems of an industrial civilization. 1945. Harvard Graduate School of Business Administration; Boston.
3. WARNER (W Lloyd) and LOW (J O). Social system of modern factory. 1947. Yale University Press; New Haven.
4. PARSONS (Talcot). Social system. 1951. Free Press; New York.
5. BEALS (Alan R) and SIEGEL (Bernard J). Divisiveness and social conflict : An anthropological approach. 1966. Stanford University Press; Standford.
6. WEBER (Max). Max Weber on the methodology of social sciences, *tr* and *ed* by Edward A. Shils and H.A. Finch. 1949. Free Press; New York. p 16.
7. SIMMEL (George). Conflict & the web of group affiliations. 1955. Free Press; New York. p 17.
8. COOLEY (Chares H). Social Process. 1918. Scribner's Son; New York. p 39.
9. ROSS (Edward A). Principles of sociology. 1920. University of Chicago Press; Chicago. p 199.
10. COOLEY (Chares H). Social Process. p 39.
11. PARK (Robert E). Social foundation of war. *American Journal of Sociology.* 46, 4; 1941; 551.
12. CHURCHILL (Winston). World crisis: The aftermath. V 4. 1928. Butter Morth; London.
13. COSER (Lewis A). Functions of social conflict. 1956. Free Press; New York.
14. FINK (C F). Some conceptual difficulties in the theory of social conflict. *Journal of Conflict Resolution.* 12, 4; 1968; 416.
15. DAHRENDORF (Ralf). Class and class conflict in industrial society. 1959. Stanford University Press; Standford. p 135.
16. LEVINE (Robert A). Anthropology and study of conflict : An Introduction. *Journal of Conflict Resolution.* 5, 1; 1961; 3-15.

17. MURRAY (Edward J). Conflict : Psychological aspect. *In* SILLS (David L), *Ed*. International encyclopedia of social sciences. V 3. 1968. Macmillan & Free Press; New York. p 220.
18. FREUD (Sigmund). General introduction to psychoanalysis. 1920. Boni and Liveright; New York.
19. LEWIN (Kurt). Dynamic theory of personality: Selected papers. 1935. McGraw Hill; New York. p 87.
20. MILLER (Neal E). Experimental study of conflict, personality and clinical disorder: A handbook based on experimental and clinical research. 1944. Ronald; New York. p 431-65.
21. DOLLARD (John) and MILLER (Neal A). Personality and psychotherapy: An analysis in terms of learning, thinking and culture. 1950. McGraw Hill; New York.
22. FREUD (Sigmund). General introduction to psychoanalysis. 1920. Boni and Liveright; New York.
23. PAVLOV (I P). Conditioned reflexes, tr. by G V Anrep. 1927. Oxford University Press; London.
24. FREUD (Sigmund). General introduction to psychoanalysis.
25. RAPOPORT (Anatol). Fights, games, and debate. 1960. University of Michigan Press; Anna Arbor. p11.
26. BROWN (David L) and CLARSON (Andrew E). Conflict. *In* NICHOLSON (Nigel), *Ed*. Blackwell encyclopedia dictionary of organization behaviour. 1997. Blackwell; Cambridge. p 92-98.
27. THOMAS (Kenneth W). Conflict and conflict management. *In* DUNNETTE (M D), *Ed*. Handbook of Industrial and organizational psychology. 1976. Rand McNally; Chicago. p 889-935.
28. LAMMERS (Cornelis J). Strikes and mutinies: Comparative study of organizational conflict between rules and ruled. *Administrative Science Quarterly*. 14, 4; 1969; 558-72.
29. JEHN (K A). Multi-method examination of the benefits and detriment of inter-group conflict. *Administrative Science Quarterly*. 40, 2; 1995; 256-85.
30. PALEN (John J). Belief in government control and displace workers. *Administrative Science Quarterly*. 14, 4; 1969; 584-93.
31. FREDERICKSON (H George). Role occupancy and attitudes towards labor relation in government. *Administrative Science Quarterly*. 14, 4; 1969; 595-606.
32. ASSAEL (Henry). Constructive role of interorganizational conflict. *Administrative Science Quarterly*. 14, 4; 1969; 573-82.

33. PETERSON (M F) and others. Role conflict ambiguity and overload : A 21 nations study. *Academy of Management Journal.* 38, 2; 1995; 429-52.
34. KAHN (R L) and others. Occupational stress : Studies in role conflict and ambiguity. 1964. John Wiley; New York.
35. WALTON (Richard E) and others. Organizational context and inter-departmental conflict. *Administrative Science Quarterly.* 14, 4; 1969; 522-42.
36. COVERMAN (S). Role overload, role conflict and stress : Addressing consequences of multiple role demands. *Social Forces.* 67, 4; 1989; 965-82.
37. WARREN (Donald I). Effects of power basis and peer groups on conformity in formal organization. *Administrative Science Quarterly.* 14, 4; 1969; 544-56.
38. RAHIM (M Afzalur). Measurement of organizational conflict. *Journal of General psychology.* 109; 1983; 189-99.
39. CORWIN (Ronald G). Pattern of organizational conflict. *Administrative Science Quarterly.* 14, 4; 1969; 507-20.
40. SUMAN (H C). Anatomy of conflict and its management. *Prashasnika.* 35, 1; 1998; 13-17.
41. FOLLETT (Mary Parker). Creative experience. 1951. Peter Smith; New York.
42. CHESLER (Mark A) and others. Power training : An alternative path to conflict management. *California Management Review.* 21, 2; 1978; 84-90.
43. DERR (C Brooklyn). Managing organizational conflict : Collaboration, bargaining, and power approaches. *California Management Review.* 21, 2; 1978; 76-83.
44. LOUIS (Meryl Reis). How individuals conceptualize conflict? Identification of steps in the process and the role of personal/developmental factors. *Human Relations.* 30, 5; 1977; 451-67.
45. ASSAEL(Henry). Constructive role; p 573-82.
46. RIDGEWAY (Valentine F). Administration of manufacturer dealer system. *Administrative Science Quarterly.* 1, 4; 1957; 466-83.
47. BERG (Thomas L). Designing the distribution system, marketing management and administrative action, ed by Stuart H Britt and Harper W. Boyd Jr. 1963. McGraw Hill; New York. p 400-08.
48. ASSAEL (Henry). Political role of trade associations in distributive conflict resolution. *Journal of Marketing.* 32, 1; 1968; 21-28.

49. THOMAS (Kenneth W). Conflict and conflict management. *In* DUNNETTE (M D), *Ed*. Handbook of Industrial and organizational psychology. 1976. Rand McNally; Chicago. p 889-935.

50. ZALEZNIK (Abraham). Power and politics in organizational life. *Harvard Business Review*. 48, 3; 1970; 47.

51. FERRARO (Vincent L) and ADAMS (Sheila A). Interdepartmental conflict: Practical ways to prevent and reduce it. *Personnel*. 61, 4; 1984; 12-23.

52. MARCH (James G) and SIMON (Herbert A). Organization. 1958. John Wiley; New York.

53. WALTON (R E). Theory of conflict in lateral organizational relationship. *In* LAWRENCE (J R), *Ed*. Operational research and social sciences. 1966. Tavisteek; London. p 409-28.

54. COSER (Lewis A). Functions of social conflict. 1956. Free Press; New York.

55. ROBBINS (Stephen P). Managing organizational conflict : A non-traditional approach. 1974. Prentice Hall; New Jersey.

56. KOLB (D M) and BARTUNEK (J M), *Eds*. Hidden conflicts in organizations. 1992. Sage; Thousand Oaks.

57. PONDY (Louis R). Organizational conflict: Concepts and models. *Administrative Science Quarterly*. 12, 2; 1967; 296-320.

58. SHEPPARD (B H). Conflict research as schizophrenia : The many faces of organizational conflict. *Journal of Organizational Behavior*. 13, 3; 1992; 325-35.

59. KANTER (R M). Men and women of the corporation. 1977. Colophon; New York.

60. CORWIN (Ronald G). Pattern of organizational conflict. *Administrative Science Quarterly*. 14, 4; 1969; 507-20.

61. MARTINS (L. Luis) and others. Moderators of the relationship between work-family conflict and career satisfaction. *Academy of Management Journal*. 45, 2; 2002; 399-409.

62. De LONG (David) and SEEMANN (Patricia). Confronting conceptual confusion and conflict in knowledge management. *Organizational Dynamics*. 29, 1; 2000; 33-44.

63. PONDY (Louis R). Organizational conflict; p 296-320.

64. SCHMIDT (Stuart M) and KOCHAN (Thomas A). Conflict : Towards conceptual clarity. *Administrative Science Quarterly*. 17, 3; 1972; 359-68.

65. PINKLEY (Robin L). Dimensions of conflict frame : Disputant

interpretations of conflict. *Journal of Applied psychology*. 75, 2; 1990; 117-26.

66. WALL (Victor) and NOLAN (Linda). Perceptions of inequality, satisfaction and conflict in task oriented groups. *Human Relations*. 39, 11; 1986; 1033-52.
67. CORWIN (Ronald G). Pattern of organizational conflict. *Administrative Science Quarterly*. 14, 4; 1969; 507-20.
68. PAUL (R J) and SCHOOLER (R D). Analysis of performance standards and generation conflict in academia. *Academy of Management Journal*. 13, 2; 1970; 212-16.
69. RAHIM (A). Management of intraorganizational conflicts : A laboratory study with organisational design. *Management International Review*. 19, 1; 1979; 97-106.
70. SHEPPARD (B H). Conflict research as schizophrenia; p 325-35.
71. LITTERER (Joseph A). Conflict in organization : A re-examination. *Academy of Management Journal*. 9, 3; 1966; 178-86.
72. ASSAEL (Henry). Constructive role; p 573-82.
73. EVAN (W M). Conflict and performance in R & D. organizations : Some preliminary findings. *Industrial Management Review*. 7, 1; 1965; 37-46.
74. HALL (J) and WILLIAM (M S). Comparison of decision making performance in established and adhoc groups. *Journal of Personality and Social Psychology*. 3, 2; 1966; 214-22.
75. JANIS (Irving L). Group think : psychological studies of policy decisions and fiascoes. Ed 2. 1982. Houghton Mifflin; Boston.
76. PELZ (D). Creative tensions in the research and development climate *Science*. 157, 3785; 1967; 160-65.
77. ROBBINS (Stephen P). Managing organizational conflict : A non-traditional approach. 1974. Prentice Hall; New Jersey.
78. ROBBINS (Stephen P). Conflict management and conflict resolution are not synonymous terms. *California Management Review*. 21, 2; 1978; 67-75.
79. KATZ (R L). Skill of effective administrator. *Harvard Business Review*. 52, 5; 1974; 90-110.
80. MAIER (N R F). Problem solving discussions and conferences : Leadership methods and skills. 1963. McGraw Hill; New York.
81. McGREGOR (D M). Professional manager. 1967. McGraw Hill; New York.

82. DEUTSCH (M). Resolution of conflict. 1973. Yale University Press; Connecticut.

83. RIZZO (John R) and others. Role conflict and ambiguity in complex organisations. *Administrative Science Quarterly.* 15, 1; 1970; 150-63.

84. TEDESCHI (J T). and others. Conflict power and game. 1973. Alden; Chicago.

85. SCHMIDT (W H). Conflict: A powerful process for (Good or Bad) change. *Management Review.* 63, 12; 1974; 4-10.

86. KING (Dennis). Three cheers for conflicts. *Personnel.* 58, 1; 1981; 13-22.

87. PAREEK (Udai). Managing conflict and collaboration.1982. Oxford and IBH Publishing; New Delhi.

88. BARON (RA). Positive effects of conflict: A cognitive perspective. *Employee Responsibilities and Rights Journal.* 4, 1; 1991; 25-35.

89. TJOSVOLD (Dean) and JOHNSON (David W). Productive conflict management perspective for organizations. 1983. Irvington Publishers; New York.

90. VAN de VLIERT (E) and De DREU (C). Optimising performance by stimulating conflict. *International Journal of Conflict Management.* 4, 2; 1994; 211-22.

91. THOMAS (Kenneth W) and others. Conflict and collaboration : Some concluding observations. *California Management Review.* 21, 2; 1978; 91-95.

92. CHANIN (M). Empirical study of problem solving techniques and conflict behavior modes. 1980. Ph.D. Thesis; City University of New York. (Unpublished).

93. MASON (R O). Dialectical approach to strategic planning. *Management Science.* 15, 3; 1969; 403-13.

94. MITROF (I I). and MASON (R O). Metaphysic of policy and planning : A reply to Cosier. *Academy of Management Review.* 6, 4; 1981; 649-51.

95. MAYO (Elton). Social problems of an industrial civilization.

96. FOX (A). Coming to terms with conflict. *Personnel Management.* 14, 1; 1972; 20-23.

97. ARGYRIS (C). Integrating the individual and organization. 1964. John Wiley; New York.

98. LIKERT (R). New patterns of management. 1961. McGraw Hill; New York.

99. MAREK (J). Battle of strategies. *In* LAWERENCE (J R), *Ed.* Operational

research and social sciences. 1966. Tavisteek; London. p 64.

100. LITTERER (Joseph A). Conflict in organization; p 178-86.
101. RAHIM (A). Management of intraorganizational conflicts; p 97-106.
102. STIMAC (Michele). Strategies for resolving conflict : Their functional and dysfunctional sides. *Personnel*. 59; 1982; 54-64.
103. BOULDING (Kenneth). Conflict and defense. 1963. Harper & Row; New York.
104. GUETZKOW (Harold) and GYR (John). Analysis of conflict in decision making groups. *Human Relations*. 7, 3; 1954; 361-81.
105. DALTON (Melville). Men who manage. 1959. Wiley; New York.
106. KAHN (R L). Role conflict and role ambiguity in organizations. *Personnel Administrator*. 9, 1; 1964; 8-13.
107. FORD (Rebecca) and JOHNSON (Cathryn). Perception of power : dependence and legitimacy in conflict. *Social Psychology Quarterly*. 61, 1; 1998; 16-32.
108. GOULDNER (Alvin). Organizational tensions. *In* MESTON (Robert), *Ed*. Sociology Today. 1959. Basic Books; New York. 400-28.
109. PRIEM (Richard) and PRICE (Kenneth). Process and outcome expectations for the dialectical inquiry, devil's advocacy, consensus, techniques of strategic decision making. *Group and Organization Studies*. 16, 2; 1991; 206-25.
110. KOLB (D) and PUTNAM (L). Multiple faces of conflict in organizations. *Journal of Organizational Behavior* . 13, 3; 1992; 311-24.
111. TJOSVOLD (D) and POON (M). Dealing with scarce resources : Open minded interaction for resolving budget conflicts. *Group & Organizational Management*. 23, 3; 1998; 237-55.
112. MARTOCCHIO (J J) and JUDGE (T A). When we don't see eye to eye: Discrepancies between supervisors and subordinates in absence disciplinary decisions. *Journal of Management*. 21, 2; 1995; 251-78.
113. FERRARO and ADAMS. Interdepartmental conflict; p 12-23.
114. WALTON (Richard E) and DUTTON (John M). Management of interdepartmental conflict: A model and review. *Administrative Science Quarterly*. 14, 1; 1969; 73-84.
115. THOMAS (Kenneth W) and SCHMIDT (Warren H). Survey of managerial interest with respect to conflict. *Academy of Management Journal*. 19, 2; 1976; 315-18.
116. PHILLIPS (Eleanor) and CHESTON (Ric). Conflict resolution: What works. *California Management Review*. 21, 4; 1979; 76-83.

117. DERR (C Brooklyn). Managing organizational conflict; p 76-83.

118. SUMAN (H C). Anatomy of conflict; p 13-17.

119. STIMAC (Michele). Strategies for resolving conflict; p 54-64.

120. BROWN and CLARSON. Conflict; p 92-98.

121. GREENBERG (Jerald) and BARON (Robert A). Behaviour in organizations : Understanding & managing the human side of work. Ed 5. 2000. Prentice Hall of India; New Delhi. p 412-50.

122. NELSON (Debra L) and QUICK (James Campbell). Organizational behavior : Foundations, realities, and challenges. Ed 3. 2003. South-Western College; Mason. p 421-57.

123. SINGH (Nirmal). Organizational behaviour: Concept theory and practice, managing people and organizations in the 21st century. 2001. Deep & Deep; New Delhi. p 399-417.

124. WHETTEN (David A) and CAMERON (Kim S). Developing management skills. Ed 2. 1991. Harper Collins; New York. p 397-99.

125. LIKERT (R) and LIKERT (J. Gibson). New ways of managing conflict. 1976. McGraw Hill; New York.

126. COOK (Curties W) and HUNSAKER (Phillips L). Management and organizational behavior. Ed 3. 2001. McGraw Hill; New York. p 372-409.

127. NEWSTROM (John W) and DAVIS (Keith). Organizational behavior: Human behaviour at work. Ed 10. 2001. Tata McGraw Hill; New Delhi. p 312-20.

128. De LONG and SEEMANN. Confronting conceptual; p 33-44.

129. NAIR (R Gangadharan). Relevance of conflict management in managing higher educational systems. *Management in Government*. 21, 4; 1990; 193-98.

130. BUNDY (Mary Lee). Conflict in libraries. *College & Research Libraries*. 27, 4; 1966; 253-62.

131. RANGANATHAN (S R) and BHATTACHARYA (G). Conflict of authorship: Person vs corporate body. *Library Science with a Slant Documentation*. 6, 2; 1969; 116-29.

132. RANGANATHAN (S R) and BHATTACHARYA (G). Conflict of authorship RANGANATHAN (S R) and BHATTACHARYA (G). Conflict of authorship: Corporate body vs corporate body. *Library Science with a Slant to Documentation*. 7, 2; 1970; 115-78.

133. RANGANATHAN (S R) and BHATTACHARYA (G). Conflict of authorship: Corporate body vs corporate body. *Library Science with a Slant to Documentation*. 7, 2; 1970; 115-78.

134. GOIL (N K). Conflict between objectives and contents : Need for enlargement and adjustment of the scheme of papers for Master of Library Science. *Library Herald*. 9, 4; 1967; 313-20.

135. ALLAWAY (SM). Conflict in Camden. *Librarian's Christian Fellowship Newsletter*. 70; 1998; 25-27.

136. FOERSTEL (H). Conflict and compromise over homosexual literature. *Emergency Librarian*. 22, 2; 1994; 28-30.

137. PETTAS (William) and GILLILAND (Steven L). Conflict in the large academic library: Friend or foe? *Journal of Academic Librarianship*. 18, 1; 1992; 24-29.

138. HUDSON (M P). Conflict and stress in time of change. *Library Management*. 20, 1 & 2; 1999; 35-38.

139. JANSSEN (B). Conflict in Hoevelaken : Library committee steps down after a disagreement with the town council. *Bibliotheek Blad*. 3, 6; 1999; 12-14.

140. RAYWARD (W Boyd). Conflict, interdependence, mediocrity : Librarians and library educators. *Library Journal*. 108, 13; 1983; 1313-17.

141. EGGLETON (Richard). Conflict in libraries revisited. *Libri*. 29, 1; 1979; 64-77.

142. LEE (Susan A). Conflict and ambiguity in the role of the academic library director. *College & Research Libraries*. 38, 5; 1977; 396-404.

143. LITTERER (Joseph A). Conflict in organization; p 178-86.

144. FOLLETT (Mary Parker). Creative experience.

145. BLAKE (Rebert R) and MOUTON (Jane S). Managerial grid. 1964. Gulf Publishing; Houston.

146. THOMAS (Kenneth W). Conflict and conflict managemen; p 889-935.

147. FILLEY (A C). Some normative issues in conflict management. *California Management Review*. 21, 2; 1978; 61-66.

148. RAHIM (M A). Measure of styles of handling interpersonal conflict. *Academy of Management Journal*. 26, 2; 1983; 365-76.

149. DERR (C Brooklyn). Managing organizational conflict; p 76-83.

150. SCHMIDT (W H) and TANNENBAUM (R). Management of differences. *Harvard Business Review*. 38, 6; 1960; 107-15.

151. PAREEK (Udai). Managing conflict and collaboration.1982. Oxford and IBH Publishing; New Delhi.

152. LIKERT and LIKERT. New ways of managing conflict.

153. BLAKE (RR) and others. Managing inter-group conflict in industry. 1964. Gulf Publishing; Houston.

154. MATHUR (H B) and SAYEED (Omer Bin). Conflict management in organizations : Development of a model. *Indian Journal of Social Work.* 44, 2; 1983; 175-83.

155. COSIER (Richard A) and RUBLE (Thomas L). Research on conflict handling behavior : An experimental approach. *Academy of Management Journal.* 24, 4; 1981; 816-31.

156. VAN de VLIERT (E) and KABANOFF (Boris). Toward theory – based measures of conflict management. *Academy of Management Journal* 33, 1; 1990; 199-209.

157. KABANOFF (Boris). Predictive validity of the mode conflict instrument. *Journal of Applied Psychology.* 72, 1; 1987; 160-63.

158. http://www.umsl.edu/~sauter/analysis/488_f01_papers/ *Ohlendorf.htm#acr*

159. RAHIM (M A). and MAGNER (N R). Confirmatory factor analysis of the style of handling interpersonal conflict : First order factor model and its invariance across groups. *Journal of Applied Psychology.* 80, 1; 1995; 122-32.

160. CHESLER (Mark A) and others. Power training; p 84.

161. RAHIM (A). Management of; p 97-106.

162. STIMAC (Michele). Strategies for resolving conflict;; p 54-64.

163. JONES (Robert E) and MELCHER (Bonita H). Personality and preference for modes of conflict resolution. *Human Relations.* 35, 8; 1982; 649-58.

164. THOMAS (Kenneth W) and others. Conflict and collaboration; p 91-95.

165. FILLEY (A C). Some normative issues; p 61-66.

166. ROBBINS (Stephen P). Conflict management; p 67-75.

167. CHESLER (Mark A) and others. Power training; p 84-90.

168. SCHEIN (D H). Organizational psychology; p 80-86.

169. FERRARO and ADAMS. Interdepartmental conflict; p 12-23.

170. THOMAS and SCHMIDT. Survey of managerial interest; p 315-18.

171. MISHRA (Prashant) and DHAR (Upinder). Liveraging functional conflict. *Indian Journal of Industrial Relations.* 38, 1; 2002; 113-19.

172. VARMA (Madhurendra K). Managing conflict at work. *Growth.* 27, 4; 2000; 7-16.

173. LAWRENCE (P R) and LORSCH (J W). Organization and environment. 1967. Irwin – Dorsey; Burr Ridge.

174. KATHMAN (Jane McGurn) and KATHMAN (Michael D). Conflict

management in the academic library. *Journal of Academic Librarianship.* 16, 3; 1990; 145-49.

175. FISHER (W) and KOUE (Glen). Conflict management. *Library Administration and Management*. 5, 3; 1991; 145-50.
176. KATHMAN (Jane McGurn) and KATHMAN (Michael D). Conflict management in libraries. *In* Allen (Kent), *Ed.* Encyclopedia of library and information science. V 51. 1993. Marcel Dekker; New York. p 190-94.
177. SINGH – SENGUPTA (Sunita). Brighter aspect of conflict. *Indian Journal of Industrial Relations.* 33, 3; 1998; 329-48.
178. GREENBERG and BARON. Behaviour in organizations; p 412-50.
179. HELLRIEGEL (Don) and others. Organizational behavior. Ed 9. 2000. South-Western; Mason. p 292-320.
180. NELSON and QUICK. Organizational behavior; p 421-57.
181. KREITNER (Robert) and KINICKI (Angelo). Organization behavior. 2000. McGraw Hill; Boston. p 444-74.
182. RAHIM (M Afzalur). Measurement of organizational conflict; p 189-99.
183. COOK and HUNSAKER. Management and; p 372-409.
184. NEWSTROM and DAVIS. Organizational behavior; p 312-20.
185. KILMANN (Ralph H) and THOMAS (Kenneth W). Developing forced choice measure of conflict handling behavior : The 'Mode' instrument. *Educational and psychological Measurement.* 37; 1977; 309-25.
186. RAHIM (M Afzalur). Strategy for managing conflict in complex organizations. *Human Relations.* 38, 1; 1985; 81-89.
187. MEYER (J P) and others. Evaluating the management of interpersonal conflict in organisations : A factor – analytic study of outcome criteria. *Candain Journal of Administrative Sciences.* 14, 1; 1997; 1-13.
188. SESSA (Valerie I). Using perspective taking to manage conflict and affect in teams. *Journal of Applied Behavioral Science.* 32, 1; 1996. 101-15.
189. RENWICK (P A). Effect of sex differences on the perceptions and management of superior-subordinate conflict: An exploratory study. *Organizational Behavior and Human Performance.* 19, 3; 1977; 403-15.
190. HOWATT (Gary) and LONDON (Manuel). Attribution of conflict management strategies in superior-subordinate dyad. *Journal of Applied Psychology.* 65, 2; 1980; 172-75.
191. BHOWON (Uma). Perceived power and interpersonal handling

strategies. *Indian Journal of Industrial Relations*. 34, 2; 1998; 183-92.

192. *http://www.computer.org/proceedings/hicss/*

193. VOLKEMA (R J) and BERGMANN (T J). Conflict styles as indicators of behavioral patterns in inter-personal conflicts. *Journal of Social Psychology. 135, 1;* 1995; 5-15.

194. SAYEED (Omer Bin). Conflict management styles : Relationship with leadership styles and moderating effect of esteem for co-worker. *Indian Journal of Industrial Relations*. 26, 1; 1990; 28-52.

195. SAMANTRA (Rabinarayan). Management of superior-subordinates conflict : An exploration. *Indian Journal of Industrial Relations*. 38, 4; 2003; 444-59.

196. BHOWON (Uma). Perceived organizational climate and interpersonal handling strategies. *Indian Journal of Industrial Relations*. 35, 1; 1999; 43-51.

197. MORRIS (Michach W) and others. Conflict management styles : Accounting for cross-national differences. *Journal of International Business Studies*. 29, 4; 1998; 729-48.

198. PARTHASARTHY (Kokila) and SINGH (P). Strategies for conflict management : An Indian experience. *Indian Management*. 23, 7; 1984; 13-22.

199. RENWICK (P A). Impact of topic and source of disagreement on conflict management *Organizational Behavior and Human Performance*. 14, 3; 1975; 416-25.

200. BHATTA (Bhim Dev). Conflict management. *Prashasan*. 19, 2; 1988; 15-23.

201. CHAN (M). Inter-group conflict and conflict management in R & D decisions of four aerospace companies. *IEEE Transaction on Engineering Management*. 36, 1; 1989; 95-104.

202. BARKER (Jeffrey) and others. Conflict approach of effective and ineffective project managers: Field study in matrix organization. *Journal of Management Studies*. 25, 2; 1988; 167-78.

203. KOZAN (M K). Cultural influence on styles of handling interpersonal conflict : Comparison among Jordanian, Turkish, and U.S. managers. *Human Relations*. 42, 9; 1989; 787-99.

204. CHANIN (Michael N) and SCHNEER (Joy A). Study of the relationship between Jungian personality dimensions and conflict - handling behaviour. *Human Relations*. 37, 10; 1984; 863-79.

205. MILLS (Joan) and others. Conflict handling and personality dimensions of project-management personnel. *Psychological Reports*. 57; 1985;

1135-43.

206. THOMAS (K W) and KILMANN (R H). Thomas-Kilmann conflict mode instrument. 1974. Xicom; New York.

207. BURKE (R F). Methods of managing superior-subordinate conflict, their effectiveness and consequences. *Canadian Journal of Behavioral Science*. 2, 1; 1971; 124-35.

208. LONDON (M) and HOWAT (G). Relationship between commitment and conflict resolution behavior. *Journal of Vocational Behavior.* 13, 1; 1978; 1-14.

209. RENWICK (P A). Perception and management of superior-subordinate conflict. *Organizational Behavior and Human Performance*. 13, 3; 1975; 444-56.

210. BLAKE (Robert R) and MOUTON (Jane S). Managerial grid. 1964. Gulf Publishing Houston.

211. BURKE (R F). Methods of resolving superior-subordinate conflict : The constructive use of subordinate differences and disagreements. *Organizational Behavior and Human Performance*. 5, 3; 1970; 393-411.

212. RAHIM (M A) and BUNTZMAN (G F). Supervisory power bases and styles of handling conflict with subordinates and subordinates compliance and satisfaction. *Journal of Psychology*. 123; 1988; 195-210.

213. MISHRA (Prashant) and others. Restrategising the management of conflict : An empirical study. *Indian Journal Industrial Relations*. 35, 2; 1999; 160-74.

214. MATHUR (H B) and SAYEED (Omer Bin). Application of conflict management strategic as perceived by the manager for himself and for his superior : Comparison. *Indian Journal of Social Work*. 41, 2-3; 1980; 163-68.

215. SAYEED (Omer Bin). Management response to handling conflict situations : An appraisal of conflict management strategies. *Decision*. 19, 1; 1990; 1-18.

216. SHARMA (R A) and SAMANTRA (R). Conflict Management in an Indian firm: A case study. *Decision*. 21, 4; 1994; 235-49.

217. SHARMA (R A) and SAMANTRA (Rabinarayan). Conflict management in an Indian firm. *Indian Journal Industrial Relations*. 30, 4; 1995; 439-53.

218. SAMANTRA (Rabindrayan). Conflict management strategies and their impact on organizational effectiveness in Indian industry. 1999. Ph.D.Thessis; Supervisor: R.A.Sharma, University of Delhi. (unpublished).

219. WEIDER-HATFIELD (Deborah) and HATFIELD (John D). Supervisors' conflict management strategies and subordinate outcomes. *Management Communication Quarterly.* 10, 2; 1996; 189-208.

220. WALL Jr. (J A) and CALLISTER (R R). Conflict and its management. *Journal of Management.* 21, 3; 1995; 515-58.

221. SINGH (P). and PARTHASARTHY (Kokila). Conflict management strategy : A scenario of avoidance. *Abhigyan.* 3, 2; 1985; 57-84.

222. DAS (S L). Conflict : Basis of collective and constructive functioning. *Indian Management.* 21, 12; 1982; 21.

223. RAHIM (M A). Organizational conflict inventory i & ii : Professional manual. 1983. Consulting Psychologists Press; Palo Alto.

224. GUPTA (S R). Institute of charted librarian : A conceptual framework. *Journal of Library and information Science.* 17, 2; 192; 43-57.

225. GUPTA (S R) and BABBAR (Parveen). Need and provision of professional library management consultancy. *Journal of Library and Information Science.* 27, 2; 2002; 142-51.

226. CHALARAGASE (Pairot). Analytical study of the professional staff with regard to their cooperation and conflict among the professional staff in the selected university libraries in Thailand. 1997. Ph.D. thesis, Supervisor: Dr. S.R. Gupta, University of Delhi. (*Unpublished.*)

227. ABBAS (S M). Managing Conflict in central university libraries in Delhi. *Library Hearld.* 46, 5, 2008; 130-37.

4

Library Management and Conflict : An Emperical View

Before managing conflict, it is very important to know about the issues and causes of conflict among library professionals. An attempt has been made to know the same. For this purpose case studies of Delhi University Library System, Jawaharlal Nehru University Library, Dr. Zakir Hussain Library, JMI, Indian Agricultural Research Institute Library, Hakim Mohd. Said Central Library, Jamia Hamdard, Tata Energy Research Institute Library and some others libraries have been undertaken.

For the purpose of data analysis, the universities which were having less then 10 library professionals, were clubbed together in one category of libraries, namely, 'Other Libraries'. The libraries of Guru Govind Singh Indraprastha University, School of Planning and Architecture, Shri Lal Bahadur Shastri Sanskrit Vidhyapeetha, National Museum Institute of History of Art, Conservation and Museology, and Indian Institute of Foreign Trade, together form the category of 'Other Libraries' in the subsequent paragraphs.

4.1. CONFLICT ISSUES

The questions were asked from the respondents about conflict issues. The responses received have been mentioned in the tables, which were analysed and interpreted with the support of tables and its findings are given below.

Table 4.1.1 : Conflict over Job Objectives

Library	Strongly Agree		Agree		Undecided		Disagree		Strongly Disagree	
	Freq.	%	Freq.	%	Freq.	%	Freq.	%	Freq.	%
DULS	5	7.35	32	47.06	5	7.35	23	33.82	3	4.41
JNUL	NIL	NIL	13	50.00	1	3.85	12	46.15	NIL	NIL
ZHL, JMI	2	10.53	14	73.68	NIL	NIL	3	15.79	NIL	NIL
IARIL	3	13.64	10	45.45	1	4.55	8	36.36	NIL	NIL
HMSCL	NIL	NIL	8	66.67	1	8.33	3	25.00	NIL	NIL
TERIL	NIL	NIL	3	30.00	2	20.00	5	50.00	NIL	NIL
OTHERS	1	4.55	9	40.91	2	9.09	9	40.91	1	4.55
TOTAL	11	6.15	89	49.72	12	6.70	63	35.20	4	2.23

N = 179

4.1.1. Conflict Over Job Objectives

The respondents were asked about their conflict issue over 'job objectives' with superiors, peers and subordinates, the data collected has been analysed and presented in Table 4.1.1.

Table 4.1.1 shows that respondents of Delhi University Library System (47.06%), JNUL (50.00%), ZHL (73.00%), IARIL (45.45%), HMSCL (66.67%) are of the view that they are having conflict on 'Job Objectives' with superiors, peers and subordinates. Further analysis of this Table reveals that respondents of TERIL (50.00%) Other Libraries (40.91%) are 'disagree' with this issue. The respondents, who 'strongly agree', 'undecided' and 'strongly disagree', their percentages are much less, such as, 7.35%, 7.35%, and 4.41% respectively. This analysis also matches with the over all percentage (49.72) of the respondents, who are of the opinion as 'agree' that conflict over job objectives is a conflict issue. It is inferred from the Table that above mentioned issue is an issue of the respondents of DULS, JNUL, ZHL, IARIL, HMSCL, wherein these are the older and bigger university libraries being studied.

4.1.2. Conflict Over Role

The library professionals play an important role in the management of university libraries, Their role becomes an issue of conflict with their superiors, peers and subordinates. The data on the issue was collected and presented in Table 4.1.2.

The responses on the conflict over role have been presented in Table 4.1.2, which reveals that respondents of the DULS (50.00%), ZHL (47.37%), IARIL (68.18), HMSCL (66.67%) and Other Libraries (54.55%) opined as 'agree', while the respondents of JNUL (34.62%) are of the view as 'disagree'. It may be noted that respondents of TERIL (40.00%) are 'agree' and in equal number 'disagree'. The over all responses received from the respondents tell the same story that (50.00%) of the respondents are 'agree' on the issue with superiors, peers and subordinates. Conclusion is drawn from the Table that

Table 4.1.2 : Conflict over Role

Library	*Strongly Agree*		*Agree*		*Undecided*		*Disagree*		*Strongly Disagree*	
	Freq.	*%*	*Freq.*	*%*	*Freq.*	*%*	*Freq.*	*%*	*Freq.*	*%*
DULS	3	4.41	34	50.00	8	11.76	23	33.82	NIL	NIL
JNUL	4	15.38	8	30.77	3	11.54	9	34.62	2	7.69
ZHL, JMI	4	21.05	9	47.37	4	21.05	2	10.53	NIL	NIL
IARIL	2	9.09	15	68.18	4	18.18	1	4.55	NIL	NIL
HMSCL	NIL	NIL	8	66.67	0	0.00	4	33.33	NIL	NIL
TERIL	NIL	NIL	4	40.00	2	20.00	4	40.00	NIL	NIL
OTHERS	2	9.09	12	54.55	3	13.64	5	22.73	NIL	NIL
TOTAL	**15**	**8.38**	**90**	**50.28**	**24**	**13.41**	**48**	**26.82**	**2**	**1.12**

N = 179

respondents from all the libraries being studied, except JNUL, 'agree' that conflict over role is a conflict issue.

4.1.3. Planning of Activities

Planning of activities is an important aspect of library administration. To know whether or not the planning of activities is a conflict issue, data for the same were received, analysed and presented in Table 4.1.3.

Table 4.1.3 : Conflict Over Planning of Activities

Library	*Strongly Agree*		*Agree*		*Undecided*		*Disagree*		*Strongly Disagree*	
	Freq.	*%*	*Freq.*	*%*	*Freq.*	*%*	*Freq.*	*%*	*Freq.*	*%*
DULS	7	10.29	40	58.82	3	4.41	17	25.00	1	1.47
JNUL	1	3.85	13	50.00	2	7.69	8	30.77	2	7.69
ZHL, JMI	6	31.58	9	47.37	2	10.53	1	5.26	1	5.26
IARIL	2	9.09	10	45.45	4	18.18	6	27.27	NIL	NIL
HMSCL	NIL	NIL	10	83.33	NIL	NIL	2	16.67	NIL	NIL
TERIL	1	10.00	7	70.00	1	10.00	1	10.00	NIL	NIL
OTHERS	2	9.09	11	50.00	4	18.18	5	22.73	NIL	NIL
TOTAL	**19**	**10.61**	**100**	**55.87**	**16**	**8.94**	**40**	**22.35**	**4**	**2.23**

N = 179

Table 4.1.3 indicates that the responses received from DULS (58.82%), JNUL (50.00%), ZHL (47.37%), HMSCL (83.33%), TERIL (70.00%) and Other Libraries (50.00%) viewed as 'agree' on the planning of activities issue, while the respondents of the JNUL (30.77%), IARIL (27.27) and Other Libraries (22.73%) responded as 'disagree'. Further analysis of this Table indicates that over all respondents of these libraries (55.87%) opined as 'agree' on the issue. It shows that this is a conflict issue of the respondents with their superiors, peers and subordinates. All the respondents of above mentioned libraries are of the view that planning of activities is a conflict issue with their superiors, peers and subordinates.

4.1.4. Distribution of Authority

Proper distribution of authority is a healthy sign in administration. To know whether or not this is an issue of conflict of the respondents with superiors, peers and subordinates, the data were collected, analysed and presented in Table 4.1.4..

Table 4.1.4 : Conflict over Distribution of Authority

Library	*Strongly Agree*		*Agree*		*Undecided*		*Disagree*		*Strongly Disagree*	
	Freq.	*%*	*Freq.*	*%*	*Freq.*	*%*	*Freq.*	*%*	*Freq.*	*%*
DULS	7	10.29	29	42.65	7	10.29	21	30.88	4	5.88
JNUL	4	15.38	11	42.31	2	7.69	9	34.62	NIL	NIL
ZHL, JMI	6	31.58	9	47.37	2	10.53	1	5.26	1	5.26
IARIL	2	8.70	9	39.13	2	8.70	9	39.13	NIL	NIL
HMSCL	2	16.67	7	58.33	1	8.33	2	16.67	NIL	NIL
TERIL	1	11.11	6	66.67	1	11.11	1	11.11	1	10.00
OTHERS	2	9.09	14	63.64	2	9.09	4	18.18	NIL	NIL
TOTAL	**24**	**13.41**	**85**	**47.49**	**17**	**9.50**	**47**	**26.26**	**6**	**3.35**

N = 179

Table 4.1.4 presents the data on 'distribution of authority' as a conflict issue. It reveals that (42.65%) of DULS, (42.31) of JNUL, (47.37%) of ZHL, (58.33%) of HMSCL, (66.67%) of TERIL, and (63.64%) of Other Libraries responded as 'agree' on the issue with their superiors, peers and subordinates. Further analysis of the Table indicates that respondents of ZHL (31.58%) are 'strongly agree', while the respondents of IARIL (39.13%) are 'agree' and in equal number 'disagree'. Over all percentage (47.49%) on this issue is in favour of 'agree' in contrast to 'disagree' (26.26%). One can draw the conclusion from the Table that respondents of all the libraries, except IARIL, have perceived that 'distribution of authority' is an issue of conflict,.

4.1.5. Reward Criteria

In any organization, the employees are rewarded when they perform extra ordinary work. To know whether or not, the reward criteria is a conflict issue, responses were collected, analysed and presented in Table 4.1.5.

Table 4.1.5 : Conflict over Reward Criteria

Library	*Strongly Agree*		*Agree*		*Undecided*		*Disagree*		*Strongly Disagree*	
	Freq.	*%*	*Freq.*	*%*	*Freq.*	*%*	*Freq.*	*%*	*Freq.*	*%*
DULS	6	8.82	18	26.47	19	27.94	22	32.35	3	4.41
JNUL	3	11.54	8	30.77	5	19.23	9	34.62	1	3.85
ZHL, JMI	4	21.05	7	36.84	5	26.32	2	10.53	1	5.26
IARIL	2	9.09	5	22.73	3	13.64	12	54.55	NIL	NIL
HMSCL	NIL	NIL	3	25.00	1	8.33	8	66.67	NIL	NIL
TERIL	NIL	NIL	6	60.00	3	30.00	1	10.00	NIL	NIL
OTHERS	NIL	NIL	12	54.55	6	27.27	4	18.18	NIL	NIL
TOTAL	**15**	**8.38**	**59**	**32.96**	**42**	**23.46**	**58**	**32.40**	**5**	**2.79**

N= 179

Table 4.1.5 shows responses received from the library professionals on the reward criteria issue. It indicates that respondents of DULS (32.35%), JNUL (34.62%), IARIL (54.55%), HMSCL (66.67%) reported as 'disagree' on this issue, while responses received from ZHL (36.84%), TERIL (60.00%) and Other Libraries (54.55%) reported as 'agree'. The over all responses on the 'agree' (32.96%) and 'disagree' (32.40%) are almost equal. It may be noted that there is no significant difference as appeared on the responses of 'agree' and 'disagree' because their percentage falls under nearly equal numbers. Further analysis of the Table reveals that respondents of ZHL (21.05%) opined as 'strongly agree'. It is inferred from the Table that reward criteria is not a conflict issue of respondents of DULS, JNUL, IARIL, and HMSCL, while the respondents of ZHL, TERIL and Other Libraries, the 'Reward Criteria' has been reported as an issue of conflict while dealing with superiors, peers and subordinates.

4.1.6. Punishment Criteria

Punitive decisions should not base on biasness and actions taken by the authority should maintain transparency. To know about the professionals' views on the issue, data was gathered, analysed, and presented in Table 4.1.6.

Table 4.1.6 : Conflict over Punishment Criteria

Library	*Strongly Agree*		*Agree*		*Undecided*		*Disagree*		*Strongly Disagree*	
	Freq.	*%*	*Freq.*	*%*	*Freq.*	*%*	*Freq.*	*%*	*Freq.*	*%*
DULS	8	11.76	13	19.12	15	22.06	26	38.24	6	8.82
JNUL	2	7.69	6	23.08	6	23.08	8	30.77	4	15.38
ZHL, JMI	2	10.53	6	31.58	4	21.05	4	21.05	3	15.79
IARIL	1	4.55	3	13.64	4	18.18	13	59.09	1	4.55
HMSCL	NIL	NIL	2	16.67	1	8.33	9	75.00	NIL	NIL
TERIL	NIL	NIL	5	50.00	5	50.00	NIL	NIL	NIL	NIL
OTHERS	2	9.09	6	27.27	9	40.91	5	22.73	NIL	NIL
TOTAL	**15**	**8.38**	**41**	**22.91**	**44**	**24.58**	**65**	**36.31**	**14**	**7.82**

N = 179

Table 4.1.6 presents 'punishment criteria' as perceived by the professionals and reveals that respondents of ZHL (31.58%) are 'agree' on this issue, while TERIL respondents (50.00%) 'agree' and equal numbers 'disagree'. The responses received from DULS (38.24%), JNUL (30.77%), IARIL (59.09%), HMSCL (75.00%) have responded as 'disagree', while respondents of TERIL (50.00%) opined as 'agree' as many as 'disagree', and Other Libraries (40.91%) as 'undecided' on the same issue. From over all responses (36.31%) received and reported as 'disagree', conclusion is drawn from the Table that punishment criteria mentioned above is not a conflict issue in DULS, JNUL, HMSCL, and Other Libraries, while ZHL professionals have opined that this is an issue of conflict with the superiors, peers and subordinates.

4.1.7. Participation In Decision Making

To involve the library professionals in decision making process is a healthy sign of administration. To know about the professionals views on this issue, the responses were received, analysed and are presented in Table 4.1.7.

Table 4.1.7 : Conflict over Participation in Decision Making

Library	*Strongly Agree*		*Agree*		*Undecided*		*Disagree*		*Strongly Disagree*	
	Freq.	*%*	*Freq.*	*%*	*Freq.*	*%*	*Freq.*	*%*	*Freq.*	*%*
DULS	6	8.82	44	64.71	3	4.41	13	19.12	2	2.94
JNUL	2	7.69	12	46.15	3	11.54	8	30.77	1	3.85
ZHL, JMI	3	15.79	14	73.68	1	5.26	1	5.26	NIL	NIL
IARIL	NIL	NIL	10	45.45	5	22.73	6	27.27	1	4.55
HMSCL	1	8.33	9	75.00	NIL	NIL	2	16.67	NIL	NIL
TERIL	2	20.00	5	50.00	1	10.00	2	20.00	NIL	NIL
OTHERS	3	13.64	17	77.27	NIL	NIL	2	9.09	NIL	NIL
TOTAL	**17**	**9.50**	**111**	**62.01**	**13**	**7.26**	**34**	**18.99**	**4**	**2.23**

N = 179

Table 4.1.7 gives the summary of the views of the respondents on the issue 'participation in decision making process, and indicates that the majority percentage of responses of the different libraries report as 'agree'. These responses include DULS (64.71%), JNUL (46.15%), ZHL (73.68%), IARIL

(45.45%), HMSCL (75.00%), TERIL (50.00%) and Other Libraries (77.27%). The respondents who have expressed as 'disagree' are from JNUL (30.77%), IARIL (27.27%) and TERIL (20.00%). Further analysis of this Table reveals that over all responses (62.01%) received for the same purpose has reported as 'agree'. The result of this Table tallies responses of all other libraries with the overall responses. It is inferred that participation in decision making is a conflict issue of the respondents with superiors, peers and subordinates in the libraries.

4.1.8. Library Policies And Procedures

In libraries, policies and procedures are framed for administration purposes. To know whether or not, there is any conflict on the library policies and procedures, data was gathered and presented in Table 4.1.8.

Table 4.1.8 : Conflict over Library Policies & Procedures

Library	*Strongly Agree*		*Agree*		*Undecided*		*Disagree*		*Strongly Disagree*	
	Freq.	*%*	*Freq.*	*%*	*Freq.*	*%*	*Freq.*	*%*	*Freq.*	*%*
DULS	8	11.76	22	32.35	5	7.35	30	44.12	3	4.41
JNUL	2	7.69	11	42.31	4	15.38	9	34.62	NIL	NIL
ZHL, JMI	3	15.79	11	57.89	1	5.26	4	21.05	NI;	NIL
IARIL	3	13.64	6	27.27	3	13.64	10	45.45	NIL	NIL
HMSCL	NIL	NIL	3	25.00	NIL	NIL	9	75.00	NIL	NIL
TERIL	2	20.00	3	30.00	2	20.00	3	30.00	NIL	NIL
OTHERS	2	9.09	13	59.09	NIL	NIL	7	31.82	NIL	NIL
TOTAL	**20**	**11.17**	**69**	**38.55**	**15**	**8.38**	**72**	**40.22**	**3**	**1.68**

N = 179

Table 4.1.8 indicates that respondents (42.31%) from JNUL, (52.89%) of ZHL, and (59.09%) of Other Libraries have viewed as 'agree', while respondents of DULS (44.12%), IARIL (45.45%), HMSCL (75.00%) have expressed their views as 'disagree'. One may note that respondents of TERIL in equal numbers (30.00%) have opined as 'agree' and 'disagree'.

Similarly, equal number of respondents (20.00%) each are divided as 'strongly agree' and 'undecided'. The overall pattern of the responses reported as 'disagree' (40.22%) and 'agree' (38.55%). It shows that value of both the views differ. It is concluded that library policies and procedures is a conflict issue among the respondents of JNUL, ZHL and Other Libraries, while the same is not a conflict issue for respondents of DULS, IARIL and HMSCL, with their superiors, peers and subordinates.

4.1.9. Promotions

It is obvious that employees feel encouraged when they get promotions. To know the real situation about this issue, the data was collected, analysed, and presented in Table 4.1.9.

Table 4.1.9 : Conflict over Promotions

Library	*Strongly Agree*		*Agree*		*Undecided*		*Disagree*		*Strongly Disagree*	
	Freq.	*%*	*Freq.*	*%*	*Freq.*	*%*	*Freq.*	*%*	*Freq.*	*%*
DULS	13	19.12	37	54.41	5	7.35	7	10.29	6	8.82
JNUL	4	15.38	12	46.15	3	11.54	5	19.23	2	7.69
ZHL, JMI	4	21.05	11	57.89	2	10.53	2	10.53	NIL	NIL
IARIL	1	4.55	5	22.73	5	22.73	9	40.91	2	9.09
HMSCL	NIL	NIL	11	91.67	NIL	NIL	1	8.33	NIL	NIL
TERIL	1	10.00	6	60.00	1	10.00	2	20.00	NIL	NIL
OTHERS	3	13.64	10	45.45	3	13.64	6	27.27	NIL	NIL
TOTAL	**26**	**14.53**	**92**	**51.40**	**19**	**10.61**	**32**	**17.88**	**10**	**5.59**

N = 179

The data in Table 4.1.9 reveals that larger number of respondents of the libraries under study are of the opinion as 'agree' on 'promotion' as a conflict issue. Such libraries include DULS (54.41%), JNUL (46.15%), ZHL (57.89%), HMSCL (91.67%), TERIL (60.00%) and Other Libraries (45.45%). On the other hand, the responses received from IARIL (40.91%) as 'disagree'. The respondents (51.40%) from all the libraries have expressed their views as 'agree' in contrast to (17.88%) as 'disagree'. It is inferred from the Table that promotion is a conflict issue amongst the respondents of all libraries, except IARIL.

4.1.10. Sanction of Leave

Provision and sanction of leave of absence to the employees is a natural requirement and almost a daily routine job. Thus availing leave, creates problem before the supervisory staff, the problem of shortage of hands on a given moment. Sometimes 'leave' is used by the employee as a tool for irritating and disturbing the staff at the top. Hence, to know whether or not 'sanction of leave' becomes a conflict issue, the data were collected, analysed and presented in Table 4.1.10..

Table 4.1.10 : Conflict Over Sanction of Leave

Library	*Strongly Agree*		*Agree*		*Undecided*		*Disagree*		*Strongly Disagree*	
	Freq.	*%*	*Freq.*	*%*	*Freq.*	*%*	*Freq.*	*%*	*Freq.*	*%*
DULS	5	7.35	18	26.47	7	10.29	33	48.53	5	7.35
JNUL	3	11.54	9	34.62	2	7.69	10	38.46	2	7.69
ZHL, JMI	4	21.05	9	47.37	4	21.05	1	5.26	1	5.26
IARIL	1	4.55	9	40.91	2	9.09	9	40.91	1	4.55
HMSCL	NIL	NIL	2	16.67	NIL	NIL	10	83.33	NIL	NIL
TERIL	NIL	NIL	8	80.00	NIL	NIL	2	20.00	NIL	NIL
OTHERS	1	4.55	10	45.45	NIL	NIL	10	45.45	1	4.55
TOTAL	**14**	**7.82**	**65**	**36.31**	**15**	**8.38**	**75**	**41.90**	**10**	**5.59**

N = 179

Table 4.1.10 shows 'sanction of leave' as a conflict issue and indicates that (47.37%) of ZHL and (80.00%) of TERIL responded that they 'agree' on the aforesaid issue, while respondents of IARIL and Other Libraries each has opined as (40.91%) as 'agree' and (45.45%) as 'disagree'. It may be observed that respondents of DULS (48.53%), JNUL (38.46%) and HMSCL (83.33%) have expressed their views as 'disagree'. Among the total respondents of all libraries (41.90%) opined that they are 'disagree' on the issue, while (36.31%) of the respondents are 'agree'. It is concluded from this Table that respondents of DULS, JNUL and HMSCL viewed that sanction of leave is not an issue of conflict, while ZHL and TERIL respondents have reported that they hold 'sanction of leave' as a conflict issue with their superiors, peers and subordinates.

4.1.11. Not Meeting Dead Lines

Supervisors allot work to their subordinates fixing some deadlines. Sometimes, subordinates do not perform their work in time. To know whether or not this becomes an issue of conflict, data was collected, analysed and presented in Table 4.1.11.

Table 4.1.11 : Conflict over Not Meeting Dead Lines

Library	*Strongly Agree*		*Agree*		*Undecided*		*Disagree*		*Strongly Disagree*	
	Freq.	*%*	*Freq.*	*%*	*Freq.*	*%*	*Freq.*	*%*	*Freq.*	*%*
DULS	5	7.35	21	30.88	12	17.65	26	38.24	4	5.88
JNUL	NIL	NIL	5	19.23	4	15.38	14	53.85	3	11.54
ZHL, JMI	2	10.53	4	21.05	11	57.89	1	5.26	1	5.26
IARIL	NIL	NIL	7	31.82	8	36.36	7	31.82	NIL	NIL
HMSCL	NIL	NIL	6	50.00	NIL	NIL	6	50.00	NIL	NIL
TERIL	NIL	NIL	3	30.00	NIL	40.00	2	20.00	1	10.00
OTHERS	NIL	NIL	8	36.36	NIL	NIL	13	59.09	1	4.55
TOTAL	**7**	**3.91**	**54**	**30.17**	**39**	**21.79**	**69**	**38.55**	**10**	**5.59**

N = 179

Table 4.1.11 presents 'not meeting deadline' as a conflict issue and indicates that larger percentage of respondents expressed their views as 'disagree', such as respondents from DULS (38.24%), JNUL (53.85%) and Other Libraries (59.09%), while responses received from ZHL (57.89%), IARIL (36.36%) and TERIL (40.10%) reported as 'undecided' on above issue. It is observed that respondents of IARIL (31.82%) and HMSCL (50.00%) opined in equal numbers as 'agree' and 'disagree' respectively. It is inferred from the Table that 'not meeting deadlines' is not a conflict issue of the respondents with their

Table 7.1.12 : Conflict over Arriving Late

Library	*Strongly Agree*		*Agree*		*Undecided*		*Disagree*		*Strongly Disagree*	
	Freq.	*%*	*Freq.*	*%*	*Freq.*	*%*	*Freq.*	*%*	*Freq.*	*%*
DULS	10	14.71	30	44.12	3	4.41	19	27.94	6	8.82
JNUL	1	3.85	10	38.46	2	7.69	9	34.62	4	15.38
ZHL, JMI	5	26.32	5	26.32	3	15.79	2	10.53	4	21.05
IARIL	1	4.55	7	31.82	3	13.64	10	45.45	1	4.55
HMSCL	NIL	NIL	7	58.33	NIL	NIL	5	41.67	NIL	NIL
TERIL	NIL	NIL	5	50.00	1	10.00	3	30.00	1	10.00
OTHERS	NIL	4.55	4	18.18	3	13.64	14	63.64	NIL	NIL
TOTAL	**18**	**10.06**	**68**	**37.99**	**15**	**8.38**	**62**	**34.64**	**16**	**8.94**

N = 179

superiors, peers and subordinates.

4.1.12. Arriving Late

Workers' arriving late on the duty in the libraries is not a good habit and develops conflict. To know whether or not this is a conflict issue, data was collected, analysed and presented in Table 4.1.12.

The data in Table 4.1.12 indicates that respondents of DULS (44.12%), JNUL (38.46%), ZHL (26.32%), HMSCL (58.33%) and TERIL (50.00%) expressed their views that they are 'agree' on the above mentioned issue, while (34.62%) of JNUL, (45.45%) of IARIL, (41.67%), of HMSCL and (63.64%) of Other Libraries responded as 'disagree'. It is also significant to note that a smaller number of respondents of ZHL (26.32%) opined as many as 'strongly agree'. It means that majority of respondents of this library are 'agree'. The highest percentage (37.99%) of the over all respondents expressed their views as 'agree' as against 'disagree (34.64%)'. It is inferred from the Table that arriving late is a conflict issue of the respondents of all libraries except IARIL and Other Libraries, with superiors, peers and subordinates.

Table 7.1.13 : Conflict over Leaving Early

Library	Strongly Agree		Agree		Undecided		Disagree		Strongly Disagree	
	Freq.	%	Freq.	%	Freq.	%	Freq.	%	Freq.	%
DULS	7	10.29	29	42.65	4	5.88	20	29.41	8	11.76
JNUL	3	11.54	9	34.62	1	3.85	8	30.77	5	19.23
ZHL, JMI	6	31.58	5	26.32	2	10.53	2	10.53	4	21.05
IARIL	1	4.55	8	36.36	2	9.09	10	45.45	1	4.55
HMSCL	1	8.33	4	33.33	NIL	NIL	7	58.33	NIL	NIL
TERIL	NIL	NIL	6	60.00	1	10.00	2	20.00	1	10.00
OTHERS	1	4.55	3	13.64	3	13.64	15	68.18	NIL	NIL
TOTAL	**19**	**10.61**	**64**	**35.75**	**13**	**7.26**	**64**	**35.75**	**19**	**10.61**

N = 179

4.1.13. Leaving Early

Leaving early from the place of duty develops conflict among co-workers. Responses on this issue were received, analysed and presented in Table 4.1.13.

Table 4.1.13 indicates that (42.65%) of professionals of DULS, (34.62%) of JNUL, (60.00%) of TERIL responded as 'agree', while (45.45%) of IARIL, (58.33%) of HMSCL and (68.18%) of Other Libraries have expressed their views as 'disagree'. Further analysis of this Table reveals that respondents of ZHL (31.58%) 'strongly agree' and (26.32%) 'agree'. It is also interesting to know that respondents (35.75%) expressed their views as 'agree' and 'disagree' equally from the over all responses. It is concluded from the Table that 'leaving early' is a conflict issue of the respondents of DULS, JNUL, ZHL and TERIL while this is not a conflict issue for the respondents of IARIL, HMSCL and Other Libraries.

4.1.14. Misinterpretation of Orders

Misinterpretation of superiors' orders by the workers in library may develop conflict. To know the views of the professionals on the issue, data was collected, analysed and

Table 7.1.14 : Conflict over Misinterpretation of Orders

Library	*Strongly Agree*		*Agree*		*Undecided*		*Disagree*		*Strongly Disagree*	
	Freq.	*%*	*Freq.*	*%*	*Freq.*	*%*	*Freq.*	*%*	*Freq.*	*%*
DULS	3	4.41	16	23.53	16	23.53	27	39.71	6	8.82
JNUL	NIL	NIL	4	15.38	5	19.23	15	57.69	2	7.69
ZHL, JMI	2	10.53	9	47.37	5	26.32	1	5.26	2	10.53
IARIL	NIL	NIL	11	50.00	NIL	NIL	10	45.45	1	4.55
HMSCL	NIL	NIL	4	33.33	1	8.33	7	58.33	NIL	NIL
TERIL	NIL	NIL	4	40.00	2	20.00	3	30.00	1	10.00
OTHERS	2	9.09	3	13.64	4	18.18	12	54.55	1	4.55
TOTAL	**7**	**3.91**	**51**	**28.49**	**33**	**18.44**	**75**	**41.90**	**13**	**7.26**

N = 179

presented in Table 4.1.14.

Table 4.1.14 reveals that respondents of ZHL (47.37%), IARIL (50.00%), TERIL (40.00%) are 'agree' on this issue, while (39.71%) respondents of DULS, (57.69%) of JNUL, (45.45%) of IARIL, (58.33%) of Other Libraries viewed as 'disagree'. It may be observed that from the over all percentage (41.90%) and (28.49%) of the respondents opined as 'disagree' and 'agree' respectively. It is inferred from the Table that 'misinterpretation of orders' is not a conflict issue of the respondents of DULS, JNUL, HMSCL, and Other Libraries, while this is a conflict issue of the respondents of ZHL, IARIL and TERIL.

4.1.15. Work Environment

For doing a good work efficiently, healthy working environment is needed. The insufficient physical conditions of work waste time, energy and skill of the workers and may develops conflict. The data collected on the same issue has been analysed and presented in Table 4.1.15.

The data in Table 4.1.15 reveals that larger percentage (42.31%) of respondents from JNUL, (36.84%) of ZHL, (60.00%) of TERIL and (40.91%) of Other Libraries have expressed their

Table 4.1.15 : Conflict over Working Environment

Library	*Strongly Agree*		*Agree*		*Undecided*		*Disagree*		*Strongly Disagree*	
	Freq.	*%*	*Freq.*	*%*	*Freq.*	*%*	*Freq.*	*%*	*Freq.*	*%*
DULS	8	11.76	22	32.35	9	13.24	26	38.24	3	4.41
JNUL	4	15.38	11	42.31	2	7.69	9	34.62	NIL	
ZHL, JMI	4	21.05	7	36.84	2	10.53	3	15.79	3	15.79
IARIL	NIL	NIL	9	40.91	2	9.09	11	50.00	NIL	NIL
HMSCL	NIL	NIL	5	41.67	1	8.33	6	50.00	NIL	NIL
TERIL	1	10.00	6	60.00	1	10.00	2	20.00	NIL	NIL
OTHERS	2	9.09	9	40.91	4	18.18	7	31.82	NIL	NIL
TOTAL	**19**	**10.61**	**69**	**38.55**	**21**	**11.73**	**64**	**35.75**	**6**	**3.35**

N = 179

views as 'agree' on the this issue, while (38.24%) of DULS, (50.00%) of IARIL and (50.00%) of HMSCL opined as 'disagree'. Further analysis of the Table reveals that (11.76%) of DULS, (15.38%) of JNUL and (21.05%) of ZHL responded as 'strongly agree'. The percentage added with 'agree' becomes higher percentage (38.55%) of the respondents of the total responses reported as 'agree' and 'disagree' (35.75%). Conclusion is drawn from the Table that working environment is a conflict issue of the respondents of the DULS, JNUL, ZHL, TERIL and Other Libraries except IARIL and HMCL.

4.1.16. Personal Habit

Every worker develops his/her own personal habits. While working together, different habits of different persons may develop conflict situations. To know whether or not conflict exists due to different personal habits of the workers, data was collected, analysed, and presented in Table 4.1.16

Table 4.1.16 shows that respondents (60.00%) of TERIL are 'agree' on this issue, while the (52.94%) of DULS, (50.00%) of JNUL, (58.33%) of HMSCL and (54.55%) of Other Libraries have responded as 'disagree'. Further analysis of this Table

Table 4.1.16 : Conflict over Personal Habits of Workers

Library	*Strongly Agree*		*Agree*		*Undecided*		*Disagree*		*Strongly Disagree*	
	Freq.	*%*	*Freq.*	*%*	*Freq.*	*%*	*Freq.*	*%*	*Freq.*	*%*
DULS	3	4.41	18	26.47	7	10.29	36	52.94	4	5.88
JNUL	1	3.85	7	26.92	4	15.38	13	50.00	1	3.85
ZHL, JMI	2	10.53	5	26.32	5	26.32	3	15.79	4	21.05
IARIL	2	9.09	7	31.82	6	27.27	7	31.82	NIL	NIL
HMSCL	NIL	NIL	3	25.00	1	8.33	7	58.33	1	8.33
TERIL	NIL	NIL	6	60.00	4	40.00	NIL	NIL	NIL	NIL
OTHERS	1	4.55	5	22.73	4	18.18	12	54.55	NIL	NIL
TOTAL	**9**	**5.03**	**51**	**28.49**	**31**	**17.32**	**78**	**43.58**	**10**	**5.59**

N = 179

reveals the views of respondents (26.32%) of ZHL are divided equally as 'agree' and 'undecided' and those of IARIL (31.82%) as 'agree' and 'disagree'. Among the total respondents, the higher percentage (43.58%) viewed as 'disagree' in contrast to 'agree' (28.49%). It is concluded from the Table that 'different personal habits' is not a conflict issue amongst the respondents of all the libraries except TERIL, with their superiors, peers and subordinates.

4.2. CONFLICT ISSUES: SUMMARISED

The views of the respondents on the various issues of conflict, though analysed and discussed separately in the preceding paragraphs, have been summarized in the form of 'At A Glance'. Such a summary of the entire data is presented in Table 4.2.

Conflict issues, their over all frequencies and percentages have been summarized and presented in Table 4.2, which reveals that the respondents 'strongly agree' and 'agree' with the conflict issues, such as, 'job objectives' (6.15%) and (47.49%); 'reward criteria' (5.38%) and (32.96%); 'participation in decision making' (9.50%) and (62.01%); 'library policies and

Table 4.2 : Summary of Data on All Sixteen Issues of Conflict

Library	Strongly Agree		Agree		Undecided		Disagree		Strongly Disagree	
	Freq.	%	Freq.	%	Freq.	%	Freq.	%	Freq.	%
1. Conflict over job objectives	11	6.15	89	49.72	12	6.70	63	35.20	4	2.23
2. Conflict over role	15	8.38	90	50.28	24	13.41	48	26.82	2	1.12
3. Planning of activities	19	10.61	100	55.87	16	8.94	40	22.35	4	2.23
4. Distribution of authority	24	13.41	85	47.49	17	9.50	47	26.26	6	3.35
5. Reward criteria	15	8.38	59	32.96	42	23.46	58	32.40	5	2.79
6. Punishment criteria	15	8.38	41	22.91	44	24.58	65	38.31	14	7.82
7. Participation in decision making	17	9.50	111	62.01	13	7.26	34	18.99	4	2.23
8. Library policies and procedures	20	11.17	69	38.55	15	8.38	72	40.22	3	1.68
9. Promotions	26	14.53	92	51.40	19	10.61	32	17.88	10	5.59
10. Sanction of leave	14	7.82	65	26.31	15	8.38	75	41.90	10	5.59
11. Not meeting deadlines	7	3.91	54	30.17	39	21.79	69	38.55	10	5.59
12. Arriving late	18	10.06	68	37.99	15	8.38	62	34.64	16	8.94
13. Leaving early	19	10.61	64	35.75	13	7.26	64	35.75	19	10.61
14. Misinterpretation of orders	7	3.91	51	28.49	33	18.44	75	41.90	13	7.26
15. Working environment	19	10061	69	38.55	21	11.73	64	35.75	6	3.35
16. Personal habit	9	5.03	51	28.49	31	17.32	78	43.58	10	5.59

N = 179

procedures' (11.17%) and (38.55%); 'promotion' (14.53%) and (51.40%); 'arriving late' (10.06%) and (37.99%); 'working environment' (10.61%) and (38.55%), and on such other conflict issues, as 'sanction of leave' (41.90%) and (5.59%); 'not meeting deadlines' (38.55%); and 'personal habits' (43.58%) and (5.59%) as 'disagree' and 'strongly disagree' respectively. Further, the responses received on the issue of 'leaving early' are equally divided as 'agree' and 'disagree'.

Conclusions may be drawn from the data in the Table 4.2 that conflict 'over job objectives', conflict over 'role', 'planning of activities', 'distribution of authority', 'reward criteria', 'participation in decision making process', 'library policies and procedures', 'promotion', 'arriving late and 'working environment' are the conflict issues with the superiors, peers and subordinates. However, some of the issues like, 'sanction of leave', 'not meeting deadlines', 'leaving early', 'misinterpretation of orders' and 'personal habits' are not the substantive conflict issues of the respondents of the libraries, being studied.

Special Observation : It may be observed that

(i) Two respondents of ZHL have mentioned their views under 'any other, please specify', raising a new conflict issue pertaining to 'volume of work expected/ to be accomplished'

(ii) Another two respondents of DULS have mentioned that 'Too much of freedom' is also an additional conflict issue.

(iii) Two respondents of Other Libraries have described 'space' as a conflict issue with their superiors, peers and subordinates.

Well, the three issues of conflict, as given above, could not be made part of the present research work. The validity of these issues, and a survey of opinion of the professionals may be studied by some other researcher in near future.

4.3. CAUSES OF INTERPERSONAL CONFLICT

Information regarding 'causes' of conflict was sought from the respondents, under this study. The data collected is being studied in the paragraphs as follows.

4.3.1. Scarce Resources

Due to financial crunch, the resources in the university libraries have been considerably squeezed. To know whether or not the 'scarce resources' cause conflict in the university libraries, the data collected, is presented in Table 4.3.1.

Table 4.3.1 : Scarce Resources: Cause of Conflict

Library	*Strongly Agree*		*Agree*		*Undecided*		*Disagree*		*Strongly Disagree*	
	Freq.	*%*	*Freq.*	*%*	*Freq.*	*%*	*Freq.*	*%*	*Freq.*	*%*
DULS	3	4.41	44	64.71	7	10.29	11	16.18	3	4.41
JNUL	1	3.85	13	50.00	3	11.54	9	34.62	NIL	NIL
ZHL, JMI	4	21.05	8	42.11	7	36.84	NIL	NIL	NIL	NIL
IARIL	1	4.45	8	36.36	1	4.55	12	54.55	NIL	NIL
HMSCL	NIL	NIL	9	75.00	NIL	NIL	2	16.67	1	8.33
TERIL	NIL	NIL	3	30.00	3	30.00	3	30.00	1	10.00
OTHERS	1	4.55	15	68.18	1	4.55	5	22.73	NIL	NIL
TOTAL	**10**	**5.59**	**100**	**55.87**	**22**	**12.29**	**42**	**23.46**	**5**	**2.79**

N = 179

Table 4.3.1 shows competition over scarce resources as a cause of interpersonal conflict, which reveals that a larger number of respondents are 'agree' on this issue; these are DULS (64.71%), JNUL (50.00%), ZHL (42.11%), HMSCL (75.00%) and Other Libraries (68.18%), while (54.55%) of IARIL have responded as 'disagree'. Further analysis of this Table reveals that respondents of TERIL have viewed as 'agree', 'undecided' and 'disagree' (30.00%) each, while (21.05%) respondents of ZHL have expressed their views as 'strongly agree'. However, higher percentage of total number of respondents 'agree' on this issue. It is inferred from the Table that competition over scarce resources perceived as a cause for conflict amongst the respondents of DULS, JNUL, ZHL, HMSCL, and Other Libraries except the IARIL and TERIL.

4.3.2. Jurisdiction Ambiguity

Jurisdiction ambiguity may cause conflict. To know whether or not this cause is prevailing, the data collected, is presented in Table 4.3.2.

Table 4.3.2 : Jurisdiction Ambiguity : Cause of Conflict

Library	*Strongly Agree*		*Agree*		*Undecided*		*Disagree*		*Strongly Disagree*	
	Freq.	*%*	*Freq.*	*%*	*Freq.*	*%*	*Freq.*	*%*	*Freq.*	*%*
DULS	7	10.29	37	54.41	3	4.41	20	29.41	1	1.47
JNUL	NIL	NIL	14	53.85	7	26.92	5	19.23	NIL	NIL
ZHL, JMI	1	5.26	11	57.89	6	31.58	1	5.26	NIL	NIL
IARIL	NIL	NIL	13	59.09	3	13.64	6	27.27	NIL	NIL
HMSCL	NIL	NIL	6	50.00	1	8.33	4	33.33	1	8.33
TERIL	NIL	NIL	5	50.00	3	30.00	2	20.00	NIL	NIL
OTHERS	NIL	NIL	6	27.27	8	36.36	8	36.36	NIL	NIL
TOTAL	8	4.47	92	51.40	31	17.32	46	25.70	2	1.12

N = 179

Data on the cause of 'jurisdiction ambiguity' presented in Table 4.3.2 Indicates that larger number of respondents have perceived the 'jurisdiction ambiguity' as the cause of conflict. Such as, (54.41%) of DULS, (53.85%) of JNUL, (57.89%) of ZHL, (59.09%) of IARIL, (50.00%) each of HMCL and TERIL, while (36.36%) respondents of Other Libraries are 'disagree' and in equal number as 'undecided'. From over all (51.40%) percentage, the respondents from all the libraries, except Other Libraries, have reported their views as 'agree' with this cause of conflict.

4.3.3. Perceptions

Different Perceptions of workers may cause interpersonal conflict. Data collected on this account is presented in Table 4.3.3.

Table 4.3.3 : Different Perceptions : Cause of Conflict

Library	*Strongly Agree*		*Agree*		*Undecided*		*Disagree*		*Strongly Disagree*	
	Freq.	*%*	*Freq.*	*%*	*Freq.*	*%*	*Freq.*	*%*	*Freq.*	*%*
DULS	3	4.41	23	33.82	12	17.65	30	44.12	NIL	NIL
JNUL	3	11.54	10	38.46	7	26.92	4	15.38	2	7.69
ZHL, JMI	6	31.58	10	52.63	2	10.53	1	5.26	NIL	NIL
IARIL	1	4.55	8	36.36	1	4.55	12	54.55	NIL	NIL
HMSCL	NIL	NIL	5	41.67	NIL	NIL	7	58.33	NIL	NIL
TERIL	NIL	NIL	6	60.00	3	30.00	1	10.00	NIL	NIL
OTHERS	NIL	NIL	9	40.91	7	31.82	6	27.27	NIL	NIL
TOTAL	**13**	**7.26**	**71**	**39.66**	**32**	**17.88**	**61**	**34.08**	**2**	**1.12**

N = 179

Table 4.3.3 reveals that respondents of JNUL (38.46%), ZHL (52.63%), TERIL (60.00%) and Other Libraries (40.91%) have found the 'different perceptions of workers' as a cause of interpersonal conflict, while respondents of DULS (44.12%), IARIL (54.55%) and HMSCL (58.33%) expressed their views as 'disagree'. The respondents (11.54%) of JNUL, (31.58%) of ZHL responded 'strongly agree'. It is significant to note that (17.65%) of DULS, (26.92%) of JNUL, (30.00%) of TERIL and (31.82%) of Other Libraries opined as 'undecided'. From the over all responses, (34.08%) respondents have viewed as 'disagree' and (39.66%) as 'agree'. Conclusion is drawn from the data so analysed that 'different perceptions' are not endorsed as a cause of conflict of the respondents of DULS, IARIL, HMSCL, while the respondents of JNUL, ZHL, TERIL and Other Libraries have seen the 'different perceptions' as a cause of interpersonal conflict.

4.3.4. Personal Differences

Personalised differences or the bias created among the respondents may cause conflict. Data was collected, analysed and presented in Table 4.3.4.

Table 4.3.4 : Personal Differences : Cause of Conflict

Library	*Strongly Agree*		*Agree*		*Undecided*		*Disagree*		*Strongly Disagree*	
	Freq.	*%*	*Freq.*	*%*	*Freq.*	*%*	*Freq.*	*%*	*Freq.*	*%*
DULS	5	7.35	17	25.00	11	16.18	27	39.71	8	11.76
JNUL	2	7.69	10	38.46	4	15.38	9	34.62	1	3.85
ZHL, JMI	2	10.53	7	36.84	2	10.53	4	21.05	4	21.05
IARIL	2	9.09	11	50.00	1	4.55	8	36.36	NIL	NIL
HMSCL	NIL	NIL	5	41.67	1	8.33	5	41.67	1	8.33
TERIL	NIL	NIL	3	30.00	3	30.00	4	40.00	NIL	NIL
OTHERS	NIL	NIL	5	22.73	4	18.18	13	59.09	NIL	NIL
TOTAL	**11**	**6.15**	**58**	**32.40**	**26**	**14.53**	**70**	**39.11**	**14**	**7.82**

N = 179

Table 4.2.4 reveals that responses received from JNUL (38.46%), ZHL (36.84%), IARIL (50.00%) reported as 'agree', while respondents of DULS (39.71%) and Other Libraries (59.09%) are of the opinion as 'disagree'. It is interesting to know that (41.67%) of the respondents 'agree' and as many 'disagree'. Among over all response (39.11%) of the respondents are 'disagree' while (32.40%) are 'agree'. It is inferred that 'personal differences' have not been found as a cause for conflict among the library professionals of DULS, HMSCL, TERIL and Other Libraries, and the same has been perceived, as a reason of conflict, by the respondents of JNUL and ZHL.

4.3.5. Differences In Value

The respondents were asked whether or not the 'differences in value' causes conflict with superiors, peers and subordinates. The data collected is presented in Table 4.3.5.

Table 4.3.5 indicates that larger number of JNUL (50.00%), ZHL (52.63%), TERIL (50.00%), and Other Libraries (45.45%) opined as 'agree' with the 'differences in value' causes conflict, while (51.47%) of DULS, (68.18%) of IARIL, (33.33%) of HMSCL responded as 'agree'. It is significant to note that

Table 4.3.5 : Differences In Value: Cause of Conflict

Library	Strongly Agree		Agree		Undecided		Disagree		Strongly Disagree	
	Freq.	%	Freq.	%	Freq.	%	Freq.	%	Freq.	%
DULS	7	10.29	14	20.59	8	11.76	35	51.47	4	5.88
JNUL	NIL	NIL	13	50.00	3	11.54	9	34.62	1	3.85
ZHL, JMI	2	10.53	10	52.63	3	15.79	3	15.79	1	5.26
IARIL	2	9.09	2	9.09	3	13.64	15	68.18	NIL	NIL
HMSCL	NIL	NIL	4	33.33	NIL	NIL	8	66.67	NIL	NIL
TERIL	NIL	NIL	5	50.00	3	30.00	2	20.00	NIL	NIL
OTHERS	1	4.55	10	45.45	3	13.64	8	36.36	NIL	NIL
TOTAL	**12**	**6.70**	**58**	**32.40**	**23**	**12.85**	**80**	**44.69**	**6**	**3.35**

N = 179

(30.00%) of TERIL are 'undecided'. The total percentage (44.69%) of respondents expressed their views as 'disagree' and (32.40%) as 'agree'. It is inferred from the Table that differences in value was not perceived as a cause of conflict by the respondents of DULS, IARIL, HMSCL, while respondents o JNUL, ZHL, TERIL, and Other Libraries perceived it as a cause of conflict.

4.3.6. Communication Barrier

Communication plays an important role in maintaining good relations among workers in any organization. To know whether or not the 'communication barriers' become the cause of conflict, data was collected, analysed and presented in Table 4.3.6..

Table 4.3.6 indicates that respondents of the most of the libraries are 'agree' that 'communication barriers' may cause conflict. These respondents include: (52.94%) of DULS, (57.69%) of JNUL, (42.11%) of ZHL, (68.18%) of IARIL, (50.00%) of HMSCL and (45.45%) of Other Libraries; while (60.00%) respondents of TERIL opined as 'disagree'. It is interesting to note that (10.29%) respondents of DULS, (15.79%) of ZHL, (10.00%) of

Table 4.3.6 : Communication Barriers : Cause of Conflict

Library	*Strongly Agree*		*Agree*		*Undecided*		*Disagree*		*Strongly Disagree*	
	Freq.	*%*	*Freq.*	*%*	*Freq.*	*%*	*Freq.*	*%*	*Freq.*	*%*
DULS	7	10.29	36	52.94	10	14.71	12	17.65	3	4.41
JNUL	1	3.85	15	57.69	4	15.38	6	23.08	NIL	NIL
ZHL, JMI	3	15.79	8	42.11	1	5.26	4	21.05	3	15.79
IARIL	1	4.55	15	68.18	NIL	NIL	5	22.73	1	4.55
HMSCL	NIL	NIL	6	50.00	1	8.33	5	41.67	NIL	NIL
TERIL	1	10.00	3	30.00	NIL	NIL	6	60.00	NIL	NIL
OTHERS	2	9.09	10	45.45	NIL	NIL	9	40.91	1	4.55
TOTAL	**15**	**8.38**	**93**	**51.96**	**16**	**8.94**	**47**	**26.26**	**8**	**4.47**

N = 179

TERIL and (9.09%) of Other Libraries responded as 'strongly agree'. Larger number (51.96%) of respondents of over all percentage are 'agree' in contrast to 'disagree' only (26.26%). It is concluded that communication barrier is one cause of conflict in all the libraries, TERIL.

4.3.7. Interdependence

Interdependence among members of a group of workers in an organization is essential element of team -work. However, it may cause conflict among them. To know whether or not 'interdependence' is a cause of conflict, the data was collected, analysed and presented in Table 4.3.7..

Table 4.3.7 indicates the larger number of respondents of all libraries 'agree' that 'interdependence' is the cause of interpersonal conflict, such as, (51.47%) of DULS, (76.92%) of JNUL, (47.37%) of ZHL, (72.73%) of IARIL, (83.33%) of HMSCL, (80.00%) of TERIL, and (72.73%) of Other Libraries. Further analysis of the Table reveals that (21.05%) of ZHL as 'strongly agree'. It is observed that respondents from all the libraries are 'agree' that 'interdependence' is a cause of interpersonal conflict of the respondents with superiors, peers and subordinates. The

Table 4.3.7 : Interdependence : Cause of Conflict

Library	*Strongly Agree*		*Agree*		*Undecided*		*Disagree*		*Strongly Disagree*	
	Freq.	*%*	*Freq.*	*%*	*Freq.*	*%*	*Freq.*	*%*	*Freq.*	*%*
DULS	6	8.82	35	51.47	6	8.82	18	26.47	3	4.41
JNUL	1	3.85	20	76.92	1	3.85	4	15.38	NIL	NIL
ZHL, JMI	4	21.05	9	47.37	4	21.05	2	10.53	NIL	NIL
IARIL	1	4.55	16	72.73	1	4.55	4	18.18	NIL	NIL
HMSCL	1	8.33	10	83.33	1	8.33	NIL	NIL	NIL	NIL
TERIL	NIL	NIL	8	80.00	1	10.00	1	10.00	NIL	NIL
OTHERS	1	4.55	16	72.73	1	4.55	4	18.18	NIL	NIL
TOTAL	**14**	**7.82**	**114**	**63.69**	**15**	**8.38**	**33**	**18.44**	**3**	**1.68**

N = 179

same view is found in the over all responses, the majority (63.69%) responded as 'agree' while 'disagree' percentage is only (18.44%).

4.3.8. Goal Differences

The goals and objectives of different workers may differ from each other in an organization. To know about 'goal difference as a cause of conflict, data was collected, analysed and presented in Table 4.3.8.

Table 7.3.8 reveals that respondents of DULS (54.41%), JNUL (46.15%), ZHL (68.42%), IARIL (59.09%), HMSCL (91.67%) and TERIL (50.00%) have expressed their views as 'agree', while respondents of Other Libraries (50.00%) responded as 'disagree'. Further analysis shows that (15.79%) of ZHL responded as 'strongly agree'. The larger number (54.19%) of respondents of the total responses fall in the same pattern. They are of the view as 'agree', while (21.23%) responded 'disagree' with the preposition. The data in this Table reveals that respondents from all libraries, except 'Other Libraries', have perceived the 'goal differences' as a cause of interpersonal conflict with superiors, peers and subordinates.

Table 4.3.8 : Goal Differences : Cause of Conflict

Library	*Strongly Agree*		*Agree*		*Undecided*		*Disagree*		*Strongly Disagree*	
	Freq.	*%*	*Freq.*	*%*	*Freq.*	*%*	*Freq.*	*%*	*Freq.*	*%*
DULS	4	5.88	37	54.41	7	10.29	16	23.53	4	5.88
JNUL	2	7.69	12	46.15	7	26.92	4	15.38	1	3.85
ZHL, JMI	3	15.79	13	68.42	3	15.79	NIL	NIL	NIL	NIL
IARIL	1	4.55	13	59.09	4	18.18	4	18.18	NIL	NIL
HMSCL	NIL	NIL	11	91.67	NIL	NIL	1	8.33	NIL	NIL
TERIL	NIL	NIL	5	50.00	3	30.00	2	20.00	NIL	NIL
OTHERS	1	4.55	6	27.27	4	18.18	11	50.00	NIL	NIL
TOTAL	**11**	**6.15**	**97**	**54.19**	**28**	**15.64**	**38**	**21.23**	**5**	**2.79**

N = 179

4.3.9. Performance Appraisal

Performance appraisal is an essential element in administration in an organization. However, the act may become a cause of conflict among the workers, if it is not handled carefully. To know whether or not the 'performance appraisal' is a cause of conflict in university libraries being studied, data collected has been analysed and presented in Table 4.3.9..

Table 4.3.9 : Performance Appraisal : Cause of Conflict

Library	*Strongly Agree*		*Agree*		*Undecided*		*Disagree*		*Strongly Disagree*	
	Freq.	*%*	*Freq.*	*%*	*Freq.*	*%*	*Freq.*	*%*	*Freq.*	*%*
DULS	8	11.76	25	36.76	7	10.29	26	38.24	2	2.94
JNUL	1	3.85	14	53.85	4	15.38	7	26.92	NIL	NIL
ZHL, JMI	2	10.53	10	52.63	5	26.32	2	10.53	NIL	NIL
IARIL	2	9.09	10	45.45	2	9.09	8	36.36	NIL	NIL
HMSCL	NIL	NIL	6	50.00	NIL	NIL	6	50.00	NIL	NIL
TERIL	NIL	NIL	6	60.00	3	30.00	1	10.00	NIL	NIL
OTHERS	2	9.09	11	50.00	2	9.09	7	31.82	NIL	NIL
TOTAL	**15**	**8.38**	**82**	**45.81**	**23**	**12.85**	**57**	**31.84**	**2**	**1.12**

N = 179

Table 4.3.9 makes evident that responses received from the DULS (36.75%), JNUL (53.85%), ZHL (52.63%), IARIL (45.45%), TERIL (60.00%) and Other Libraries (50.00%) reported as 'agree', while respondents of HMSCL (50.00%) responded 'agree' and equal numbers 'disagree'. It is significant to note that (11.76%) of DULS, (10.53%) of ZHL and (9.09%) each of IARIL and Other Libraries have responded as 'strongly agree'. The larger number (31.84%) of over all responses has viewed as 'disagree'. It is inferred from the Table that 'performance appraisal' is perceived as a cause for conflict with superiors, peers and subordinates.

4.3.10. Differences In Expertise

To know whether or not the 'differences in expertise' of workers creates the cause of interpersonal conflict among the workers, the data was collected, analysed and presented in Table 4.3.10.

Table 4.3.10 : Differences In Expertise : Cause of Conflict

Library	*Strongly Agree*		*Agree*		*Undecided*		*Disagree*		*Strongly Disagree*	
	Freq.	*%*	*Freq.*	*%*	*Freq.*	*%*	*Freq.*	*%*	*Freq.*	*%*
DULS	6	8.82	17	25.00	12	17.65	32	47.06	1	1.47
JNUL	NIL	NIL	11	42.31	6	23.08	9	34.62	NIL	NIL
ZHL, JMI	4	21.05	9	47.37	5	26.32	1	5.26	NIL	NIL
IARIL	2	9.09	9	40.91	1	4.55	10	45.45	NIL	NIL
HMSCL	NIL	NIL	3	25.00	2	16.67	7	58.33	NIL	NIL
TERIL	1	10.00	4	40.00	3	30.00	2	20.00	NIL	NIL
OTHERS	NIL	NIL	13	59.09	3	13.64	6	27.27	NIL	NIL
TOTAL	**13**	**7.26**	**66**	**36.87**	**32**	**17.88**	**67**	**37.43**	**1**	**0.56**

N = 179

Table 4.3.10 indicates that (42.31%) respondents of JNUL, (47.37%) of ZHL, (40.00%) of TERIL and (59.09%) of Other Libraries have viewed as 'agree' while (47.06%) of DULS, (34.62%) of JNUL, (45.45%) of IARIL and (58.33%) of HMSCL have expressed their views as 'disagree'. It is also interesting to note that (21.05%) of ZHL, (9.09%) of IARIL and (10.00%) of TERIL have opined as 'strongly agree'. The overall percentage (44.13%) of respondents are 'agree' and 'strongly agree'; whereas the total percentage of respondents is (37.99%) when 'disagree' and 'strongly disagree' are put together.

4.3.11. Distrust

It has been observed that mutual trust among workers results into better work environment. Distrust of any kind may develop conflict. To know whether or not 'distrust' is cause of conflict in the libraries being studied, the data collected was analysed and presented in Table 4.3.11.

Table 4.3.11 : Distrust : Cause of Conflict

Library	*Strongly Agree*		*Agree*		*Undecided*		*Disagree*		*Strongly Disagree*	
	Freq.	*%*	*Freq.*	*%*	*Freq.*	*%*	*Freq.*	*%*	*Freq.*	*%*
DULS	3	4.41	12	17.65	14	20.59	32	47.06	7	10.29
JNUL	2	7.69	4	15.38	7	26.92	10	38.46	3	11.54
ZHL, JMI	2	10.53	5	26.32	6	31.58	4	21.05	2	10.53
IARIL	NIL	NIL	2	9.09	4	18.18	16	72.73	NIL	NIL
HMSCL	NIL	NIL	3	25.00	NIL	NIL	9	75.00	NIL	NIL
TERIL	NIL	NIL	3	30.00	4	40.00	3	30.00	NIL	NIL
OTHERS	2	9.09	4	18.18	5	22.73	11	50.00	NIL	NIL
TOTAL	**9**	**5.03**	**33**	**18.44**	**40**	**22.35**	**85**	**47.49**	**12**	**6.70**

N = 179

Table 4.3.11 indicates that respondents of DULS (47.06%), JNUL (38.46%), IARIL (72.73%), HMSCL (75.00%) and Other Libraries (50.00%) opined as 'disagree', while respondents of ZHL (26.32%) responded as 'agree' and (10.53%) 'strongly agree'. It is also interesting to note that respondents (30.00%) of TERIL have viewed as 'agree' and in equal numbers 'disagree' leaving (40.00%) 'undecided'. The large number (47.49%) of over all percentage of the respondents are of the view as 'disagree' and (18.44%) 'agree'. It is concluded that distrust did not perceive as a cause of conflict for all libraries, except ZHL. It may be of interest for someone to know that when total 'agree' and 'strongly agree' are put together, the percentage in favour of the preposition comes to only (23.47%), and on the other hand when 'disagree' and 'strongly disagree' are put together, the percentage reaches on the higher side of (54.19%), leaving 'undecided' at (22.35%). Hence, one may conclude that the larger number of respondents are in disagreement and are of the view that distrust among workers is not the cause of conflict among them.

4.3.12. Technological Changes

Rapid changes and up-grading in technology adopted by the libraries, may cause conflict. To know whether or not the 'technological changes' are the cause of conflict in the libraries being studied, the data was collected, analysed and presented in Table 4.3.12.

Table 4.3.12 : Technological Changes : Cause of Conflict

Library	*Strongly Agree*		*Agree*		*Undecided*		*Disagree*		*Strongly Disagree*	
	Freq.	*%*	*Freq.*	*%*	*Freq.*	*%*	*Freq.*	*%*	*Freq.*	*%*
DULS	11	16.18	29	42.65	9	13.24	16	23.53	3	4.41
JNUL	3	11.54	16	61.54	3	11.54	3	11.54	1	3.85
ZHL, JMI	5	26.32	7	36.84	2	10.53	4	21.05	1	5.26
IARIL	2	9.09	7	31.82	3	13.64	10	45.45	NIL	NIL
HMSCL	1	8.33	9	75.00	NIL	NIL	2	16.67	NIL	NIL
TERIL	1	10.00	3	30.00	2	20.00	4	40.00	NIL	NIL
OTHERS	4	18.18	12	54.55	2	9.09	4	18.18	NIL	NIL
TOTAL	27	15.08	83	46.37	21	11.73	43	24.02	5	2.79

N = 179

Table 4.3.12 shows the 'technological changes' as a cause of interpersonal conflict and indicates that a good number of the respondents of DULS (42.65%), JNUL (61.54%), ZHL

(36.84%), HMSCL (75.00%) and Other Libraries (54.55%) opined as 'agree', while respondents of IARIL (45.45%) and TERIL (40.00%) expressed their views as 'disagree'. Further analysis of this Table shows that (16.18%) of DULS, (11.54%) of JNUL, (26.32) of ZHL, (10.00%) of TERIL and (18.18%) of Other Libraries viewed as 'strongly agree'. The respondents (46.37%) of total responses opined as 'agree'. It is concluded from Table 4.3.12 that 'technological changes' forms a cause of conflict of the respondents with superiors, peers and subordinates, except in IARIL. and TERIL.

4.3.13. Participation In Professional Meetings

Professional meetings offer an opportunity to the workers to understand various professional issues and the latest know-how. But, the opportunity provided and availed by them may cause conflict. To know whether or not it is cause of conflict, data was collected, analysed and presented in Table 4.3.13..

Table 4.3.13 : Participation in Professional Meetings : Cause of Conflict

Library	*Strongly Agree*		*Agree*		*Undecided*		*Disagree*		*Strongly Disagree*	
	Freq.	*%*	*Freq.*	*%*	*Freq.*	*%*	*Freq.*	*%*	*Freq.*	*%*
DULS	12	17.65	42	61.76	9	13.24	3	4.41	2	2.94
JNUL	5	19.23	16	61.54	3	11.54	2	7.69	NIL	NIL
ZHL, JMI	5	26.32	9	47.37	4	21.05	NIL	NIL	1	5.26
IARIL	3	13.64	12	54.55	NIL	NILD	7	31.82	NIL	NIL
HMSCL	1	8.33	6	50.00	1	8.33	4	33.33	NIL	NIL
TERIL	2	20.00	3	30.00	1	10.00	4	40.00	NIL	NIL
OTHERS	2	9.09	15	68.18	2	9.09	3	13.64	NIL	NIL
TOTAL	**30**	**16.76**	**103**	**57.54**	**20**	**11.17**	**23**	**12.85**	**3**	**1.68**

N = 179

Table 4.3.13 indicates that majority of respondents of DULS (61.76%), JNUL (61.54%), ZHL (47.37%), IARIL (54.55%), HMSCL (50.00%) and Other Libraries (68.18%) are of the view that they 'agree' with the preposition 'participation in professional meetings', while (40.00) of TERIL respondents opined as 'disagree'. Further analysis of this Table show that (17.65%) of DULS, (19.23%) of JNUL, (26.32%) of ZHL, (13.64%) of IARIL and (20.00%) of TERIL have responded as 'strongly agree'. Conclusion is drawn from the Table that 'participation in professional meetings' is perceived as a cause of interpersonal conflict amongst the respondents with superiors, peers and subordinates.

4.3.14. Vacant Posts

It has been observed that in university libraries, several vacant posts are not filled. This situation may also cause of conflict. The data collected and analysed, is presented in Table 4.3.14.

Table 4.3.14 : Vacant Posts : Cause of Conflict

Library	*Strongly Agree*		*Agree*		*Undecided*		*Disagree*		*Strongly Disagree*	
	Freq.	*%*	*Freq.*	*%*	*Freq.*	*%*	*Freq.*	*%*	*Freq.*	*%*
DULS	16	23.53	33	48.53	9	13.24	7	10.29	3	4.41
JNUL	6	23.08	7	26.92	3	11.54	6	23.08	4	15.38
ZHL, JMI	2	10.53	10	52.63	3	15.79	NIL	NIL	4	21.05
IARIL	2	9.09	3	13.64	5	22.73	12	54.55	NIL	NIL
HMSCL	1	8.33	9	75.00	0	0.00	2	16.67	NIL	NIL
TERIL	NIL	NIL	2	20.00	6	60.00	1	10.00	1	10.00
OTHERS	1	4.55	10	45.45	4	18.18	7	31.82	NIL	NIL
TOTAL	**28**	**15.64**	**74**	**41.34**	**30**	**16.76**	**35**	**19.55**	**12**	**6.70**

N = 179

Table 4.3.14 reveals that (48.53%) respondents of DULS, (26.92%) of JNUL, (52.63%) of ZHL, (75.00%) of HMSCL, and (45.45%) of Other Libraries, are 'agree', while (54.55%) of IARIL and (60.00%) of TERIL expressed their views as 'undecided'. It is also significant to note that respondents of DULS (23.53%), JNUL (23.00%) and ZHL (10.53%) have viewed as 'strongly agree'. The large number (41.34% + 15.64%)) of over all percentage of the respondents are 'agree' and 'strongly agree'. It is inferred from that 'vacant posts' is perceived as a cause for interpersonal conflict amongst the respondents of all the libraries, except IARIL and TERIL.

4.4. SUMMARY OF CAUSES OF INTERPERSONAL CONFLICT

Data regarding all of the 14 causes of conflict, discussed individually in the preceding paragraphs, has been put together and with a view to the details at a glance, the summary is presented in Table 4.4.

Table 4.4 indicates that a larger number of respondents are "strongly agree" and "agree" with the causes of conflict with their superiors, peers and subordinates, such as,' competition over scarce resources', 'Jurisdiction ambiguity', 'Different Perceptions', 'communication barriers', 'interdependence', 'goal differences', 'performance appraisal', 'differences in expertise', 'technical changes', 'participation in professional meetings', and 'vacant posts'; while respondents opined as 'disagree' with such causes as 'personal differences', 'differences in value', and 'distrust'. We can draw the conclusion from the summary presentation thåt 'competition over scarce resources', 'jurisdiction ambiguity', 'perceptions', 'communication barriers', 'interdependence', 'goal differences', 'performance appraisal', 'difference in expertise', 'technological changes', 'participation in professional meetings', and 'vacant posts' are the major source of conflict by the respondents with their superiors, peers and subordinates in the university libraries being studied..

It may be observed that in the case of interpersonal conflict, (i) 'participation in professional meetings', and (ii) 'vacant posts', the higher percentage of over all respondents are 'strongly agree' and 'agree'.

Further, under 'others, please specify', three respondents from DULS have specified the 'differences in

Table 4.4 : Summary of 14 Causes of Conflict

Causes of International Conflict	Strongly Agree		Agree		Undecided		Disagree		Strongly Disagree	
	Freq.	%	Freq.	%	Freq.	%	Freq.	%	Freq.	%
1. Competition over scarce resources	10	5.58	100	55.80	22	12.29	42	23.46	5	2.79
2. Jurisdiction ambiguity	8	4.47	92	51.40	31	17.32	46	25.70	2	1.12
3. Perceptions	13	7.26	71	39.66	32	17.88	61	34.08	2	1.12
4. Personal differences	11	6.15	58	32.40	26	14.53	70	39.11	14	7.82
5. Differences in value	12	6.70	58	32.40	23	12.85	80	44.69	6	3.35
6. Communi- cation barrier	15	8.38	93	51.96	16	8.94	47	26.26	8	4.47
7. Interdepen- dence	14	7.82	114	63.69	15	8.38	33	18.44	3	1.68
8. Goal differences	11	6.15	97	54.19	28	15.64	38	21.23	5	2.79
9. Performance appraisal	15	8.38	82	45.81	23	12.85	57	31.84	2	1.12
10. Differences in Expertise	13	7.26	66	36.87	32	17.88	67	37.43	1	0.56
11. Distrust	9	.503	33	18.44	40	22.35	85	47.49	12	6.70
12. Techno- logical changes	27	15.08	83	46.37	21	11.73	43	24.02	5	2.79
13. Participation in professional meetings	30	16.76	103	57.54	20	11.17	23	12.85	3	1.68
14. Vacant posts	28	15.64	74	41.34	30	16.76	35	19.55	12	6.70

N=179

opinions' as a cause of conflict, while two respondents from JNUL have mentioned that 'hierarchical differences in status' is also one of the causes of conflict with the superiors, peers and subordinates.

4.5. CONCLUSION

Conflict issues and causes of the conflict its responses and their interpretation have been given in this chapter. When the library professionals interact with their superiors, peers and subordinates, some conflict issues develop. Such conflict issues include 'conflict over job objectives', 'conflict over role', 'planning of activities', 'distribution of authority', 'reward criteria', 'participation in decision making process', 'library policies and procedures', 'promotion', 'arriving late', and 'working environment'.

Causes of conflict may be highlighted, such as, 'competition over scarce resources', 'jurisdiction ambiguity', 'different perceptions', 'communication barriers', 'interdependence', 'goal differences', 'performance appraisal', 'difference in expertise', 'technological changes', 'participation in professional meetings', and 'vacant posts'.

5

Managing Conflict in Libraries : Styles and Strategies

The conflict management behavior of the professionals working in the libraries of the universities in Delhi has been studied in this chapter. It presents results of analysis of data made available by the respondents, interpretation of data. The various choices applicable to the strategies of managing conflict with superiors, peers and subordinates have been worked out, Mean Value and Standard Deviation have been calculated, and presented in various relevant Tables. Management of conflict with superiors, peers and subordinates.

ROCI-II (Rahim Organizational Conflict Inventory – II)

In order to measure the conflict management, Rahim has devised five styles of handling interpersonal conflict, such a. integrating, obliging, avoiding, compromising and dominating styles. National sample was taken for designing the scale. Its validity, reliability were tested by him. The scale was validated and its topology was found to be easy to understand and the results were found more accurate in Indian context.

The choices adopted by different groups of the respondents have also been presented.

5.1. STYLES OF CONFLICT MANAGEMENT

The five well known managerial styles, namely, (i) Integrating, (ii) Obliging, (iii) Avoiding, (iv) Compromising, and (v) Dominating have been studied and their 'Mean Value' and Standard Deviation' worked out on the data collected from the library professionals. This is being discussed in the paragraphs as follows.

5.2. STYLES OF CONFLICT MANAGEMENT : DESIGNATION-WISE

The respondents, who have participated in the present study, fall in various categories of library professionals, namely, Librarians, Deputy Librarians, Assistant Librarians and Professional Assistants, and in similar and equivalent positions/ designations. The data collected from them is being studied in the paragraphs as follows.

5.2.1. Librarians' Styles Of Conflict Management

The term 'Librarian' stands for the senior most position in the library staff. He is the In-Charge/Chief Executive or the top most Library Manager. To know about the preferences and practices of managerial styles of this category of Library Managers, in managing conflict, the data collected has been analysed and presented in Table 5.2.1.

Table 5.2.1 :Librarians' Styles of Conflict Management

S.No.	*Conflict Management Styles*	*Mean Value*	*Standard Deviation*
1.	Integrating	3.48	0.79
2.	Obliging	2.91	0.97
3.	Avoiding	2.72	0.96
4.	Compromising	2.51	1.02
5.	Dominating	3.18	0.87

N = 11

Table 5.2.1 examines the prevalent five strategies of conflict management while dealing with the subordinates. It may be observed that 'integrating' style is the primary style with (3.48) Mean Value, followed by 'dominating' with (3.18) Mean Value. 'Compromising' with (2.51) Mean Value is preferred least, while 'obliging' (2.91) and 'avoiding' (2.72) are the methods preferred low. The value of standard deviation calculated for this purpose is found high (1.02) in 'compromising' style and low (0.79) in 'integrating' style. Trend emerged is that 'integrating' is the primary style of the library professionals while dealing with subordinates, followed by the 'dominating' style.

5.2.2. Deputy Librarians' Styles Of Conflict Management

Deputy Librarians play a vital role in the university libraries. They stand second in the hierarchy of top management in university libraries. They form the second line managerial support to the Chief Librarian, and at times have to act in that position whenever the man at the top is away. To know about the preferences and practices of managerial styles of this category of Library Managers towards their (i) superiors, (ii) peers, and (iii) subordinates, the data collected has been analysed and presented in Table 5.2.2.1, Table 5.2.2.2, and Table 5.2.2.3 and in the paragraphs as follow.

5.2.2.1. Styles of Conflict Management with Superiors

The Deputy Librarians have the University Librarian, members of Library Committee, and other high-ups, as their superiors. To know about the preferences and practices of managerial styles of Deputy Librarians, towards their superiors, the data collected has been analyzed and presented in Table 5.2.2.1.

Table 5.2.2.1 reveals conflict management styles of the Deputy Librarians with their superiors. It is noted that 'integrating' (3.28) is the most preferred managerial strategy of resolving conflict with superiors, followed by 'dominating' (3.27), which is also having almost equal mean value. The other methods, in order of preference are: 'compromising' (2.83), 'obliging' (2.77) and 'avoiding' (2.76). It is significant to note

Table 5.2.2.1 : Styles of Conflict Management with Superiors

S.No.	*Conflict Management Styles*	*Mean Value*	*Standard Deviation*
1.	Integrating	3.28	0.99
2.	Obliging	2.77	0.86
3.	Avoiding	2.72	0.96
4.	Compromising	2.83	0.69
5.	Dominating	3.27	0.88

N = 6

that 'integrating' and 'dominating' are preferred almost equally, followed by 'compromising' and 'obliging'. Here 'avoiding' is least preferred. However, the standard deviation value found high 0.99 in 'integrating' and low 0.69 in 'compromising'. Findings of this Table are; 'integrating' and 'dominating' are the styles, which are preferred by the respondents.

5.2.2.2. *Styles of Conflict Management with Peers*

To know about the preferences and practices of managerial styles of Deputy Librarians, towards their peers, the data collected has been analyzed and presented in Table 5.2.2.2.

Table 5.2.2.2 : Styles of Conflict Management with Peers

S.No.	*Conflict Management Styles*	*Mean Value*	*Standard Deviation*
1.	Integrating	1.72	1.66
2.	Obliging	3.25	1.02
3.	Avoiding	1.39	1.43
4.	Compromising	1.38	1.20
5.	Dominating	1.94	2.13

N = 6

It can be seen from Table 5.2.2.2 that deputy librarians rely upon the 'obliging' mode for resolving conflict with peers to the maximum extent. .It has the highest mean value (3.25). It is very significant to note that no other methods are preferred as their mean value varies from (1.94) to (1.38). The standard deviation also varies 1.02 to 2.13, highest is found in 'dominating' and lowest in 'obliging'. Thus, it is clear that 'obliging' is being utilized frequently for resolving conflict.

5.2.2.3. Styles of Conflict Management with Subordinates

The data collected from Deputy Librarians on their styles of conflict management towards their subordinates is analysed and presented in Table 5.2.2.3.

Table 5.2.2.3 : Styles of Conflict Management with Subordinates

S.No.	*Conflict Management Styles*	*Mean Value*	*Standard Deviation*
1.	Integrating	3.05	0.79
2.	Obliging	2.61	1.02
3.	Avoiding	2.39	0.77
4.	Compromising	2.44	0.93
5.	Dominating	3.11	1.00

N = 6

It may be noted from Table 5.2.2.3 that 'dominating' (3.11) is the primary method for resolving conflict. The backup method is 'integrating' (3.05). The other methods, being used, are 'obliging' (2.61), 'compromising' (2.44) and 'avoiding' (2.39). The value of standard deviation for each method of conflict management ranges from 0.77 to 1.02, tends more of reliability. Conclusion is drawn from the Table that primary method is 'dominating' and back up method is 'integrating', that are being relied upon by the respondents.

5.2.2.4. Styles of Conflict Management with Superiors/ Peers/ Subordinates

A comparative picture of conflict managerial styles of the Deputy Librarians with superiors/ peers/ subordinates is given in Table 5.2.2.4 and Figure 5.2.2.4 as follow.

Table 5.2.2.4 : Styles of Conflict Management with Superiors/ Peers/ Subordinates

S. No.	*Conflict Management Styles*	*Superiors*		*Peers*		*Subordinates*	
		Mean Value	*Standard Deviation*	*Mean Value*	*Standard Deviation*	*Mean Value*	*Standard Deviation*
1.	Integrating	3.28	0.99	1.72	1.66	3.05	0.79
2.	Obliging	2.77	0.86	3.25	1.02	2.61	1.02
3.	Avoiding	2.72	0.96	1.39	1.43	2.39	0.77
4.	Compromising	2.83	0.69	1.38	1.20	2.44	0.93
5.	Dominating	3.27	0.88	1.94	2.13	3.11	1.00

N = 6

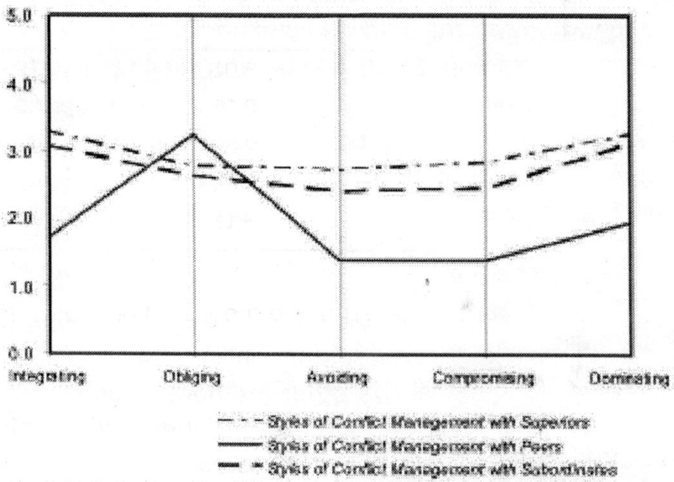

Fig. 5.2.2.4 : Graphical Presentation of Mean Value and Standard Deviation of Deputy Librarians' Styles of Conflict Management

It may be observed from Table 5.2.2.4 and Figure 5.2.2.4 that while dealing with superiors, as per the Mean Value 'integrating' and 'dominating' are preferred to the maximum extent, but standard deviation differs from 0.88 to 0.99, and 'Obliging' is being utilized fairly high; while dealing with peers. 'Dominating' and 'Integrating' methods are being preferred by the respondents, when they are dealing with subordinates. 'Integrating' method is preferred, while dealing with superiors; 'obliging' is used to maximum extent, dealing with peers; and 'dominating' is primary choice of the respondents dealing with subordinates. Findings of this Table are that no homogeneity is found in the methods of resolving conflict with superiors/ peers/ subordinates.

5.2.3. Assistant Librarians' Styles Of Conflict Management

Assistant Librarians play a vital role in day to day administration of the university libraries. They stand at the third ladder in the hierarchy of top management in university libraries. They form the essential managerial support to the Chief Librarian/Deputy Librarians, and at times have to act in that position whenever the man in higher position is away. To know about the preferences and practices of managerial styles of this category of Library Managers towards their (i) superiors, (ii) peers, and (iii) subordinates, the data collected has been analysed and presented in Table 5.2.3.1, Table 5.2.3.2, and Table 5.2.3.3 and in the relevant paragraphs as follow.

5.2.3.1. Styles of Conflict Management with Superiors

The Assistant Librarians have the Deputy Librarians and above, as their superiors. To know about the preferences and practices of managerial styles of Assistant Librarians, towards their superiors, the data collected has been analyzed and presented in Table 5.2.3.1.

Table 5.2.3.1 : Styles of Conflict Management with Superiors

S. No.	*Conflict Management Styles*	*Mean Value*	*Standard Deviation*
1.	Integrating	4.02	0.76
2.	Obliging	3.39	0.91
3.	Avoiding	2.77	1.00
4.	Compromising	2.90	0.86
5.	Dominating	2.56	1.05

N = 44

Table 5.2.3.1 reveals that there is a dominance of

integrating (4.02) strategy, which is followed by obliging (3.39). Compromising (2.90), avoiding (2.77) and dominating (2.56), while dealing with the superiors. The standard deviation varies from 0.76 to 1.05. The value found more in dominating and less in integrating. It is concluded from the Table that integrating is preferred, which is followed by obliging.

5.2.3.2. Styles of Conflict Management with Peers

To know about the preferences and practices of managerial styles of Assistant Librarians towards their peers, the data collected has been analyzed and presented in Table 5.2.3.2.

Table 5.2.3.2 : Styles of Conflict Management with Peers

S. No.	*Conflict Management Styles*	*Mean Value*	*Standard Deviation*
1.	Integrating	3.77	1.13
2.	Obliging	3.25	1.02
3.	Avoiding	2.81	1.10
4.	Compromising	2.82	1.05
5.	Dominating	2.47	1.03

N = 44

Table 5.2.3.2 reveals that integrating (3.77) is the method, in which the assistant librarians rely upon to the maximum extent. The back up method is obliging (3.25). The strategies of compromising (2.82) and avoiding (2.81) are the medium preferred strategies and dominating is the least utilized method for resolving conflict. The standard deviation value of each conflict resolution method calculated. Deviation is found less 1.02 in obliging and more 1.13 in integrating. Findings of this Table brings out that assistant librarians utilize integrating style highly, while dealing with the peers, followed by obliging.

5.2.3.3. Styles of Conflict Management with Subordinates

The data collected from Assistant Librarians on their styles of conflict management towards their subordinates is analysed and presented in Table 5.2.3.3.

Table 5.2.3.3 : Styles of Conflict Management with Subordinates

S.No.	Conflict Management Styles	Mean Value	Standard Deviation
1.	Integrating	3.69	0.78
2.	Obliging	3.28	0.88
3.	Avoiding	2.84	1.05
4.	Compromising	2.84	0.89
5.	Dominating	2.67	0.93

N = 44

Table 5.2.3.3 indicates that integrating (3.69) is the first choice of the respondents followed by obliging (3.28). Avoiding (2.84) and compromising (2.84) methods are being utilized equal number of respondents, while dominating (2.67) behaviour preferred least by the assistant librarians while dealing with subordinates. The standard deviation calculated for each method ranges from 0.78 to 1.05. We can draw conclusion from the Table that integrating mode of resolving conflict is predominant one, which is followed by obliging, avoiding, compromising and dominating.

5.2.3.4. Styles of Conflict Management with Superiors/ Peers/ Subordinates

A comparative picture of conflict managerial styles of the Assistant Librarians with superiors/ peers/ subordinates is given in Table 5.2.3.4 and Figure 5.2.3.4 as follows.

Table 5.2.3.4 and Figure 5.2.3.4 reveal much interestingly that integrating method for resolving conflict is dominant one, which is followed by dominating, while dealing with superiors. Integrating is also preferred and followed by obliging, while dealing with superiors, peers and subordinates. Further analysis of this Table clarifies that integrating method is the first order of choice dealing with all the three groups, and followed by

Table 5.2.3.4 : Styles of Conflict Management with Superiors/ Peers / Subordinates

S. No.	*Conflict Management Styles*	*Superiors*		*Peers*		*Subordinates*	
		Mean Value	*Standard Deviation*	*Mean Value*	*Standard Deviation*	*Mean Value*	*Standard Deviation*
1.	Integrating	4.02	0.76	3.77	1.13	3.69	0.78
2.	Obliging	3.39	0.91	3.25	1.02	3.28	0.88
3.	Avoiding	2.77	1.00	2.81	1.10	2.84	1.05
4.	Compromising	2.90	0.86	2.82	1.05	2.84	0.89
5.	Dominating	2.56	1.05	2.47	1.03	2.67	0.93

N = 44

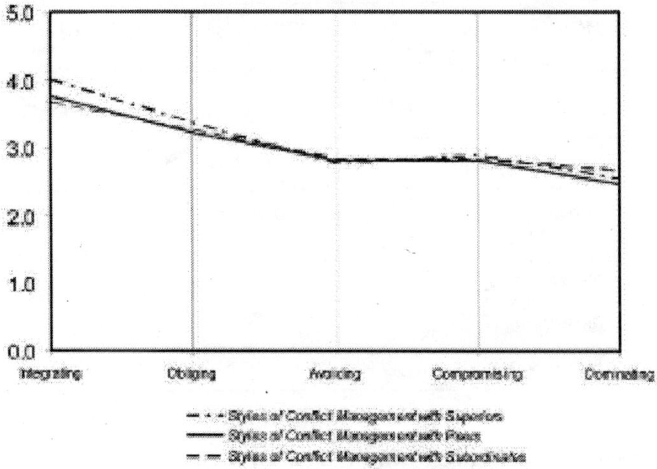

Fig. 5.2.3.4 : Presentation of Styles of Conflict Management by Assistant Librarians with Superiors/ Peers/ Subordinates

obliging, with superiors, peers and subordinates. It is significant to note that dominating style is being utilized least with the three groups. The value of standard deviation is found less in compromising method, and more in integrating. The preferred order is observed for resolving conflict, while dealing with the superiors, peers and subordinates is integrating method in all the three groups.

5.2.4. Prof. Assistants' Styles Of Conflict Management

Professional Assistants are important link of the hierarchy of library managers in university libraries. They help their seniors by performing various library jobs of repetitive nature. To know as to how they are managing conflict with their superiors, peers and subordinates, the data was collected, analysed and is presented in Tables, Figures and paragraphs as follow.

5.2.4.1. Styles of Conflict Management with Superiors

The Professional Assistant have the Assistant Librarians and above, as their superiors. To know about the preferences and practices of managerial styles of Professional Assistants, towards their superiors, the data collected has been analyzed and presented in Table 5.2.4.1.

Table 5.2.4.1 Styles of Conflict Management with Superiors

S. No.	*Conflict Management Styles*	*Mean Value*	*Standard Deviation*
1.	Integrating	3.54	0.88
2.	Obliging	3.36	0.85
3.	Avoiding	2.88	0.82
4.	Compromising	3.14	0.79
5.	Dominating	2.79	1.07

N = 118

Table 5.2.4.1 examines the conflict management strategies utilized by the Professional Assistants, while dealing with superiors. It indicates that Professional Assistants tend to make a considerably greater use of integrating (3.54), obliging (3.36) and compromising (3.14) than that of avoiding (2.88) and dominating (2.79) methods. The standard deviation calculated for each method and its value varies from 0.79 to 1.07. Deviation is found less in compromising method and more in dominating method. It is observed from the Table that integrating is preferred method, which is followed by obliging and compromising.

5.2.4.2. *Styles of Conflict Management with Peers*

To know about the preferences and practices of managerial styles of Professional Assistants towards their peers, the data collected has been analyzed and presented in Table 5.2.4.2.

Table 5.2.4.2 : Styles of Conflict Management with Peers

S. No.	*Conflict Management Styles*	*Mean Value*	*Standard Deviation*
1.	Integrating	3.52	0.96
2.	Obliging	3.20	0.86
3.	Avoiding	2.94	0.84
4.	Compromising	3.20	0.82
5.	Dominating	2.68	1.01

N = 118

Table 5.2.4.2 presents the prevalent strategies of conflict management and indicates that integrating (3.52) style is being utilized by the Professional Assistants, while dealing with peers, to the maximum extent, followed by obliging (3.20) and compromising (3.20) which are preferred equally. Dominating (2.68) method of resolving conflict is preferred least than avoiding (2.94). Standard deviation calculated for this purpose ranges its value from 0.82 to 1.01. Deviation is found more in dominating and less in integrating. Conclusion is drawn from the Table that the Professional Assistants prefer integrating style followed by obliging and compromising.

5.2.4.3. *Styles of Conflict Management with Subordinates*

The data collected from Professional Assistants on their styles of conflict management towards their subordinates, is analysed and presented in Table 5.2.4.3.

Table 5.2.4.3 shows modes of professional assistants' for managing conflict with subordinates. It has been observed that Professional Assistants mostly rely upon integrating (3.59)

Table 5.2.4.3 : Styles of Conflict Management with Subordinates

S. No.	*Conflict Management Styles*	*Mean Value*	*Standard Deviation*
1.	Integrating	3.59	0.87
2.	Obliging	3.24	0.85
3.	Avoiding	2.92	0.84
4.	Compromising	3.14	0.79
5.	Dominating	2.74	1.02

N = 118

method for resolving conflict, which is followed by obliging (3.24) and compromising (3.14). Avoiding (2.92) and dominating (2.74) are being utilized at rather low preference. The value of standard deviation is found high (1.02) in dominating method and low (0.79) in compromising method. The picture emerged from the Table is that integrating method is primary behaviour of the Professional Assistants, and followed by obliging and compromising.

5.2.4.4. Styles of Conflict Management with Superiors/ Peers/ Subordinates

A comparative picture of conflict managerial styles of the Assistant Librarians with superiors/ peers/ subordinates is given in Table 5.2.4.4 and Figure 5.2.4.4 as follows.

Table 5.2.4.4 and Figure 5.2.4.4 present the profile of the managerial conflict resolution strategies adopted by the Professional Assistants with their superiors, peers and subordinates. It is revealed from the analysis that there is a dominance of integrating strategy followed by obliging and compromising, while dealing with the superiors, peers and subordinates. It is also noted that the equal mean value (3.14) is found in compromising method while dealing with superiors and subordinates and obliging (3.20) and compromising (3.20) in case of peers. The standard deviation ranges from 0.79 to 1.07, its value is found lowest in compromising method, while

Table 5.2.4.4 : Styles of Conflict Management with Superiors/ Peers/ Subordinates

S. No.	Conflict Management Styles	Superiors Mean Value	Superiors Standard Deviation	Peers Mean Value	Peers Standard Deviation	Subordinates Mean Value	Subordinates Standard Deviation
1.	Integrating	3.54	0.88	3.52	0.96	3.59	0.87
2.	Obliging	3.36	0.85	3.20	0.86	3.24	0.85
3.	Avoiding	2.88	0.82	2.94	0.84	2.92	0.84
4.	Compromising	3.14	0.79	3.20	0.82	3.14	0.79
5.	Dominating	2.79	1.07	2.68	1.01	2.74	1.02

N = 118

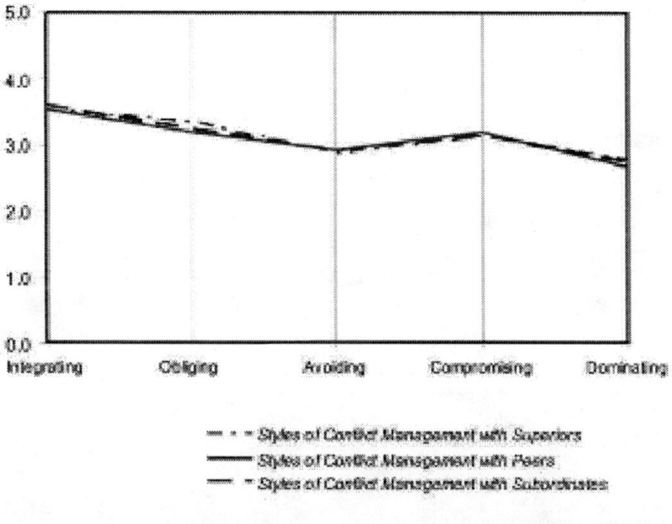

Figure 5.2.4.4 : Graphical Presentation of Styles of Conflict Management by Professional Assistants with Superiors/ Peers /Subordinates

dealing with superiors and subordinates, and highest in dominating method, while dealing with superiors. Conclusion is drawn from the Table that there is uniformity in applying conflict resolution methods by the Professional Assistants, wherein integrating is followed by obliging and compromising.

5.3. CONFLICT MANAGEMENT STYLES : ACROSS THE HIERARCHY

An organization is formed by an hierarchy of authority flowing from top to bottom. In university libraries, the hierarchy may be represented, such as, Library Committee, Librarian, Deputy Librarians, Assistant Librarians, Professional Assistants, Semi-Professional Assistants and Library Attendants. The positions up-to Assistant Librarians belong to top level management, the Professional Assistants at the mid level and below them the bottom level management. To study the conflict management styles across the hierarchy, the data was collected and analysed, and the same is presented and discussed in the paragraphs as follow.

5.3.1. Styles of Conflict Management with Superiors

The data pertaining to styles of managing conflict with superiors by the Deputy Librarians, Assistant Librarians and Professional Assistants have been analyzed and presented in Table 5.3.1 and Figure 5.3.1.

Table 5.3.1 : Styles of Conflict Management with Superiors

S. No.	*Conflict Management Styles*	*Deputy Librarian (N = 6)*		*Assistant Librarian (N = 44)*		*Professional Asst. (N = 118)*	
		Mean Value	*Standard Deviation*	*Mean Value*	*Standard Deviation*	*Mean Value*	*Standard Deviation*
1.	Integrating	3.28	0.99	4.02	0.76	3.54	0.88
2.	Obliging	2.77	0.86	3.39	0.91	3.36	0.85
3.	Avoiding	2.72	0.96	2.77	1.00	2.88	0.82
4.	Compromising	2.83	0069	2.90	0.86	3.14	0.79
5.	**Dominating**	**3.27**	**0.88**	**2.56**	**1.05**	**2.79**	**1.07**

Table 5.3.1 and Figure 5.3.1 show a uniformity in adopting integrating style by all the three categories of respondents, and having the highest mean value (3.28), (4.02) and (3.54) respectively. It is followed by obliging (3.39) and (3.36) in case of Assistant Librarians and Professional Assistants and

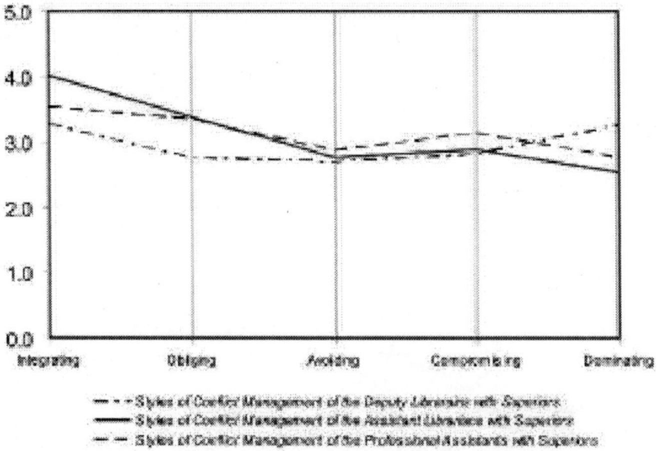

Fig. 5.3.1 : Graphical Presentation of Styles of Conflict Management with Superiors : Across the Hierarchy

dominating (3.27) in case of Deputy Librarians. Further analysis reveals that similarity is found also in case of Assistant Librarians and Professional Assistants, while their least preferred style is dominating with mean value (2.56) and (2.79) respectively. However, avoiding with mean value (2.72) is preferred least in case of Deputy Librarians. The value of standard deviation computed for each method in these categories varies from 0.69 to 1.07, and is found less in compromising method in case of Deputy Librarians and high in dominating in case of Professional Assistants. Findings of this Table are that Deputy Librarians, Assistant Librarians and Professional Assistant prefer integrating method for resolving conflict with superiors.

5.3.2. Styles of Conflict Management with Peers

The data pertaining to styles of managing conflict with peers by the Deputy Librarians, Assistant Librarians and Professional Assistants has been analyzed and presented in Table 5.3.2 and Figure 5.3.2.

Table 5.3.2 : Styles of Conflict Management with Peers

S. No.	Conflict Management Styles	Deputy Librarian (N = 6)		Assistant Librarian (N = 44)		Professional Asst. (N = 118)	
		Mean Value	Standard Deviation	Mean Value	Standard Deviation	Mean Value	Standard Deviation
1.	Integrating	1.72	1.66	3.77	1.13	3.52	0.96
2.	Obliging	3.25	1.02	3.25	1.02	3.20	0.86
3.	Avoiding	1.39	1.43	2.81	1.10	2.94	0.84
4.	Compromising	1.38	1.20	2.82	1.05	3.20	.0.82
5.	**Dominating**	**1.94**	**2.13**	**2.47**	**1.03**	**2.68**	**1.01**

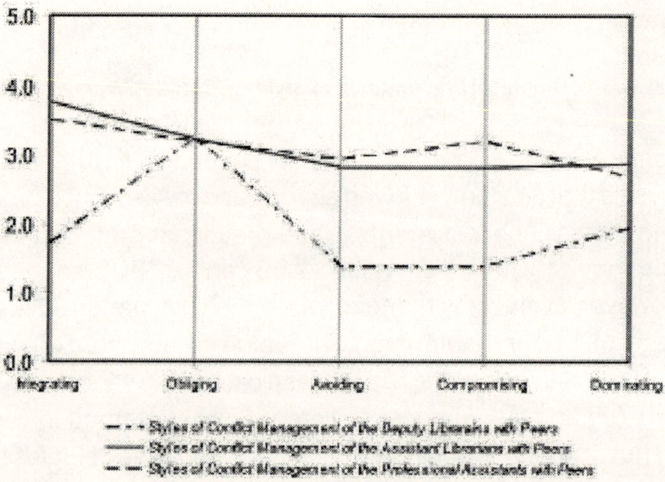

Fig. 5.3.2 : Graphical Presentation of Styles of Conflict Management with Peers : Across the Hierarchy

Table 5.3.2 and Figure 5.3.2 show that Assistant Librarians and Professional Assistants utilizes integrating style most as their mean value (3.77) and (3.52) respectively. It is followed by obliging (3.25) and (3.20) in case of Assistant Librarians and Professional Assistants. Obliging with mean value (3.27) is relied upon to the maximum extent by Deputy Librarians. Further analysis reveals that similarity is found also in applying the conflict methods by the Assistant Librarians and

Professional Assistants, while avoiding and compromising are medium preference and dominating is least preferred in these cases. The lowest 0.82 standard deviation is found in compromising method in case of Assistant Librarians and highest 2.13 in dominating method in case of Deputy Librarians, primary style is obliging, while Assistant Librarians and Professional Assistants prefer integrating method.

5.3.3. Styles of Conflict Management with Subordinates

The data pertaining to styles of managing conflict with subordinates by the Librarians, Deputy Librarians, Assistant Librarians and Professional Assistants has been analyzed and presented in Table 5.3.3 and Figure 5.3.3.

Table 5.3.3 and Figure 5.3.3 indicate that there is uniformity in utilizing the primary style in case of Librarians, Assistant Librarians and Professional Assistants because they apply integrating method as their preferred method for resolving conflict, and its mean value is found highest (3.48), (3.69) and (3.59) in these three categories of library managers, but, in the case of Deputy Librarians, the dominating method is relied upon the most. Librarians and Deputy Librarians are utilizing dominating (3.18) method and integrating method (3.05) respectively as a back up style, while Assistant Librarians and Professional Assistants are following obliging (3.28) and (3.24) respectively. The least preferred method is compromising (2.51) in case of Librarians, avoiding (2.39) in case of Deputy Librarians, and dominating (2.67), (2.74) in case of Assistant Librarians and Professional Assistants. The standard deviation calculated for each method for each category is found less, i.e., 0.78 in integrating and more, i.e., 1.05 in avoiding method in case of Assistant Librarians. It is inferred that Librarians, Assistant Librarian, and Professional Assistants prefer integrating while Deputy Librarians prefer dominating while managing conflict with their subordinates.

Table 5.3.3 : Styles of Conflict Management with Subordinates

S. No.	Conflict Management Styles	Librarian (N = 11)		Deputy Librarian (N = 6)		Assistant Librarian (N = 44)		Professional Asst. (N = 118)	
		Mean Value	*Standard Deviation*	*Mean Value*	*Standard Deviation*	*Mean Value*	*Standard Deviation*	*Mean Value*	*Standard Deviation*
1.	Integrating	3.48	0.79	3.05	0.79	3.69	0.78	3.59	0.87
2.	Obliging	2.91	0.97	2.61	1.02	3.28	0.88	3.24	0.85
3.	Avoiding	2.72	0.96	2.39	0.72	2.84	1.05	2.92	0.84
4.	Compromising	2.51	1.02	2.44	0.93	2.84	0.89	3.14	0.79
5.	Dominating	3.18	0.87	3.11	1.00	2.67	0.93	2.74	1.02

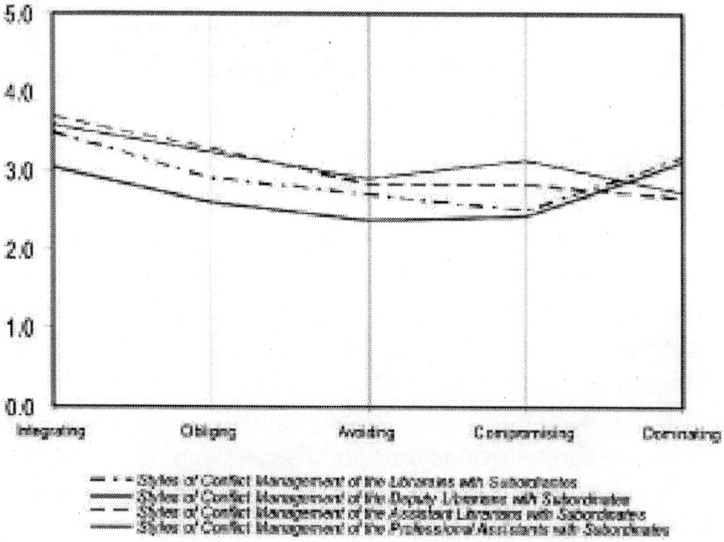

Fig. 5.3.3 : Graphical Presentation of Styles of Conflict Management with Subordinates : Across the Hierarchy

5.4. STYLES OF CONFLICT MANAGEMENT : LIBRARY WISE ANALYSIS

In the present study, all the twelve university libraries located in Delhi/New Delhi have been included. These 12 university libraries, with the number of professionals working with them, are listed below:

1. DULS (71 professionals in staff)
2. JNUL (32 professionals in staff)
3. ZHL (20 professionals in staff)
4. IARIL (28 professionals in staff)
5. HMSCL (13 professionals in staff)
6. TERIL (10 professionals in staff), and
7. OTHER LIBRARIES (University Libraries with less than 10 professionals on their staff). These are:
   (i) UIRC, GGSI University (07 professionals in staff)

(ii) IGNOUL (04 professionals in staff)

(iii) SPAL (02 professionals in staff)

(iv) Dr. MML, SLBSS Vidyapeeth (03 professionals in staff)

(v) Dr. LPSRC, NMIHACM (01 professionals in staff), and

(vi) IIFTL (05 professional in staff)

Out of these 12 university libraries, six libraries under the category of 'Other Libraries', are being studied for the styles of managing conflict among the library staff (up-to the level of Professional Assistants) in (i) an individual library (including the category 'Other Libraries'), (ii) all the libraries compared together as per the Mean Value and Standard Deviation, (iii) all the university libraries (other than libraries of 'Deemed Universities'), (iv) styles of conflict management by the library professionals (Male/Female staff), (v) library professionals in different age groups, (vi) qualifications possessed by the library professionals, and (vii) finally, in a summary form, the data made available on the styles of conflict management by all the respondents, in the paragraphs as follow..

5.4.1. Styles of Conflict Managemen in DULS

Delhi University Library System is one of the oldest university library in Delhi serving the students, researchers and academicians. To know as to how the library professionals in this library, are managing conflict with their superiors, peers and subordinates, the data collected was analysed, and the same is presented and discussed in the paragraphs as follow.

5.4.1.1. Styles of Conflict Management with Superiors

To know about the preferences and practices of managerial styles of Library Managers in DULS towards their superiors, the data collected has been analyzed and presented in Table 5.4.1.1.

Table 5.4.1.1 : Styles of Conflict Management with Superiors (DULS)

S. No.	*Conflict Management Styles*	*Mean Value*	*Standard Deviation*
1.	Integrating	3.58	0.95
2.	Obliging	3.18	0.96
3.	Avoiding	2.93	0.87
4.	Compromising	2.98	0.94
5.	Dominating	2.63	1.13

N = 68

Table 5.4.1.1 indicates that respondents make use of integrating method (3.58) as their primary choice. Obliging method (3.18) is being utilized as a back up method of conflict management. Avoiding (2.93) and compromising (2.98) are in medium use by the respondents of the DULS. The value of standard deviation ranges from 0.94 to 1.13. Lesser value of standard deviation is found in compromising, and more standard deviation in dominating. The pattern emerged is that integrating mode is highly preferred than other modes by professionals in DULS.

5.4.1.2. Styles of Conflict Management with Peers

The Mean Value and Standard Deviation in five styles of conflict management with peers in DULS are presented in Table 5.4.1.2.

Table 5.4.1.2 : Styles of Conflict Management with Peers

S. No.	*Conflict Management Styles*	*Mean Value*	*Standard Deviation*
1.	Integrating	3.53	0.99
2.	Obliging	3.07	0.97
3.	Avoiding	2.94	0.88
4.	Compromising	3.08	0.94
5.	Dominating	2.58	1.02

N = 68

Table 5.4.1.2 indicates that integrating mode (3.53) as

their primary choice for resolving conflict with peers is being utilized to the maximum extent by the professionals in DULS. It is followed by compromising method (3.08) and obliging method (3.07). It may be noted that both the methods have got almost equal mean value. The other methods avoiding and dominating with mean value (2.94) and (2.58) respectively, are relied less. The standard deviation varies from 0.88 to 1.02, and is found lowest in avoiding method and highest in dominating method. It is found that integrating is the method upon which the respondents of DULS rely to the maximum extent, followed by compromising and obliging modes in DULS.

5.4.1.3. Styles of Conflict Management with Subordinates

The Mean Value and Standard Deviation in five styles of conflict management with subordinates in DULS are presented in Table 5.4.1.3.

Table 5.4.1.3 : Styles of Conflict Management with Subordinates

S. No.	*Conflict Management Styles*	*Mean Value*	*Standard Deviation*
1.	Integrating	3.57	0.88
2.	Obliging	3.09	0.91
3.	Avoiding	2.88	0.89
4.	Compromising	3.00	0.90
5.	Dominating	2.75	1.05

N = 68

Table 5.4.1.3 reveals that integrating mode of resolving conflict has been assigned the higher priority as it has got the highest mean value (3.57). Integrating is followed by obliging (3.09) and compromising (3.00) modes. The respondents prefer less to avoiding (2.88) and least to dominating (2.75) methods. The standard deviation for each method ranges from 0.88 to 1.05, and it means that deviation is less in integrating (0.88) and more in dominating (1.05) method. The conclusion drawn is that respondents are making use of the integrating method on the highest priority, followed by compromising and dominating modes.

5.4.1.4. Styles of Conflict Management with Superiors / Peers / Subordinates

A comparative picture of conflict managerial styles of the Library Professionals with superiors/ peers/ subordinates is given in Table 5.4.1.4 and Figure 5.4.1.4 as follows.

Table 5.4.1.4 : Styles of Conflict Management with Superiors/ Peers/ Subordinates

S. No.	*Conflict Management Styles*	*Superiors*		*Peers*		*Subordinates*	
		Mean Value	*Standard Deviation*	*Mean Value*	*Standard Deviation*	*Mean Value*	*Standard Deviation*
1.	Integrating	3.58	0.95	3.53	0.99	3.57	0.88
2.	Obliging	3.18	0.96	3.07	0.97	3.09	0.91
3.	Avoiding	2.93	0.87	2.94	0.88	2.88	0.89
4.	Compromising	2.98	0.94	3.08	0.94	3.00	0.90
5.	Dominating	2.63	1.13	2.58	1.02	2.75	1.05

N = 68

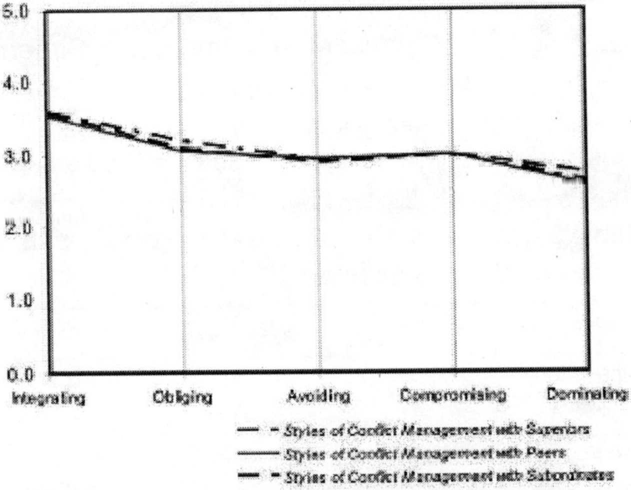

Fig. 5.4.1.4 : Graphical Presentation of Styles of Conflict Management with Superiors/Peers/Subordinates in DULS

Table 5.4.1.4 and Figure 5.4.1.4 present the profile of the managerial conflict resolution strategies adopted by the Library Professionals with their superiors/peers/subordinates in DULS. It indicates that integrating method is preferred while dealing with superiors/ peers/subordinates with mean value (3.58)/(3.53)/(3.57) respectively. The same trend is emerged in obliging method with mean value (3.18)/ (3.07)/ (3.09). The dominating style with mean value (2.63)/ (2.58)/ (2.75) has been least preferred in all the three groups. Standard deviation is found high 1.13 in dominating method and low 0.87 in avoiding method. Finding is that there is a homogeneity in the method of managing conflict with superiors/ peers/ subordinates in the behaviour of the respondents. They prefer integrating, followed by obliging modes.

5.4.2. Styles of Conflict Management in JNUL

Jawaharlal Nehru University is a central university, well supported by its library. To know as to how the library professionals in this library, are managing conflict with their superiors, peers and subordinates, the data collected was analysed, and the same is presented and discussed in the paragraphs as follow.

5.4.2.1. Styles of Conflict Management with Superiors

To know about the preferences and practices of managerial styles of Library Managers in JNUL towards their superiors, the data collected has been analyzed and presented in Table 5.4.2.1.

Table 5.4.2.1: Styles of Conflict Management with Superiors (JNUL)

S. No.	*Conflict Management Styles*	*Mean Value*	*Standard Deviation*
1.	Integrating	3.51	1.24
2.	Obliging	3.11	1.01
3.	Avoiding	2.55	0.96
4.	Compromising	3.15	0.97
5.	Dominating	2.62	1.33

N = 26

Table 5.4.2.1 indicates that respondents make use of integrating method with mean value (3.51) to the maximum extent, followed by compromising method (3.15) and obliging method (3.11), whereas avoiding (2.55) is least preferred by respondents of JNUL, while dealing with the superiors. The value of standard deviation varies from 0.96 to 1.33. Deviation is less in avoiding method and more in dominating method. It is inferred that integrating method is the first choice of the respondents.

5.4.2.2. Styles of Conflict Management with Peers

The Mean Value and Standard Deviation in five styles of conflict management with peers in JNUL are presented in Table 5.4.2.2.

Table 5.4.2.2 : Styles of Conflict Management with Peers

S. No.	*Conflict Management Styles*	*Mean Value*	*Standard Deviation*
1.	Integrating	3.65	1.12
2.	Obliging	3.10	0.93
3.	Avoiding	2.78	1.02
4.	Compromising	3.28	0.96
5.	Dominating	2.66	1.26

N = 26

Table 5.4.2.2 indicates that integrating mode with mean value (3.65) is the primary choice of respondents from JNUL for resolving conflict with peers. Compromising method (3.28) is being utilized as a backup style, which is followed by obliging (3.10). The least used method is dominating (2.66). The value of standard deviation is higher (1.26) in dominating method and lower (0.93) in obliging method. Conclusion drawn is that respondents rely upon the integrating method, followed by compromising and obliging methods.

5.4.2.3. Styles of Conflict Management with Subordinates

The Mean Value and Standard Deviation in five styles of

conflict management with subordinates in JNUL are presented in Table 5.4.2.3.

Table 5.4.2.3 : Styles of Conflict Management with Subordinates

S. No.	*Conflict Management Styles*	*Mean Value*	*Standard Deviation*
1.	Integrating	3.74	0.74
2.	Obliging	3.25	0.82
3.	Avoiding	2.96	0.86
4.	Compromising	3.26	0.81
5.	Dominating	2.70	1.25

N = 26

Table 5.4.2.3 indicates that respondents have assigned top priority to the integrating method with (3.74) mean value, followed by compromising (3.26) and obliging (3.25) methods. The least priority has been assigned to the dominating method (2.70). The lowest value (0.74) of standard deviation is found in integrating method, in contrast to the highest (1.25) in dominating method. The conclusion drawn is that integrating method is being preferred, followed by compromising and obliging methods.

5.4.2.4. Styles of Conflict Management with Superiors/ Peers/ Subordinates

A comparative picture of conflict managerial styles of the Library Professionals with superiors/ peers/ subordinates is given in Table 5.4.2.4 and Figure 5.4.2.4 as follows.

Table 5.4.2.4 and Figure 5.4.2.4 show a similarity in styles of conflict management adopted by the respondents because integrating method is found on the top priority while considering all the three groups of library managers in JNUL, and it possesses the highest mean value (3.51), followed by the compromising method (3.15) and obliging method (3.11). The similar pattern has emerged in backup style. The least preferred methods are avoiding while dealing with the superiors, and dominating while

Table 5.4.2.4 : Styles of Conflict Management with Superiors/ Peers/ Subordinates

S. No.	*Conflict Management Styles*	*Superiors*		*Peers*		*Subordinates*	
		Mean Value	*Standard Deviation*	*Mean Value*	*Standard Deviation*	*Mean Value*	*Standard Deviation*
1.	Integrating	3.51	1.24	3.65	1.12	3.74	0.74
2.	Obliging	3.11	1.01	3.10	0.93	3.25	0.82
3.	Avoiding	2.55	0.96	2.78	1.02	2.96	0.86
4.	Compromising	3.15	0.97	3.28	0.96	3.26	0.81
5.	Dominating	2.62	1.33	2.66	1.26	2.70	1.25

N = 26

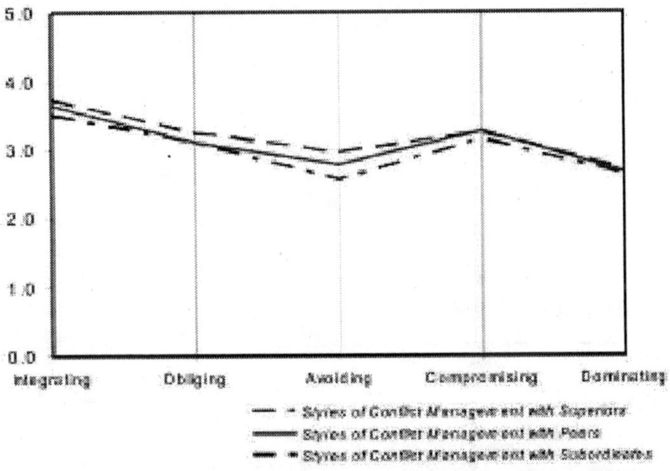

Fig. 5.4.2.4 : Graphical Presentation of Styles of Conflict Management with Superiors/Peers/Subordinates in JNUL

dealing with peers and subordinate. The standard deviation value is found lesser 0.81 in compromising while dealing with subordinates, and higher 1.33 in dominating while dealing with superiors. Homogeneity is found in styles of conflict management. It is inferred that integrating method is the primary style of conflict management, while dealing with superiors/ peers/ subordinates.

5.4.3. Styles of Conflict Management In ZHL

Dr. Zakir Husain Library is a central university library. To know as to how the library professionals in this library, are managing conflict with their superiors, peers and subordinates, the data collected was analysed, and the same is presented and discussed in the paragraphs as follow.

5.4.3.1. Styles of Conflict Management with Superiors

To know about the preferences and practices of managerial styles of Library Managers in ZHL towards their superiors, the data collected has been analyzed and presented in Table 5.4.3.1.

Table 5.4.3.1 : Styles of Conflict Management with Superiors (ZHL)

S. No.	*Conflict Management Styles*	*Mean Value*	*Standard Deviation*
1.	Integrating	3.52	1.28
2.	Obliging	3.56	1.21
3.	Avoiding	2.63	1.32
4.	Compromising	3.03	1.11
5.	Dominating	2.56	1.14

N = 19

Table 5.4.3.1 indicates that respondents make use of obliging with mean value of (3.56) to the maximum extent, followed by integrating (3.52) and compromising (3.03). Avoiding (2.63) and dominating (2.56) are such methods on which respondents rely the least. The standard deviation possesses higher value (1.32) in avoiding method and lower value (1.11) in compromising. Findings are obliging is preferred method, followed by integrating while dealing with superiors.

5.4.3.2. Styles of Conflict Management with Peers

The Mean Value and Standard Deviation in five styles of conflict management with peers in ZHL are presented in Table 5.4.3.2.

Table 5.4.3.2 : Styles of Conflict Management with Peers

S. No.	*Conflict Management Styles*	*Mean Value*	*Standard Deviation*
1.	Integrating	3.61	1.28
2.	Obliging	3.43	1.18
3.	Avoiding	2.71	1.32
4.	Compromising	3.03	1.15
5.	Dominating	2.59	1.29

N = 19

Table 5.4.3.2 show that integrating method with mean value (3.61) is being utilized upto maximum extent, followed by obliging (3.43) and compromising (3.03). Dominating (2.59) and avoiding (2.71) methods are relied upon least. Standard deviation varies from 1.15 to 1.32. Deviation is found less in compromising, and more in avoiding. One may concluded that respondents of Dr. Zakir Husain Library rely upon the integrating method, followed by obliging and compromising methods, while dealing with peers.

5.4.3.3. Styles of Conflict Management with Subordinates

The Mean Value and Standard Deviation in five styles of conflict management with subordinates in ZHL are presented in Table 5.4.3.3.

Table 5.4.3.3 : Styles of Conflict Management with Subordinates

S. No.	*Conflict Management Styles*	*Mean Value*	*Standard Deviation*
1.	Integrating	3.80	0.87
2.	Obliging	3.52	0.81
3.	Avoiding	2.94	1.03
4.	Compromising	3.22	0.78
5.	Dominating	2.85	0.93

N = 19

Table 5.4.3.3 reveals that the integrating method of resolving conflict is predominant as it has the highest mean value (3.80), followed by obliging (3.52) and compromising (3.22).modes. The respondents are making less utilization of the avoiding (2.94) and dominating (2.85). The standard deviation varies from 0.78 to 1.03. The highest value (1.03) is found in avoiding method, while compromising method possesses lowest standard deviation (0.78). One may concluded that respondents are making use of integrating method, followed by obliging and compromising methods.

5.4.3.4. Styles of Conflict Management with Superiors/ Peers/ Subordinates

A comparative picture of conflict managerial styles of the Library Professionals with superiors/ peers/ subordinates is given in Table 5.4.3.4 and Figure 5.4.3.4 as follows.

Table 5.4.3.4 : of Conflict Management with Superiors/ Peers/ Subordinates

S. No.	*Conflict Management Styles*	*Superiors*		*Peers*		*Subordinates*	
		Mean Value	*Standard Deviation*	*Mean Value*	*Standard Deviation*	*Mean Value*	*Standard Deviation*
1.	Integrating	3.52	1.28	3.61	1.28	3.80	0.87
2.	Obliging	3.56	1.21	3.43	1.18	3.52	0.81
3.	Avoiding	2.63	1.32	2.71	1.32	2.94	1.03
4.	Compromising	3.03	1.11	3.03	1.15	3.22	0.78
5.	Dominating	2.56	1.14	2.59	1.29	2.85	0.93

N = 19

Table 5.4.3.4 and Figure 5.4.3.4 indicate that while dealing with superiors/peers/subordinates, obliging method with mean value (3.56) is preferred, followed by integrating method (3.52), The respondents in ZHL are making use of integrating method to the maximum extent. while dealing with peers and subordinates. Standard deviation is found lowest (1.11) in compromising, while dealing with subordinates and

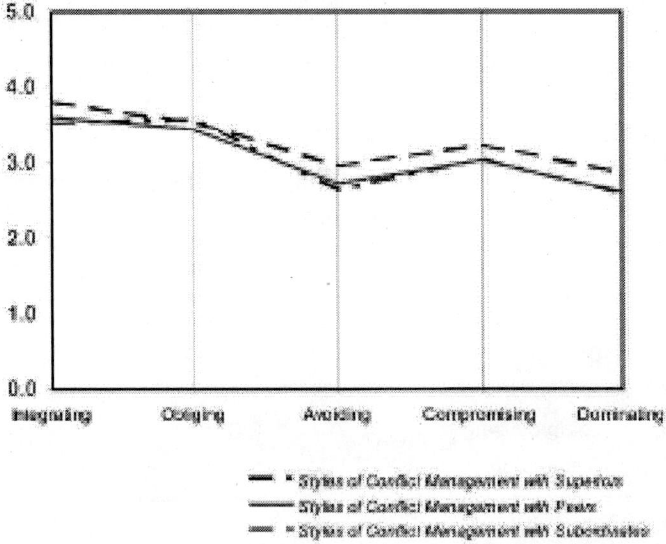

Fig. 5.4.3.4 : Graphical Presentation of Styles of Conflict Management with Superiors/Peers/Subordinates in ZHL

highest (1.32) in avoiding, while dealing with superiors and peers. It shows a minor change in the conflict management behaviour of the respondents. The other conflict management styles, such as, compromising, avoiding and dominating are found to be in the similar pattern, while dealing with the superiors, peers and subordinates. Conclusion drawn is that obliging is preferred, while dealing with superiors and integrating is being utilized most by the respondents, while dealing with the peers and subordinates.

5.4.4. Styles of Conflict Management in IARIL

The Indian Agricultural Research Institute has attained the status of a deemed university and its library has occupied the status of National Library in Agricultural Sciences (like National Medical Library). IARI Library is a special library. To know as to how the library professionals in this library, are managing conflict with their superiors, peers and subordinates, the data collected was analysed, and the same is presented and discussed in the paragraphs as follow.

5.4.4.1. Styles of Conflict Management with Superiors

To know about the preferences and practices of managerial styles of Library Managers in IARIL towards their superiors, the data collected has been analyzed and presented in Table 5.4.4.1.

Table 5.4.4.1 : Styles of Conflict Management with Superiors (IARIL)

S. No.	Conflict Management Styles	Mean Value	Standard Deviation
1.	Integrating	3.18	1.16
2.	Obliging	3.03	1.16
3.	Avoiding	2.62	1.02
4.	Compromising	2.87	0.94
5.	Dominating	2.81	1.05

N = 22

Table 5.4.4.1 indicates that integrating method, with mean value (3.18), is given the top priority by the library professionals in IARIL for resolving the conflict with superiors, which is followed by obliging method (3.03). The respondents of this library have given low preference to compromising (2.87) and dominating (2.81), and the lowest to avoiding (2.62). The standard deviation varies from 0.94 to 1.16. Conclusion drawn is that integrating method is being relied upon by the respondents to the maximum extent, followed by obliging method.

5.4.4.2. Styles of Conflict Management with Peers

The Mean Value and Standard Deviation in five styles of conflict management with peers in IARIL are presented in Table 5.4.4.2.

Table 5.4.4.2 shows that integrating method with mean value (2.93) is being utilized upto maximum extent, followed by obliging (2.92) and compromising (2.77). Dominating (2.60) and avoiding (2.66) methods are relied upon least. Standard deviation varies from 1.12 to 1.33, it is least (1.12) i in avoiding

Table 5.4.4.2 : Styles of Conflict Management with Peers

S. No.	*Conflict Management Styles*	*Mean Value*	*Standard Deviation*
1.	Integrating	2.93	1.33
2.	Obliging	2.92	1.14
3.	Avoiding	2.66	1.12
4.	Compromising	2.77	1.13
5.	Dominating	2.60	1.13

N = 22

and most (1.33) in integrating. One may conclude that respondents of IARIL rely upon the integrating method, followed by obliging and compromising methods, while dealing with their peers.

5.4.4.3. Styles of Conflict Management with Subordinates

The Mean Value and Standard Deviation in five styles of conflict management with subordinates in IARIL are presented in Table 5.4.4.3.

Table 5.4.4.3 : Styles of Conflict Management with Subordinates

S. No.	*Conflict Management Styles*	*Mean Value*	*Standard Deviation*
1.	Integrating	3.22	0.88
2.	Obliging	2.96	0.74
3.	Avoiding	2.75	0.81
4.	Compromising	2.96	0.61
5.	Dominating	2.90	0.64

N = 22

Table 5.4.4.3 shows that the respondents rely maximum upon the integrating method with mean value (2.93) in resolving conflict with their subordinates. It is also observed that obliging and compromising methods with mean value (2.92) are also being utilized almost equal to integrating. Standard deviation for each method varies from 0.61 to 0.88, it is lowest (0.61) in compromising and highest (0.88) in integrating methods. One may infer that primary style of conflict management by professionals in IARIL is integrating, followed by obliging methods.

5.4.4.4. Styles of Conflict Management with Superiors/ Peers/ Subordinates

A comparative picture of conflict managerial styles of the Library Professionals with superiors/ peers/ subordinates in IARIL is given in Table 5.4.4.4 and Figure 5.4.4.4 as follows.

Table 5.4.4.4 : Styles of Conflict Management with Superiors/ Peers/ Subordinates

S. No.	*Conflict Management Styles*	*Superiors*		*Peers*		*Subordinates*	
		Mean Value	*Standard Deviation*	*Mean Value*	*Standard Deviation*	*Mean Value*	*Standard Deviation*
1.	Integrating	3.18	1.16	2.93	1.33	3.22	0.88
2.	Obliging	3.03	1.16	2.92	1.14	2.96	0.74
3.	Avoiding	2.62	1.02	2.66	1.12	2.75	0.81
4.	Compromising	2.82	0.94	2.77	1.13	2.96	0.61
5.	Dominating	2.81	1.05	2.60	1.13	2.90	0.64

N = 22

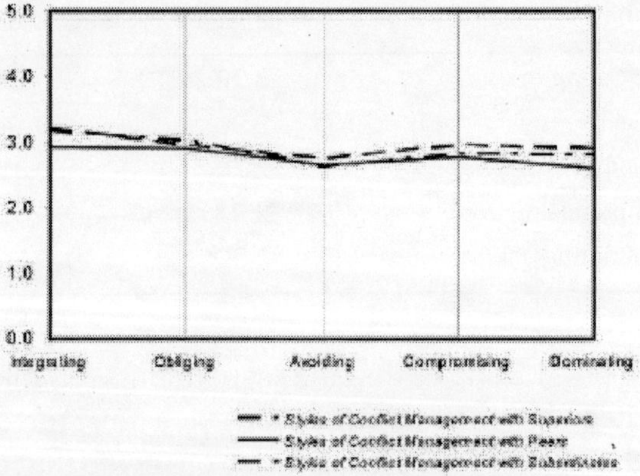

Fig. 5.4.4.4 : Graphical Presentation of Styles of Conflict Management with Superiors/ Peers/ Subordinates in IARIL

Table 5.4.4.4 and Figure 5.4.4.4 reveal uniformity in the choice of conflict management styles while dealing with all the three groups of respondents in IARIL. Integrating method with highest mean value (3.18) is preferred by the respondents in the case of their superiors, (2.93) in the case of peers, and (3.22) in the case of subordinates. All the mean values are high in all the respective styles. Further analysis also indicates the similarity in the various styles of conflict management. The integrating method is followed by the obliging method. The least operative methods is avoiding while dealing with superiors, and dominating while dealing with peers and subordinates. One may note that standard deviation is on higher side in case of superiors and peers and on the lower side in case of subordinates. It is concluded that integrating is the most prevalent style, followed by obliging mode.

5.4.5. Styles of Conflict Management in HMSCL

Hakim Mohd. Said Central Library is the main University Library of Jamia Hamdard which serves to the user community, such as, students, researchers and academic staff. To know as to how the library professionals in this library, are managing conflict with their superiors, peers and subordinates, the data collected was analysed, and the same is presented and discussed in the paragraphs as follow.

5.4.5.1. Styles of Conflict Management with Superiors

To know about the preferences and practices of managerial styles of Library Managers in HMSCL towards their superiors, the data collected has been analyzed and presented in Table 5.4.5.1.

Table 5.4.5.1 reveals that integrating mode with mean value (3.41) is the most operative style, while dealing with superiors, followed by obliging (3.08) and compromising (3.05). One may note that both the methods have almost equal mean value. The least preferred methods are avoiding and dominating with their mean value (2.50) and (2.44) respectively. The

Table 5.4.5.1 : Styles of Conflict Management with Superiors (HMSCL)

S. No.	*Conflict Management Styles*	*Mean Value*	*Standard Deviation*
1.	Integrating	3.41	1.26
2.	Obliging	3.08	1.23
3.	Avoiding	2.50	1.19
4.	Compromising	3.05	1.09
5.	Dominating	2.44	1.24

N = 12

standard deviation value is found highest (1.26) in integrating method. It is inferred that respondents from HMSCL assign the highest priority to the integrating method, followed by obliging method.

5.4.5.2. *Styles of Conflict Management with Peers*

The Mean Value and Standard Deviation in five styles of conflict management with peers in HMSCL are presented in Table 5.4.5.2.

Table 5.4.5.2 : Styles of Conflict Management with Peers

S. No.	*Conflict Management Styles*	*Mean Value*	*Standard Deviation*
1.	Integrating	3.30	1.64
2.	Obliging	2.86	1.46
3.	Avoiding	2.36	1.38
4.	Compromising	2.66	1.31
5.	Dominating	2.05	1.20

N = 12

Table 5.4.5.2 indicates that integrating mode with mean value (3.30) is the most preferred style of the respondents of HMSCL, followed by obliging (2.86). On the other hand, compromising (2.66) and avoiding (2.36) methods are being utilized with low priority, and the dominating method enjoys the least priority. Further analysis of the data shows that the standard deviation for each method varies from 1.20 to 1.64. It is concluded that integrating method is being utilized at the top priority, followed by obliging method while dealing with peers for resolving the conflict.

5.4.5.3. Styles of Conflict Management with Subordinates

The Mean Value and Standard Deviation in five styles of conflict management with subordinates in HMSCL are presented in Table 5.4.5.3.

Table 5.4.5.3 : Styles of Conflict Management with Subordinates

S. No.	*Conflict Management Styles*	*Mean Value*	*Standard Deviation*
1.	Integrating	3.72	0.66
2.	Obliging	3.27	1.01
3.	Avoiding	2.86	1.11
4.	Compromising	3.00	0.89
5.	Dominating	2.55	0.89

N = 12

Table 5.4.5.3 reveals that integrating method with mean value (3.72) has been assigned the highest priority, and is followed by obliging (23.27) and compromising (3.00) methods. The lowest priority has been assigned to the dominating method (2.55). The minimum standard deviation is 0.66 in integrating method, while maximum standard deviation 1.11 is in avoiding method. It is inferred that the respondents rely maximum upon the integrating method, followed by obliging method, while dealing with the subordinates.

5.4.5.4. Styles of Conflict Management with Superiors/ Peers/ Subordinates

A comparative picture of conflict managerial styles of the Library Professionals with superiors/ peers/ subordinates in IARIL is given in Table 5.4.5.4 and Figure 5.4.5.4 as follows.

Table 5.4.5.4 : Styles of Conflict Management with Superiors/ Peers/ Subordinates

S. No.	*Conflict Management Styles*	*Superiors*		*Peers*		*Subordinates*	
		Mean Value	*Standard Deviation*	*Mean Value*	*Standard Deviation*	*Mean Value*	*Standard Deviation*
1.	Integrating	3.41	1.26	3.30	1.64	3.72	0.66
2.	Obliging	3.08	1.23	2.86	1.46	3.27	1.01
3.	Avoiding	2.50	1.19	2.36	1.38	2.86	1.11
4.	Compromising	3.05	1.09	2.66	1.31	3.00	0.89
5.	Dominating	2.44	1.24	2.05	1.20	2.55	0.89

N = 12

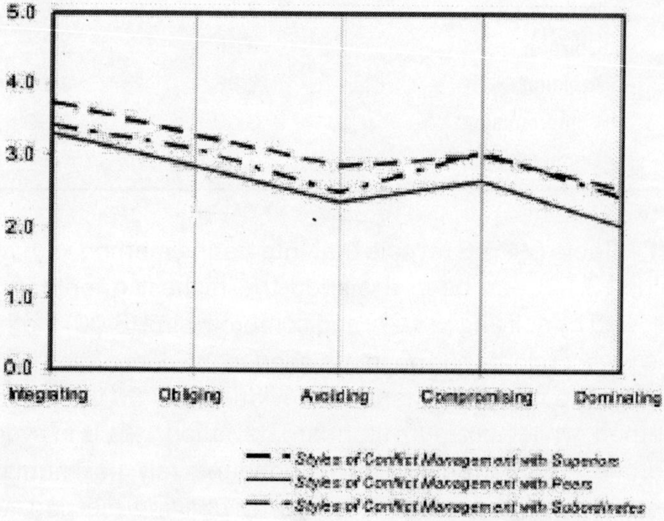

Fig. 5.4.5.4 : Graphical Presentation of Styles of Conflict Management with Superiors/ Peers/ Subordinates in HMSCL

Table 5.4.5.4 and Figure 5.4.5.4 reveal that the homogeneity is found in the styles of conflict management dealing with all three groups, which indicates that integrating is being utilized most, while dealing with the superiors, peers and subordinates which is also being followed by obliging in all these three groups. Further analysis of the table brings out a similarly in least preferred method, which is found to be dominating method in all the three groups. The standard deviation also adopt the same pattern found more than one, while dealing with superiors, and peers while it is 0.66 to 1.11 while dealing with subordinates. It is concluded that integrating is most preferred method of resolving conflict followed by obliging while dealing with all the three groups, namely, superiors, peers and subordinates.

5.4.6. Styles of Conflict Management in TERIL

Tata Energy Research Institute is devoted to research in the field of energy and attained the status of a deemed university. Hence, TERIL is a special library, which serves to the user community, such as, students, researchers and scientists. To know as to how the library professionals in this library, are managing conflict with their superiors, peers and subordinates, the data collected was analysed, and the same is presented and discussed in the paragraphs as follow.

5.4.6.1. Styles of Conflict Management with Superiors

To know about the preferences and practices of managerial styles of Library Managers for managing conflict with their superiors, the data collected has been analyzed and presented in Table 5.4.6.1.

Table 5.4.6.1 : Styles of Conflict Management with Superiors (TERIL)

S. No.	*Conflict Management Styles*	*Mean Value*	*Standard Deviation*
1.	Integrating	3.60	1.45
2.	Obliging	3.13	1.23
3.	Avoiding	2.46	1.02
4.	Compromising	2.36	1.17
5.	Dominating	2.26	1.10

N = 10

Table 5.4.6.1 indicates that integrating style with mean value (3.60) is the top most method of resolving conflict, which is adopted by the respondents in TERIL. It is followed by obliging

(3.13), avoiding (2.46), and compromising (2.36) modes. The respondents rely least (2.26) upon the dominating method. The standard deviation value varies from 1.10 to 1.45, which shows low (1.02) deviation in avoiding method, and high (1.45) in integrating method. It is inferred that respondents most rely upon the integrating method, followed by obliging method.

5.4.6.2. *Styles of Conflict Management with Peers*

The Mean Value and Standard Deviation in five styles of conflict management with peers in TERIL are presented in Table 5.4.6.2.

Table 5.4.6.2 : Styles of Conflict Management with Peers

S. No.	*Conflict Management Styles*	*Mean Value*	*Standard Deviation*
1.	Integrating	3.13	1.77
2.	Obliging	2.63	1.42
3.	Avoiding	2.33	1.32
4.	Compromising	2.26	1.50
5.	Dominating	2.00	1.20

N = 10

Table 5.4.6.2 reveals that choice of integrating with mean value (3.13) for resolving conflict is preferred by the respondents in TERIL, and is followed by obliging (2.63). The strategies of avoiding (2. 33) and compromising (2.26) are lowly preferred. The choice of dominating is least relied upon. The value of standard deviation ranges from 1.20 to 1.77 and minimum (1.20) deviation is found in dominating method, while the maximum deviation (1.77) is in integrating method. Conclusion is drawn that respondents are making use of integrating method to the maximum extent, followed by obliging method while dealing with the peers.

5.4.6.3. *Styles of Conflict Management with Subordinates*

The Mean Value and Standard Deviation in five styles of

conflict management with subordinates in TERIL are presented in Table 5.4.6.3.

Table 5.4.6.3 : Styles of Conflict Management with Subordinates

S.No.	*Conflict Management Styles*	*Mean Value*	*Standard Deviation*
1.	Integrating	3.53	0.78
2.	Obliging	3.66	0.64
3.	Avoiding	2.90	0.68
4.	Compromising	2.60	0.91
5.	Dominating	2.76	0.82

N = 10

Table 5.4.6.3 indicates that respondents highly rely upon obliging method with mean value (3.66), followed by integrating (3.53). Avoiding (2.90) and dominating (2.76) are less relied upon and the least priority is assigned to compromising (2.60). Standard deviation varies from 0.64 to 0.91. It has been found lowest (0.64) in obliging and highest (0,78) in compromising method. It is concluded that obliging method is being utilized by the respondent at the top most, followed by integrating.

5.4.6.4. Styles of Conflict Management with Superiors/ Peers/ Subordinates

A comparative picture of conflict managerial styles of the Library Professionals with superiors/ peers/ subordinates in TERIL is given in Table 5.4.6.4 and Figure 5.4.6.4 as follows.

Table 5.4.6.4 and Figure 5.4.6.4 indicate that integrating method is preferred while dealing with superiors and peers, but in case of subordinates, obliging is adopted at most, followed by the obliging in case of superiors and peers and integrating, while dealing with subordinates. Further analysis of indicates that respondents are making lesser use of avoiding and compromising methods with their superiors and peers and subordinates. It is interesting to note that homogeneity is found in case of dominating method which is least preferred in all

Table 5.4.6.4 : Styles of Conflict Management with Superiors/ Peers/ Subordinates

S. No.	*Conflict Management Styles*	*Superiors*		*Peers*		*Subordinates*	
		Mean Value	*Standard Deviation*	*Mean Value*	*Standard Deviation*	*Mean Value*	*Standard Deviation*
1.	Integrating	3.60	1.45	3.13	1.77	3.53	0.78
2.	Obliging	3.13	1.23	2.63	1.42	3.66	0.64
3.	Avoiding	2.46	1.02	2.33	1.32	2.90	0.68
4.	Compromising	2.36	1.17	2.26	1.50	2.60	0.91
5.	Dominating	2.26	1.10	2.00	1.20	2.76	0.82

N = 10

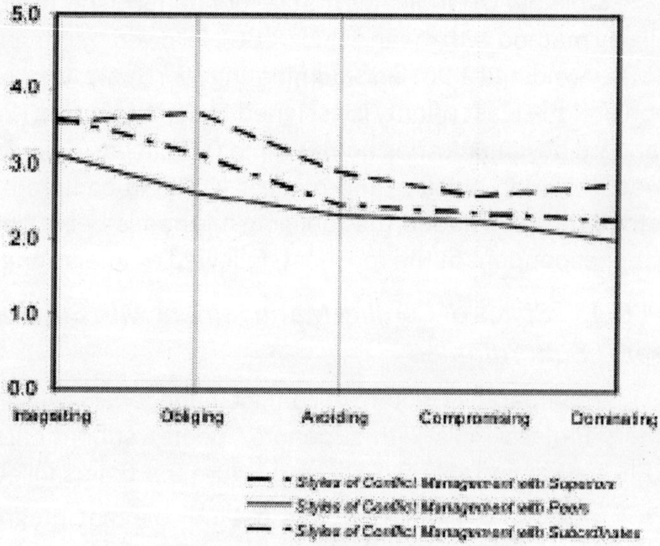

Fig. 8.4.6.4 : Graphical Presentation of Styles of Conflict Management with Superiors/ Peers/ Subordinates in TERIL

three groups superiors, peers and subordinates. The value of standard deviation is found less in obliging 0.64 in case of subordinates and more in integrating method 1.77 in case of peers. It is concluded that the primary style is integrating while dealing with superiors and peers, and obliging while dealing with subordinates.

5.4.7. Styles of Conflict Management in 'Other Libraries'

University Libraries, which are having less than 10 professionals on their staff, were clubbed together as a category, namely, 'Other Libraries' for the purpose of analysis in the present study. Data from the respondents of 'Other Libraries' was gathered to investigate their styles of conflict management with superiors, peers and subordinates. The respondents' behaviour with their superiors, peers and subordinates has been studied individually and collectively in the paragraphs as follow.

5.4.7.1. Styles of Conflict Management with Superiors

The data pertaining to styles of conflict management with the superiors in Other Libraries have been presented in Table 5.4.7.1.

Table 5.4.7.1 : Styles of Conflict Management with Superiors

S. No.	*Conflict Management Styles*	*Mean Value*	*Standard Deviation*
1.	Integrating	3.01	1.77
2.	Obliging	2.83	1.73
3.	Avoiding	2.19	1.45
4.	Compromising	2.42	1.43
5.	Dominating	2.37	1.66

N = 22

Table 5.4.7.1 indicates that respondents of 'Other Libraries' are making use of integrating mode with mean value (3.01) to the maximum extent for resolving conflict with superiors, followed by obliging mode. The respondents prefer less to compromising (2.42) and dominating (2.37) and least to avoiding method (2.19). Further analysis shows that value of standard deviation is found highest (1.77) in integrating method, and lowest (1.43) in compromising method. It is concluded that respondents are make use of integrating method at their top priority, followed by obliging method.

5.4.7.2. Styles of Conflict Management with Peers

The Mean Value and Standard Deviation in five styles of conflict management with peers in Other Libraries are presented in Table 5.4.7.2.

Table 5.4.7.2 : Styles of Conflict Management with Peers

S. No.	*Conflict Management Styles*	*Mean Value*	*Standard Deviation*
1.	Integrating	2.37	1.88
2.	Obliging	2.30	1.75
3.	Avoiding	2.03	1.60
4.	Compromising	1.92	1.48
5.	Dominating	1.83	1.54

N = 22

Table 5.4.7.2 reveals that integrating with mean value (2.37) is preferred most, followed by obliging (2.30). Avoiding (2.03) and compromising (1.92) modes are relied upon, by the respondents, at a low priority, while dominating with mean value (1.83) enjoys their least favour. The standard deviation ranges from 1.48 to 1.88, making it high (1.88) in integrating method. It is concluded that integrating is utilized by the respondents in Other Libraries, to the maximum extent, followed by the obliging method.

5.4.7.3. Styles of Conflict Management with Subordinates

The Mean Value and Standard Deviation in five styles of conflict management with subordinates in 'Other Libraries' are presented in Table 5.4.7.3.

Table 5.4.7.3 indicates that respondents are making use of integrating (3.65) which has got highest mean value, is being followed by obliging (3.24). Further analysis of this table shows that avoiding (2.78) and dominating (2.77) and compromising (2.71) are being applied least as their mean values do not significantly vary. Standard deviation varies from 0.91 to 1.02. But it is observed from the table that value of standard deviation

Table 5.4.7.3 : Styles of Conflict Management with Subordinates

S. No.	*Conflict Management Styles*	*Mean Value*	*Standard Deviation*
1.	Integrating	3.65	0.91
2.	Obliging	3.24	0.96
3.	Avoiding	2.78	1.02
4.	Compromising	2.71	0.91
5.	Dominating	2.77	1.02

N = 22

is equal in case of integrating and compromising, avoiding and dominating. Conclusion is drawn from the table that integrating is primary style and obliging as back up.

5.4.7.4. *Styles of Conflict Management with Superiors/ Peers/ Subordinates*

A comparative picture of conflict managerial styles of the Library Professionals with superiors/ peers/subordinates in 'Other Libraries' is given in Table 5.4.7.4 and Figure 5.4.7.4 as follows.

Table 5.4.7.4 : Styles of Conflict Management with Superiors/ Peers/ Subordinates

S. No.	*Conflict Management Styles*	*Superiors*		*Peers*		*Subordinates*	
		Mean Value	*Standard Deviation*	*Mean Value*	*Standard Deviation*	*Mean Value*	*Standard Deviation*
1.	Integrating	3.01	1.77	2.37	1.88	3.65	0.91
2.	Obliging	2.83	1.73	2.30	1.75	3.24	0.96
3.	Avoiding	2.19	1.45	2.03	1.60	2.78	1.02
4.	Compromising	2.42	1.43	1.92	1.48	2.71	0.91
5.	Dominating	2.37	1.66	1.83	1.54	2.77	1.02

N = 22

Table 5.4.7.4 and Figure 5.4.7.4 show a similar pattern emerging in all the three categories. The respondents' choice integrating as dominance one while dealing with superiors, peers

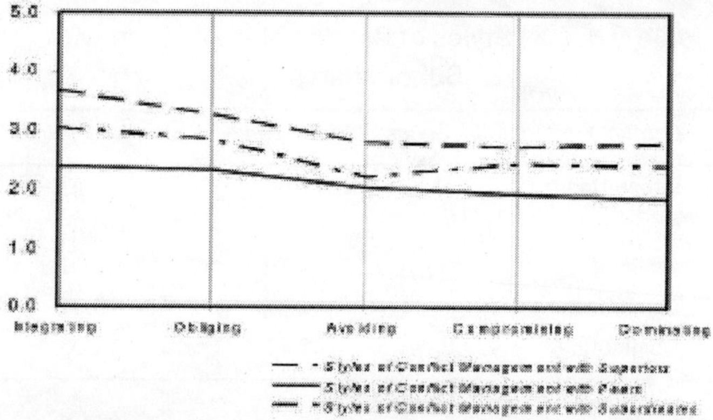

Fig. 5.4.7.4 : Graphical Presentation of Styles of Conflict Management with Superiors/ Peers/ Subordinates in 'Other Libraries'

and subordinates. But it has less than 3 mean values, while dealing with the peers. Obliging method is being used as back up method in all categories. Table shows a similar pattern but behaviour of conflict management differs as compromising and dominating strategies prefer less and least to avoiding while dealing with superiors, avoiding and dominating are less utilized and compromising is least preferred while dealing with peers and subordinates. The standard deviation is found more than one in case of superiors, and peers and one and less than one in case of subordinates. It is inferred that integrating is primary style, followed by obliging.

5.5. STYLES OF CONFLICT MANAGEMENT IN UNIVERSITY LIBRARIES: SUMMARY

The views of the respondents on the various styles of conflict management in the twelve university libraries, have been analysed and discussed separately in the preceding paragraphs. To make available the data analysis of all the twelve university libraries **'At A Glance'**, the entire data analysis is presented in a summary form in Tables and/or Figures 5.5.1, 5.5.2 and 5.5.3.

Table 5.5.1 and Figure 5.5.1 show the conflict management styles of the library professionals of all the twelve university libraries in Delhi, being studied in the present research

Table 5.5.1 : Styles of Conflict Management with Superiors in University Libraries in Delhi : SUMMARY

S. No.	Conflict Management Styles	DULS N = 68		JNUL N = 26		ZHL N = 19		IARL N = 22		HMSCL N = 12		TERIL N = 10		Other Libraries N = 22	
		Mean	*S.D.*	*Mean*	*S.D.*	*Mean*	*S.D.*	*Mean*	*S.D.*	*Mean*	*S.D.*	*Mean*	*S.D.*	*Mean*	*S.D.*
1.	Integrating	3.58	0.95	3.51	1.24	3.52	1.28	3.18	1.16	3.41	1.26	3.60	1.45	3.01	1.77
2.	Obliging	3.18	0.96	3.11	1.01	3.56	1.21	3.03	1.16	3.08	1.23	3.13	1.23	2.83	1.73
3.	Avoiding	2.93	0.87	2.55	0.96	2.63	1.32	2.62	1.02	2.50	1.19	2.46	1.02	2.19	1.45
4.	Compromising	2.98	0.94	3.15	0.97	3.03	1.11	2.82	0.94	3.05	1.09	2.36	1.17	2.42	1.43
5.	Dominating	2.63	1.13	2.62	1.33	2.56	1.14	2.81	1.05	2.44	1.24	2.26	1.10	2.37	1.66

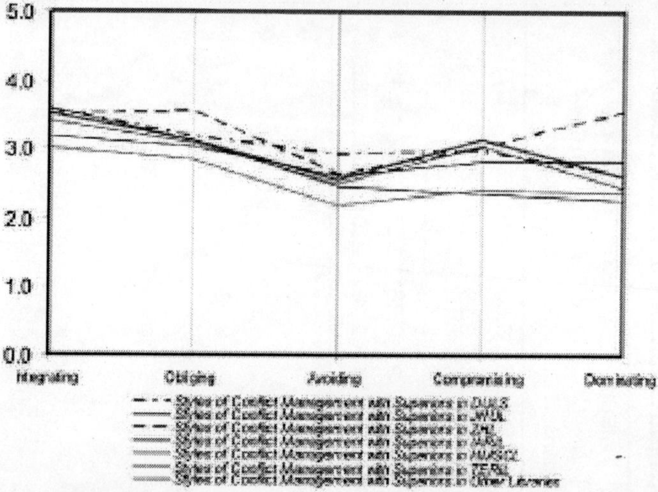

Fig. 5.5.1 : Graphical Presentation of Styles of Conflict Management with Superiors in University Libraries in Delhi : Summary

work. The data analysis reveals that the respondents, while dealing with superiors, have preference for integrating styles with mean value (3.58), (3.51), (3.18), (3.41), (3.60) and (3.01) respectively. The ZHL is an exception with mean value (3.56) of obliging over the mean value (3.52) of integrating. Avoiding is preferred least by the respondents of JNUL, IARIL, HMSCL and 'Other libraries', while dominating (2.63), (2.56) and (2.26) is preferred least by the respondents of DULS, ZHL and TERIL respectively. Compromising is being preferred medium. The standard deviation calculated for each method ranges from 0.94 to 1.77. The lowest deviation is found in compromising method and the highest in integrating method in DULS and Other Libraries respectively. An amount of uniformity may be seen in respondents' preference for integrating style in all the libraries, except ZHL as back up method, however, their behaviour vary. It is concluded that integrating is preferred to the maximum extent by the larger number of respondents.

Table 5.5.2 : Styles of Conflict Management with Peers in University Libraries In Delhi : Summary

S. No.	Conflict Management Styles	DULS N = 68		JNUL N = 26		ZHL N = 19		IARIL N = 22		HMSCL N = 12		TERIL N = 10		Other Libraries N = 22	
		Mean	S.D.	Mean	S.D.	Mean	S.D.	Mean	S.D.	Mean	S.D.	Mean	S.D.	Mean	S.D.
1.	Integrating	3.53	0.93	3.65	1.12	3.61	1.28	2.93	1.33	3.30	1.64	3.13	1.77	2.37	1.88
2.	Obliging	3.08	0.97	3.10	0.93	3.43	1.18	2.92	1.14	2.86	1.46	2.63	1.42	2.30	1.75
3.	Avoiding	2.94	0.88	2.78	1.02	2.71	1.32	2.66	1.12	2.36	1.38	2.33	1.32	2.03	1.60
4.	Compromising	3.08	0.94	3.28	0.96	3.03	1.15	2.77	1.13	2.66	1.31	2.26	1.50	1.92	1.48
5.	Dominating	2.58	1.02	2.66	1.26	2.59	1.29	2.60	1.13	2.05	1.20	2.00	1.20	1.83	1.54

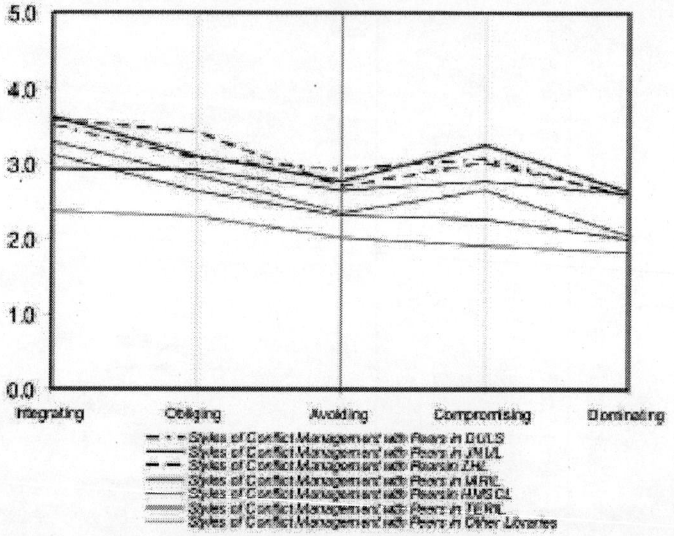

Fig. 5.5.2 : Graphical Presentation of Styles of Conflict Management with Peers in University Libraries in Delhi : Summary

Table 5.5.2 and Figure 5.5.2 show the conflict management styles of the library professionals while dealing with their peers in the libraries undertaken for the present study. The analysis of data reveals that the respondents of DULS,JNUL, ZHL, IARIL, HMSCL, TERIL, and Other Libraries utilize integrating method with mean value (3.53), (3.65), (3.61), (2.93), (3.13) and (2.37) respectively to the maximum extent. Integrating method is followed by compromising method with mean value (3.08), (3.28) of the respondents of DULS and JNUL, and the obliging method with mean value (3.43), (2.92), (2.86), (2.63) and (2.30) by the respondents of ZHL, IARIL, HMSCL, TERIL, and Other Libraries respectively. It is further observed that respondents of all the libraries rely least upon dominating method. The standard deviation calculated for this purpose varies from 0.88 to 1.88. It is found less 0.88 in avoiding in DULS and more 1.88 in integrating in Other Libraries, while dealing with the peers. It is inferred that that respondents of all the libraries are utilizing the integrating method to the maximum extent.

Table 5.5.3 : Styles of Conflict Management with Subordinates of University Libraries in Delhi : Summary

S. No.	Conflict Management Styles	DULS N = 68		JNUL N = 26		ZHL N = 19		IARIL N = 22		HMSCL N = 12		TERIL N = 10		Other Libraries N = 22	
		Mean	*S.D.*	*Mean*	*S.D.*	*Mean*	*S.D.*	*Mean*	*S.D.*	*Mean*	*S.D.*	*Mean*	*S.D.*	*Mean*	*S.D.*
1.	Integrating	3.57	0.88	3.74	0.74	3.80	0.87	3.22	0.88	3.72	0.66	3.53	0.78	3.65	0.91
2.	Obliging	3.09	0.91	3.25	0.82	3.52	0.81	2.96	0.74	3.27	1.01	3.66	0.64	3.24	0.96
3.	Avoiding	2.88	0.89	2.96	0.86	2.94	1.03	2.75	0.81	2.86	1.11	2.90	0.68	2.78	1.02
4.	Compromising	3.00	0.90	3.26	0.81	3.22	0.78	2.96	0.61	3.00	0.89	2.60	0.91	2.71	0.91
5.	Dominating	2.75	1.05	2.70	1.25	2.85	0.93	2.90	0.64	2.55	0.89	2.76	0.82	2.77	1.02

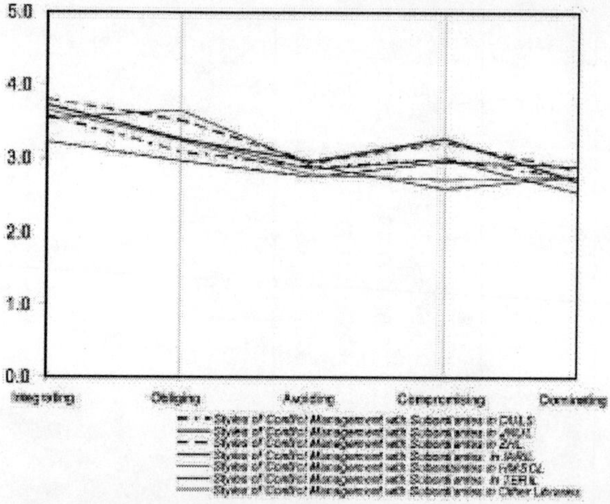

Fig. 5.5.3 : Graphical Presentation of Styles of Conflict Management with Subordinates in University Libraries in Delhi : Summary

Table 5.5.3 and Figure 5.5.3 present the comparative strategies of respondents of the university libraries being studied in the present research work. The analysis of data reveals uniformity in the pattern of behaviour of the respondents while resolving conflict with subordinates. Integrating is being utilized most by the respondents of all the libraries, such as, DULS with mean value (3.57), JNUL (3.74), ZHL (3.80), IARIL (3.22), HMSCL (3.72) and 'Other Libraries (3.65). The only exception is TERIL, respondents of the same prefer maximum the obliging mode with a mean value (3.66), followed by obliging mode by the library professionals of all the libraries. The integrating mode is being given second priority by the respondents of TERIL. The respondents of DULS, JNUL, ZHL, prefer least the dominating mode with mean value (2.75), (2.70), (2.85) respectively. It has been further observed that while the respondents of TERIL and Other Libraries prefer least the compromising mode with mean value (2.60) and (2.71) respectively. On the other hand, the avoiding mode (2.75) is utilized least by the respondents of IARIL. Standard deviation value computed for each method is found less 0.74 in integrating and more 1.11 in avoiding mode while dealing with subordinates in JNUL, HMSCL. It is concluded that integrating is being utilized by the respondents of all the libraries, except TERIL in which obliging mode is preferred.

5.6. STYLES OF CONFLICT MANAGEMENT IN DIFFERENT CATEGORIES OF UNIVERSITY LIBRARIES

The universities In Delhi, have been grouped in two categories, namely, (i) Central/State universities, and (ii) Deemed universities. The responses from library professionals in each category, were analysed and are presented in the paragraphs as follow.

5.6.1. Styles of Conflict Management in Central/State University Libraries

Central/State University libraries were analysed on the basis of respondents' styles of conflict management with their superiors / peers / subordinates, as presented and discussed in the paragraphs as follow.

5.6.1.1. Styles of Conflict Management with Superiors

The data collected from library professionals' behaviour with their superiors in the Central/State university libraries, is presented in Table 5.6.1.1.

Table 5.6.1.1 : Styles of Conflict Management with Superiors

S. No.	*Conflict Management Styles*	*Mean Value*	*Standard Deviation*
1.	Integrating	3.54	1.14
2.	Obliging	3.22	1.08
3.	Avoiding	2.72	1.04
4.	Compromising	3.00	1.02
5.	Dominating	2.63	1.21

N = 124

Table 5.6.1.1 shows that most preferred method for resolving conflict is integrating (3.54), while obliging (3.22) and compromising (3.00) are less utilized methods. Avoiding and dominating methods are least preferred. The value of standard deviation is highest in dominating 1.21 and lowest in avoiding 1.02. Findings of this table bring out integrating is most favoured tactics followed by obliging and compromising.

5.6.1.2. *Styles of Conflict Management with Peers*

The data collected from library professionals' behaviour with their peers in the Central/State university libraries, is presented in Table 5.6.1.2.

Table 5.6.1.2 : Styles of Conflict Management with Peers

S. No.	*Conflict Management Styles*	*Mean Value*	*Standard Deviation*
1.	Integrating	3.49	1.20
2.	Obliging	309	1.09
3.	Avoiding	2.84	1.06
4.	Compromising	3.04	1.06
5.	Dominating	2.56	1.19

N = 124

Table 5.6.1.2 makes clear that most relied method of resolution of conflict in university libraries is integrating (3.49) followed by obliging (3.09) and compromising (3.04). Avoiding (2.84) and dominating (2.56) are least methods which are adopted by the respondents. Conclusion is drawn from the table that integrating, obliging and compromising are the preferred than avoiding and dominating methods of resolution of conflict, while dealing with the peers.

5.6.1.3. *Styles of Conflict Management with Subordinates*

The data collected on library professionals' behaviour with their subordinates in the Central/State university libraries, is presented in Table 5.6.1.3.

Table 5.6.1.3 indicates that integrating is the most preferred method of managing conflict as it has mean value of (3.66). The other two methods, which have been relied upon by

Table 5.6.1.3 : Styles of Conflict Management with Subordinates

S. No.	Conflict Management Styles	Mean Value	Standard Deviation
1.	Integrating	3.66	1.08
2.	Obliging	3.22	0.88
3.	Avoiding	2.92	0.92
4.	Compromising	3.09	0.86
5.	Dominating	2.77	1.07

N = 124

the respondents are obliging (3.22) and compromising (3.09) followed by avoiding (2.92) and dominating (2.77). The standard deviation calculated is ranging from 0.86 to 1.08. The lowest variations are in compromising method and highest variation found in integrating. It is inferred from the above table that integrating is most preferred method followed by obliging and compromising.

5.6.1.4. Styles of Conflict Management with Superiors/ Peers/ Subordinates

The data collected on library professionals' behaviour with their superiors/peers/subordinates in the Central/State university libraries, is compared and presented in Table 5.6.1.4 and Figure 5.6.1.4.

Table 5.6.1.4: of Conflict Management with Superiors/ Peers/ Subordinates

S. No.	Conflict Management Styles	Superiors		Peers		Subordinates	
		Mean Value	Standard Deviation	Mean Value	Standard Deviation	Mean Value	Standard Deviation
1.	Integrating	3.54	1.14	3.49	1.20	3.66	0.88
2.	Obliging	3.22	1.08	3.09	1.09	3.22	0.88
3.	Avoiding	2.72	10.4	2.84	1.06	2.92	0.92
4.	Compromising	3.00	1.02	3.04	1.06	3.09	0.86
5.	Dominating	2.63	1.21	2.56	1.19	2.77	1.07

N = 124

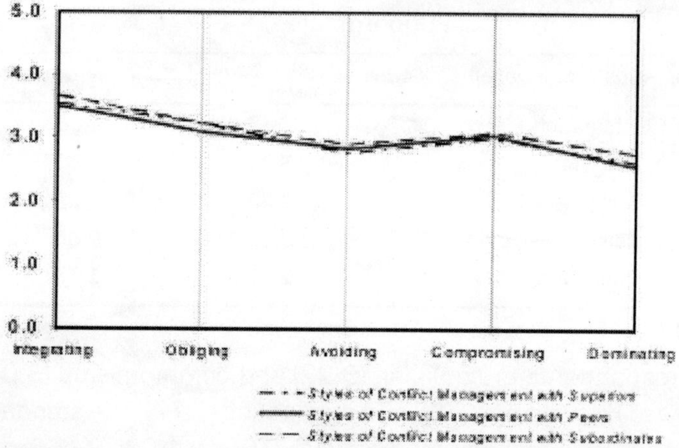

Fig. 5.6.1.4: Graphical Presentation of Styles of Conflict Management with Superiors/Peers/Subordinates

Table 5.6.1.4 and Figure 5.6.1.4 bring out a significant similarity in all three groups. It also indicates that library professionals assign a high priority to the integrating (3.54), (3.49) and (3.66) obliging (3.22), (3.09) and (3.22) and compromising (3.00), (3.04) and (3.09) respectively followed by the avoiding and dominating. The standard deviation calculated lowest 0.84 in integrating method, while dealing with subordinates and highest is 1.21 in dominating, while dealing with the superiors. The conclusion is drawn from the table that the strategies is more or less same are applied for resolving the conflict while dealing with superiors, peers and subordinates. Integrating is preferred most followed by obliging.

5.6.2. *Styles of Conflict Management in Deemed University Libraries*

Deemed universities are those Institutions of higher education and research in some specialiased field, which have been given recognition by the UGC equivalent to be deemed universities. The data collected from the library professionals working such deemed university libraries has been analysed on the bases of respondents' styles of conflict management with their superiors/ peers/ subordinates, as presented and discussed in the paragraphs as follow.

5.6.2.1. *Styles of Conflict Management with Superiors*

The data collected from library professionals' behaviour with their superiors in the Deemed university libraries, is presented in Table 5.6.2.1.

Table 5.6.2.1 : Styles of Conflict Management with Superiors

S. No.	*Conflict Management Styles*	*Mean Value*	*Standard Deviation*
1.	Integrating	3.20	1.37
2.	Obliging	2.96	1.32
3.	Avoiding	2.41	1.14
4.	Compromising	2.59	1.16
5.	Dominating	2.47	1.25

N = 55

Table 5.6.2.1 makes clear that integrating with mean value (3.20) preferred by the respondents, while the other methods obliging (2.96), compromising (2.59), dominating (2.47) and avoiding (2.41) are less or more similar used because their mean value slightly differs from each other. The standard deviation calculated ranging 1.14 to 1.37. Conclusion is drawn from the table that integrating is used most followed by obliging and compromising and least preferred method is avoiding.

5.6.2.2. *Styles of Conflict Management with Peers*

The data collected from library professionals' behaviour with their peers in the Deemed University libraries, is presented in Table 5.6.2.2.

Table 5.6.2.2 indicates that integrating with mean value (2.87), obliging (2.67) and compromising (2.30) are the styles adopted by the library professionals. The mean value of avoiding (2.30) and dominating (2.15) is slightly differs from the other methods. The standard deviation value varies from 1.23 to 1.58

Table 5.6.2.2 : Styles of Conflict Management with Peers

S. No.	*Conflict Management Styles*	*Mean Value*	*Standard Deviation*
1.	Integrating	2.87	1.58
2.	Obliging	2.67	1.41
3.	Avoiding	2.30	1.31
4.	Compromising	2.43	1.35
5.	Dominating	2.15	1.23

N = 55

having the lowest value in dominating and highest value is integrating. It is inferred from the table as there is no clear cut picture comes out, all the five methods are being utilized but integrating and obliging are slightly preferred.

5.6.2.3. Styles of Conflict Management with Subordinates

The data collected from library professionals' behaviour with their subordinates in the Deemed University libraries, is presented in Table 5.6.2.3.

Table 5.6.2.3 : Styles of Conflict Management with Subordinates

S. No.	*Conflict Management Styles*	*Mean Value*	*Standard Deviation*
1.	Integrating	3.44	0.85
2.	Obliging	3.18	0.87
3.	Avoiding	2.80	1.31
4.	Compromising	2.80	0.82
5.	Dominating	2.75	0.79

N = 55

Table 5.6.2.3 shows that integrating having mean value (3.44) is the most prevalent method adopted by library professionals while dealing with their subordinates followed by obliging (3.18) mean value. It is interesting to note that avoiding and compromising are preferred equally as their mean value (2.80) each is found. Dominating having mean value (2.75) is the least preferred method. The value calculated of standard deviation in between 0.79 to 1.31, less in dominating. Conclusion is drawn from the table integrating and obliging are preferred methods of managing conflict.

5.6.2.4. Styles of Conflict Management with Superiors/ Peers/ Subordinates

The data collected on library professionals' behaviour with their superiors/peers/subordinates in the deemed university libraries, is compared and presented in Table 5.6.2.4 and Figure 5.6.2.4.

Table 5.6.2.4 : Styles of Conflict Management with Superiors/ Peers/ Subordinates

S. No.	*Conflict Management Styles*	*Superiors*		*Peers*		*Subordinates*	
		Mean Value	*Standard Deviation*	*Mean Value*	*Standard Deviation*	*Mean Value*	*Standard Deviation*
1.	Integrating	3.20	1.37	2.87	1.58	3.44	0.85
2.	Obliging	2.96	1.32	2.67	1.41	3.18	0.87
3.	Avoiding	2.41	1.14	2.30	1.31	2.80	1.31
4.	Compromising	2.59	1.16	2.43	1.35	2.80	0.82
5.	Dominating	2.47	1.25	2.15	1.23	2.75	0.79

N = 55

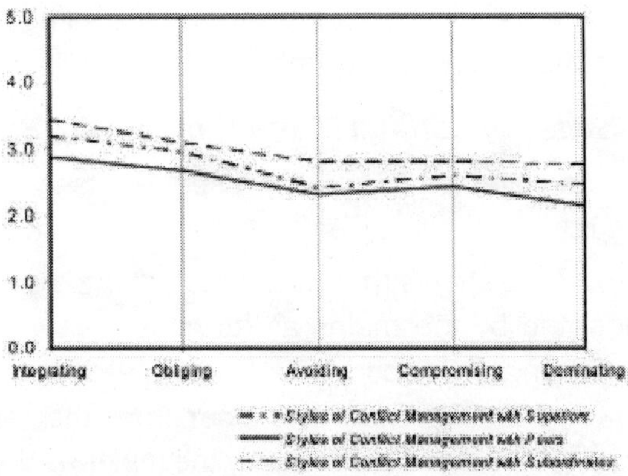

Fig. 5.6.2.4: Graphical Presentation of Styles of Conflict Management with Superiors/Peers/Subordinates

Table 5.6.2.4 and Figure 5.6.2.4 indicate that integrating is most preferred choice of the respondents while dealing with superiors, peers and subordinates with highest mean value (3.20), (2.87) and (3.44), which is followed by obliging (2.96), (2.67) and (3.18) mean value respectively. The standard deviation value ranges from 0.79 to 1.58. The lowest value of standard deviation 0.79 in dominating method while dealing with subordinates and highest 1.58 in integrating method while dealing with peers are found. This table reveals a significant uniformity in the choice of conflict management, while dealing with the superiors, peers and subordinates. It is concluded that integrating is the most preferred choice, followed by obliging and compromising modes.

5.7. STYLES OF CONFLICT MANAGEMENT: MALE/ FEMALE WISE

The data collected from the respondents was analysed sex-wise to know the male/female respondents' behaviour for managing conflict with their superiors, peers and subordinates.

5.7.1. Styles of Conflict Management by Males

Data gathered from the male respondents to investigate their managing conflict behaviour with superiors/ peers/ subordinates was analysed separately and the same has been presented in the paragraphs as follow.

5.7.1.1. Styles of Conflict Management with Superiors

The data collected from male respondents is presented in Table 5.7.1.1.

Table 5.7.1.1 shows that preference of integrating style, which is adopted by the males as its mean value is (3.29), followed by obliging (2.97), compromising (2.79), avoiding (2.57) and dominating (2.46). Thus it is clear from the table that obliging is being utilizing as a backup by the males as their mean value differs. The avoiding and dominating styles utilizing by the males has been rather low. The standard deviation

Table 5.7.1.1 : Styles of Conflict Management With Superiors

S. No.	*Conflict Management Styles*	*Mean Value*	*Standard Deviation*
1.	Integrating	3.29	1.39
2.	Obliging	2.97	1.30
3.	Avoiding	2.52	1.16
4.	Compromising	2.79	1.20
5.	Dominating	2.46	1.32

N = 100

calculated for each specific method of conflict resolution ranging from 1.16 to 1.39. The variation is found highest in integrating method 1.39 and lowest in avoiding 1.16. It is inferred from the table that primary style adopted by the males is integrating and backup style is obliging.

5.7.1.2. *Styles of Conflict Management with Peers*

The data collected has been analysed and presented in Table 5.7.1.2.

Table 5.7.1.2: Styles of Conflict Management with Peers

S. No.	*Conflict Management Styles*	*Mean Value*	*Standard Deviation*
1.	Integrating	3.21	1.46
2.	Obliging	2.87	1.28
3.	Avoiding	2.57	1.21
4.	Compromising	2.76	1.25
5.	Dominating	2.38	1.29

N = 100

Table 5.7.1.2 indicates that Integrating with mean value (3.21) is most prominent one. It is followed by obliging (2.87) and compromising (2.76) modes. The least adopted methods are avoiding (2.57) and dominating (2.30). The standard deviation varies from 1.29 to 1.46. It indicates that variation is managing conflict is higher 1.46 in integrating and lower 1.29 in dominating. The picture emerged from the table that integrating method is preferred over the obliging, avoiding, compromising and dominating.

5.7.1.3. *Styles of Conflict Management with Subordinates*

The data collected has been analysed and presented in Table 5.7.1.3.

Table 5.7.1.3: Styles of Conflict Management with Subordinates

S. No.	*Conflict Management Styles*	*Mean Value*	*Standard Deviation*
1.	Integrating	3.52	0.88
2.	Obliging	3.11	0.89
3.	Avoiding	2.84	0.90
4.	Compromising	2.96	0.90
5.	Dominating	2.72	1.00

N = 100

Table 5.7.1.3 reveals that integrating with mean value (3.52) is the prominent styles adopted by the males of the library staff. Obliging (3.11) is also utilized by the males library staff. The other preference of the styles of conflict resolution are compromising (2.96), avoiding (2.84) and dominating (2.72). The standard deviation varies from 1.00 to 0.88. The variation 0.88 in integrating method of conflict resolution is less and more. 1.00 in dominating, while it will be significant to note that variation in obliging 0.89, avoiding 0.90, and compromising 0.90 are almost equal. The preferred style used by the males is integrating followed by obliging.

5.7.1.4. *Styles of Conflict Management with Superiors/ Peers/ Subordinates*

To make a comparative study of the data collected from male respondents, the same has been analysed and presented in Table 5.7.1.4 and Figure 5.7.1.4.

Table 5.7.1.4 : Styles of Conflict Management with Superiors/Peers/ Subordinates

S. No.	Conflict Management Styles	Superiors		Peers		Subordinates	
		Mean Value	Standard Deviation	Mean Value	Standard Deviation	Mean Value	Standard Deviation
1.	Integrating	3.29	1.39	3.21	1.46	3.52	0.88
2.	Obliging	2.97	1.30	2.87	1.28	3.11	0.89
3.	Avoiding	2.52	1.16	2.57	1.21	2.84	0.90
4.	Compromising	2.79	1.20	2.76	1.25	2.96	0.90
5.	Dominating	2.46	1.32	2.38	1.29	2.72	1.00

N = 100

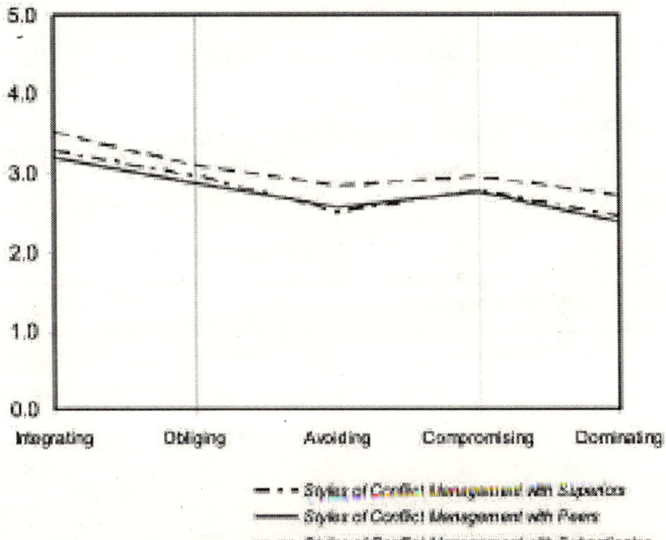

Fig. 5.7.1.4 : Graphical Presentation of Styles of Conflict Management with Superiors/Peers/ Subordinates of the Male Respondents

Table 5.7.1.4 and Figure 5.7.1.4 makes clear that integrating with mean value (3.29), (3.21) and (3.52) is the dominant style of managing conflict with the superiors/peers/ subordinates, followed by obliging style. The compromising style, adopted by male professionals, is preferred less with superiors, peers and subordinates, while least preferred styles are dominating and avoiding. The standard deviation calculated for the each method, while dealing with superiors, peers and subordinates are higher in integrating 1.46 and lower also in integrating 0.88 dealing with peers and subordinate respectively. It is also interesting that integrating, obliging and compromising are the styles of resolving conflict while avoiding is the less and dominating is the least used methods by the males with the superiors/ peers/ subordinates.

5.7.2. Styles of Conflict Management by Females

The data collected from the female respondents has been analysed as per their behaviour regarding managing conflict with superiors, peers and subordinates, and the same is presented in the paragraphs as follow.

5.7.2.1. Styles of Conflict Management with Superiors

The data collected pertaining to styles of conflict management by female respondents, while dealing with the superiors in university libraries in Delhi, is being presented in Table 5.7.2.1.

Table 5.7.2.1 : Styles of Conflict Management with Superiors

S. No.	*Conflict Management Styles*	*Mean Value*	*Standard Deviation*
1.	Integrating	3.62	0.94
2.	Obliging	3.35	0.93
3.	Avoiding	2.83	0.95
4.	Compromising	2.98	0.88
5.	Dominating	2.73	1.08

N = 79

Table 5.7.2.1 presents that the females prefer integrating styles having mean value of (3.62), followed by the obliging (3.35). The least preferred method, which is used by the females in university libraries in Delhi, is dominating (2.73). The other two methods, namely, avoiding (2.83) and compromising (2.98), are also used by the females. The standard deviation values vary from 0.94 to 1.08. There is standard variation 0.94 in integrating whereas, obliging 0.93 and avoiding 0.95 are almost similar. The lowest variation is in obliging and highest variation is in dominating are found. It is inferred that female professionals tend to considerably greater use of integrating, obliging and compromising than the avoiding and dominating.

5.7.2.2. Styles of Conflict Management with Peers

The data collected has been presented in Table 5.7.2.2.

Table 5.7.2.2: Styles of Conflict Management with Peers

S. No.	*Conflict Management Styles*	*Mean Value*	*Standard Deviation*
1.	Integrating	3.42	1.19
2.	Obliging	3.08	1.11
3.	Avoiding	2.81	1.11
4.	Compromising	2.97	1.10
5.	Dominating	2.51	1.10

N = 79

Table 5.7.2.2 shows that integrating with mean value (3.42) is the preferred style, which is followed by the obliging (3.00). The others styles adopted by the females are compromising (2.97), avoiding (2.81) and dominating (2.51). The standard deviation calculated for this purpose varies from 1.19 to 1.10. It is further noticed that from obliging to dominating variation are almost similar with the 1.11, 1.11, 1.10 and 1.10 except 1.19 who is having variation slightly higher. It is drawn from the above table that females prefer integrating and obliging styles than the avoiding, compromising and dominating while dealing with the peers.

5.7.2.3. Styles of Conflict Management with Subordinates

The data collected has been presented in Table 5.7.2.3.

Table 5.7.2.3 shows that the preferred method of conflict management by female library managers while dealing with their

Table 5.7.2.3 Styles of Conflict Management with Subordinates

S. No.	Conflict Management Styles	Mean Value	Standard Deviation
1.	Integrating	3.69	0.80
2.	Obliging	3.33	0.84
3.	Avoiding	2.91	0.90
4.	Compromising	3.06	0.79
5.	Dominating	2.82	0.98

N = 79

subordinates is integrating with mean value (3.69), which is followed by obliging (3.33) and compromising (3.06). The least methods utilized by the females are dominating (2.82) and avoiding (2.91). The highest variation found in dominating 0.98 and lowest in compromising 0.79. The other methods are having variation almost same is integrating 0.80 and obliging 0.84. It is concluded from this table that females' tend to prefer integrating, obliging and compromising while dealing with subordinates than the avoiding and compromising.

5.7.2.4. *Styles of Conflict Management with Superiors/ Peers/ Subordinates*

To make a comparative study of the data collected from male respondents, the same has been analysed and presented in Table 5.7.2.4 and Figure 5.7.2.4.

Table 5.7.2.4 and Figure 5.7.2.4 indicate that the most preferred strategies of female library managers are integrating and obliging having the mean value (3.62), (3.42) and (3.69) and (3.35), (3.08) and (3.33) followed by the compromising having the mean value of (2.98), (2.97) and (3.06). The least preferred method tend by the females with superiors, peers and subordinates is dominating which is having the mean value of (2.73), (2.51) and (2.82). Avoiding is less utilizing method in resolving conflict. The standard deviation varies from 0.79 to 1.19. The lowest variation is 0.79 in compromising, while dealing

Table 5.7.2.4 : Styles of Conflict Management with Superiors/Peers/ Subordinates

S. No.	*Conflict Management Styles*	*Superiors*		*Peers*		*Subordinates*	
		Mean Value	*Standard Deviation*	*Mean Value*	*Standard Deviation*	*Mean Value*	*Standard Deviation*
1.	Integrating	3.62	0.94	3.42	1.19	3.69	0.80
2.	Obliging	3.35	0.93	3.08	1.11	3.33	0.84
3.	Avoiding	2.83	0.95	2.81	1.11	2.91	0.90
4.	Compromising	2.98	0.88	2.97	1.10	3.06	0.79
5.	Dominating	2.73	1.08	2.51	1.10	2.82	0.98

N = 79

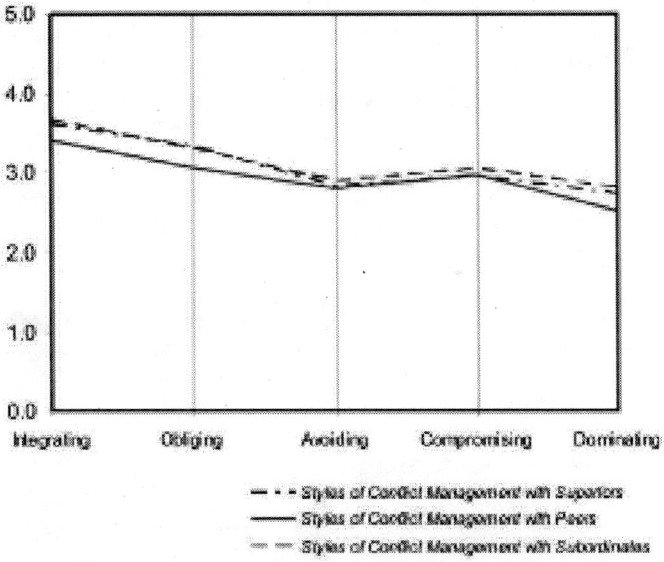

Fig. 5.7.2.4: Graphical Presentation of Styles of Conflict Management with Superiors/ Peers/Subordinates of Females

with subordinates and highest variation is in 1.19 integrating, while dealing with the peers. It is inferred from the above table that females tend to use integrating, obliging and compromising than the avoiding and dominating while dealing with superiors, peers and subordinates. Homogeneity is found in the styles of conflict management of the female professionals in all the three groups.

5.8. STYLES OF CONFLICT MANAGEMENT : AGE WISE

To know the styles of conflict management by the library managers in different age-groups, the data collected from the libraries under study, has been analysed and interpretated forming two groups of respondents, names, (i) library managers falling in the age-group upto 40 years, and (ii) library managers in the age group of 41-60 years. The results of the study are presented and discussed in the paragraphs as follow.

5.8.1. Styles of Conflict Management of Respondents Upto 40 Years of Age

Responses from the library managers (in the age group of upto 40 years) dealing with their superiors, peers and subordinates has been analysed and studied in the paragraphs as follow.

5.8.1.1. Styles of Conflict Management with Superiors

The data collected is analysed and presented in the Table 5.8.1.1.

Table 5.8.1.1: Styles of Conflict Management with Superiors

S. No.	*Conflict Management Styles*	*Mean Value*	*Standard Deviation*
1.	Integrating	3.68	1.11
2.	Obliging	3.36	0.95
3.	Avoiding	2.64	0.93
4.	Compromising	2.85	0.92
5.	Dominating	2.66	1.17

N = 32

Table 5.8.1.1 shows the preference of respondents on their conflict management with their superiors for integrating with mean value (3.68), followed by obliging (3.36) and compromising (2.85). The two methods which are preferred less are avoiding (2.64) and dominating (2.66) having almost equal mean value. The deviation is found less 0.92 in compromising and more 1.17 in dominating. It is inferred from the table that library professionals preferred integrating method followed by obliging.

5.8.1.2. *Styles of Conflict Management with Peers*

The data collected has been analysed and is being presented in Table 5.8.1.2.

Table 5.8.1.2 : Styles of Conflict Management with Peers

S. No.	*Conflict Management Styles*	*Mean Value*	*Standard Deviation*
1.	Integrating	3.16	1.54
2.	Obliging	2.87	1.25
3.	Avoiding	2.58	1.20
4.	Compromising	2.63	1.25
5.	Dominating	2.22	1.25

N = 32

Table 5.8.1.2 indicates that integrating mode is most prevalent among the respondents as it has the highest mean value (3.16). The obliging (2.87) and compromising (2.63) modes are found to be medium preferred. Avoiding (2.58) and dominating (2.22) are least preferred modes while dealing with the peers. The value of standard deviation is higher 1.54 in integrating and lowers in avoiding 1.20. It shows variation is found more in integrating and less in avoiding. It is inferred that integrating is prevalent mode adopted by the respondents.

5.8.1.3. *Styles of Conflict Management with Subordinates*

The data collected is being presented in Table 5.8.1.3.

Table 5.8.1.3 makes clear that integrating with mean value (3.61) is having the highest mean value. Obliging (3.36) is the other method which is preferred after the integrating. Compromising (2.95) and avoiding (2.89) are being utilized after

Table 5.8.1.3: Styles of Conflict Management with Subordinates

S.No.	Conflict Management Styles	Mean Value	Standard Deviation
1.	Integrating	3.61	0.94
2.	Obliging	3.36	0.79
3.	Avoiding	2.89	0.95
4.	Compromising	2.95	0.79
5.	Dominating	2.63	0.98

N = 32

the integrating and obliging as their mean value less and slightly differs. Dominating is being utilized least but it possesses greater variation 0.98 than others. It is concluded from the table that integrating is a prevalent method, which is being followed by obliging and compromising.

5.8.1.4. Styles of Conflict Management with Superiors/ Peers/ Subordinates

To make a comparative study of the data collected from library managers, the same has been analysed and presented in Table 5.8.1.4 and Figure 5.8.1.4.

Table 5.8.1.4: Styles of Conflict Management with Superiors/Peers/ Subordinates

S. No.	Conflict Management Styles	Superiors		Peers		Subordinates	
		Mean Value	Standard Deviation	Mean Value	Standard Deviation	Mean Value	Standard Deviation
1.	Integrating	3.68	1.11	3.16	1.54	3.61	0.94
2.	Obliging	3.36	0.95	2.87	1.25	3.36	0.79
3.	Avoiding	2.64	0.93	2.58	1.20	2.89	0.95
4.	Compromising	2.85	0.92	2.63	1.25	2.95	0.79
5.	Dominating	2.66	1.17	2.22	1.25	2.63	0.98

N = 32

Table 5.8.1.4 and Figure 5.8.1.4 show that integrating mode of resolving conflict is the most dominant as it has highest

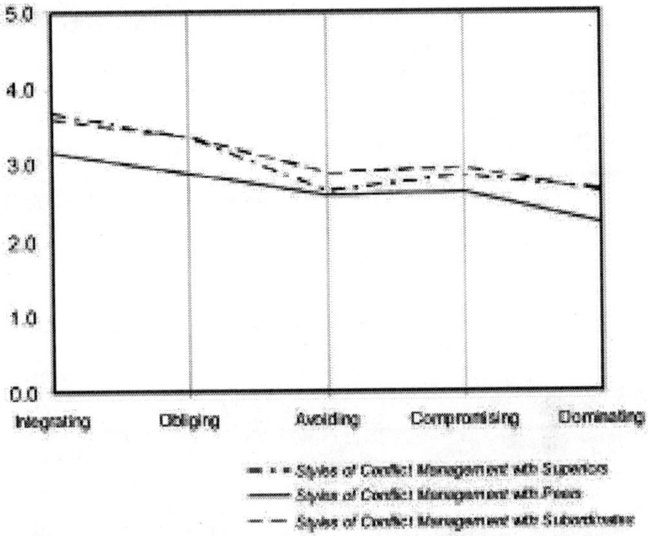

Fig. 5.8.1.4: Graphical Presentation of Styles of Conflict Management with Superiors/Peers/Subordinates Upto 40 Years of Age

mean value (3.68), (3.16) and (3.61), while dealing with superiors, peers and subordinates. The other preference orders of the respondents are obliging (3.36), (2.87) and (3.36) and compromising (2.85), (2.63) and (2.95). It is interesting to know that mean value of obliging while dealing with peer is less than 3 even though it was preferred after integrating. The standard deviation varies from 0.79 to 1.54, is found less in obliging and compromising while dealing with subordinates and more in integrating while dealing with peers. The pictured emerged from the table that similarly of adoption of modes of conflict resolution, while dealing with superiors, peers and subordinates. The preferred pattern is integrating followed by obliging.

5.8.2. Styles of Conflict Management of Respondents of 40 To 60 Years Age

Responses from the library managers (in the age group of 40-60 years) dealing with their superiors, peers and subordinates are analysed and studied in the paragraphs as follow.

5.8.2.1. *Styles of Conflict Management with Superiors*

The data collected is analysed and presented in the Table 5.8.2.1.

Table 5.8.2.1: Styles of Conflict Management with Superiors

S. No.	Conflict Management Styles	Mean Value	Standard Deviation
1.	Integrating	3.38	1.24
2.	Obliging	3.09	1.21
3.	Avoiding	2.66	1.11
4.	Compromising	2.88	1.11
5.	Dominating	2.56	1.24

N = 147

Table 5.8.2.1 indicates that the integrating with mean value (3.38) is most preferred method. The second preference has been assigned to obliging method, which is having the mean value (3.09). The other three methods adopted by the respondents are compromising (2.88) avoiding (2.66) and dominating (2.56), which are having mean value slightly differ from each other. The standard deviation ranges from 1.11 to 1.24. It is significant to note that value of standard deviation is similar1.24 in integrating and dominating methods, and 1.11 in avoiding and compromising methods, the highest and the lowest respectively. This analysis highlights the dominance of integrating and obliging followed by compromising, avoiding and dominating.

5.8.2.2. *Styles of Conflict Management with Peers*

The data collected is presented in Table 5.8.2.2.

Table 5.8.2.2 shows that the respondents relied on integrating (3.33). They also use the obliging (2.98) and compromising (2.90) methods of resolving conflict, while dealing with the peers. Avoiding (2.69) is less preferred method and dominating (2.48) is being utilized least. The value of standard deviation is higher in integrating 1.31 and lesser in avoiding 1.16. Obliging 1.20 and dominating 1.20 possesses the equal

Table 5.8.2.2: Styles of Conflict Management with Peers

S. No.	*Conflict Management Styles*	*Mean Value*	*Standard Deviation*
1.	Integrating	3.33	1.31
2.	Obliging	2.98	1.20
3.	Avoiding	2.69	1.16
4.	Compromising	2.90	1.17
5.	Dominating	2.48	1.20

N = 147

value of standard deviation. Deviation is found high in integration and less in avoiding and compromising, which is almost equal. It is inferred from the table that integrating is preferred than obliging and compromising.

5.8.2.3. *Styles of Conflict Management with Subordinates*

The data collected is presented in Table 5.8.2.3.

Table 5.8.2.3 : Styles of Conflict Management with Subordinates

S. No.	*Conflict Management Styles*	*Mean Value*	*Standard Deviation*
1.	Integrating	3.59	0.83
2.	Obliging	3.17	0.89
3.	Avoiding	2.87	0.89
4.	Compromising	3.01	0.87
5.	Dominating	2.79	1.00

N = 147

Table 5.8.2.3 indicates that integrating with mean value (3.59) is being utilized by the respondents frequently as against the dominating (2.79) is least in practice, followed by obliging (3.17) and compromising (3.01). The value of standard deviation starting from 0.83 to 1.00 is found less in integrating and more in dominating. It is inferred that integrating is the most favoured method adopted by the respondents, followed by obliging and compromising methods.

5.8.2.4. Styles of Conflict Management with Superiors/ Peers/ Subordinates

To make a comparative study of the data collected from library managers, the same has been analysed and presented in Table 5.8.2.4 and Figure 5.8.2.4.

Table 5.8.2.4 : Styles of Conflict Management with Superiors/Peers/ Subordinates

S. No.	*Conflict Management Styles*	*Superiors*		*Peers*		*Subordinates*	
		Mean Value	*Standard Deviation*	*Mean Value*	*Standard Deviation*	*Mean Value*	*Standard Deviation*
1.	Integrating	3.38	1.24	3.33	1.31	3.59	0.83
2.	Obliging	3.09	1.21	2.98	1.20	3.17	0.89
3.	Avoiding	2.66	1.11	2.69	1.16	2.87	0.89
4.	Compromising	2.88	1.11	2.90	1.17	3.01	0.87
5.	Dominating	2.56	1.24	2.48	1.20	2.79	1.00

N = 147

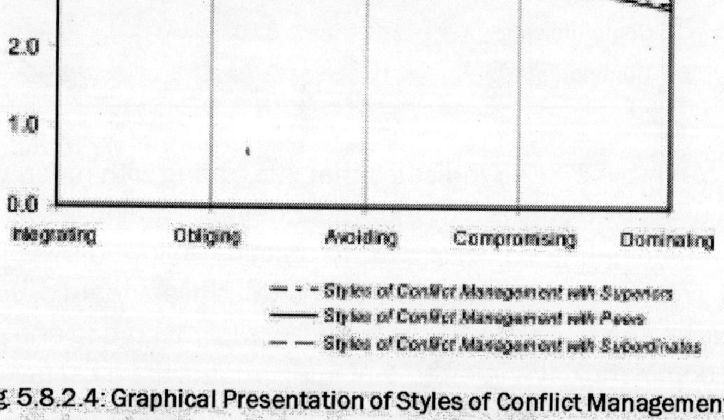

Fig. 5.8.2.4: Graphical Presentation of Styles of Conflict Management with Superiors/Peers/Subordinates (40 To 60 Years Age Group)

Table 5.8.2.4 and Figure 5.8.2.4 presents the overall

analysis and indicate among all the three groups of respondents that integrating with mean values (3.38), (3.33) and (3.59) is the first choice of resolving conflict. Obliging method (3.09), (2.98) and (3.17) is the second most preferred method followed by compromising (2.88), (2.90) and (3.01). The standard deviation varies from 0.83 to 1.31 found highest and lowest in integrating while dealing with superiors and subordinates respectively. Conclusion is drawn from the table that preference of this age group of the library professionals is similar in dealing with superiors, peers and subordinates. The most frequent choices applied by respondents is integrating, followed by obliging and compromising methods.

5.9. STYLES OF CONFLICT MANAGEMENT : QUALIFICATIONS- WISE

During the course of study, it was observed that library managers working in university libraries in Delhi, possess different sets of academic and professional qualifications. Hence, to know about the styles of conflict management of the respondents possessing different sets of qualifications, namely, (i) graduation with B.L.I.Sc.. and its equivalent, (ii) post graduation with B.L.I.Sc.. and its equivalent, (iii) post graduation with M.L.I.Sc.. and its equivalent, (iv) M.Phil./Ph.D. in a subject other than Library and Information Scienc with B.L.I.Sc../ M.L.I.Sc.. and their equivalent, and (v) M.Phil./Ph.D. in Library and Information Science. The data collected were analysed, also in the various categories of library managers' behaviour with their superiors, peers, and subordinates. The study and its results are presented and discussed in the paragraphs as follow.

5.9.1. Styles of the Conflict Management (Grad.+ B.L.I.Sc.)

The data collected from the library managers with this set of qualifications, while dealing with their superiors, peers and subordinates has been analysed and studied in the paragraphs as follow.

5.9.1.1. *Styles of Conflict Management with Superiors*

The data collected is presented in Table 5.9.1.1.

Table 5.9.1.1: Styles of Conflict Management with Superiors

S. No.	*Conflict Management Styles*	*Mean Value*	*Standard Deviation*
1.	Integrating	3.56	0.77
2.	Obliging	3.34	0.67
3.	Avoiding	2.94	0.76
4.	Compromising	3.36	0.77
5.	Dominating	2.31	1.00

N = 23

Table 5.9.1.1 indicates that integrating with mean value (3.56) viewed as most preferred strategy for resolving conflict with their superiors which is followed by compromising (3.36) and obliging (3.34). Avoiding (2.94) and dominating (2.31) modes have been rather insignificant falling above the "on a few occasions" response category. Value of standard deviation is found high is 1.00 and low is 0.67. It is therefore, inferred that most prevalent method is integrating, followed by compromising mode.

5.9.1.2. *Styles of Conflict Management with Peers*

The data collected has been presented in Table 5.9.1.2.

Table 5.9.1.2: Styles of Conflict Management with Peers

S. No.	*Conflict Management Styles*	*Mean Value*	*Standard Deviation*
1.	Integrating	3.44	0.78
2.	Obliging	3.31	0.76
3.	Avoiding	2.81	0.84
4.	Compromising	3.69	0.41
5.	Dominating	2.34	0.95

N = 23

Table 5.9.1.2 indicates that compromising with mean value (3.69) method is being utilized to the maximum extent.

Integrating (3.44) and obliging (3.31) are the other methods preferred after the compromising method for resolving the conflict. The respondents adopt avoiding (2.81) and dominating (2.34) least compromising method which is preferred by the respondents possess standard value low 0.41 and high is dominating method, upon which the respondents relied least. It is inferred from table that compromising strategy is preferred, followed by integrating mode.

5.9.1.3. Styles of Conflict Management with Subordinates

The data collected has been presented in Table 5.9.1.3.

Table 5.9.1.3 Styles of Conflict Management with Subordinates

S. No.	*Conflict Management Styles*	*Mean Value*	*Standard Deviation*
1.	Integrating	3.59	0.65
2.	Obliging	3.33	0.64
3.	Avoiding	2.98	0.81
4.	Compromising	3.57	0.49
5.	Dominating	2.43	0.95

N = 23

Table 5.9.1.3 brings out observations that integrating with mean value (3.59) is the primary strategy of the respondents, which is being followed by compromising (3.57) and obliging (3.33) methods. The least utilized method is dominating (2.43). The standard deviation value varied from 0.49 to 0.95. The lowest deviation is found in compromising and highest in dominating. Conclusion is drawn from the table that integrating is being preferred followed by compromising.

5.9.1.4. Styles of Conflict Management with Superiors/ Peers/ Subordinates

To make a comparative study of the conflict management strategies used by the library professionals while dealing with their superiors/peers/subordinates, based on the mean value and standard deviation worked out for various styles of conflict management, the data has been analysed and is presented in Table 5.9.1.4 and Figure 5.9.1.4.

Table 5.9.1.4 : Styles of Conflict Management with Superiors/ Peers/ Subordinates

S. No.	*Conflict Management Styles*	*Superiors*		*Peers*		*Subordinates*	
		Mean Value	*Standard Deviation*	*Mean Value*	*Standard Deviation*	*Mean Value*	*Standard Deviation*
1.	Integrating	3.56	0.77	3.44	0.78	3.59	0.65
2.	Obliging	3.34	0.67	3.31	0.76	3.33	0.64
3.	Avoiding	2.94	0.76	2.81	0.84	2.98	0.81
4.	Compromising	3.36	0.77	3.69	0.41	3.57	0.49
5.	Dominating	2.31	1.00	2.34	0.95	2.43	1.06

N = 23

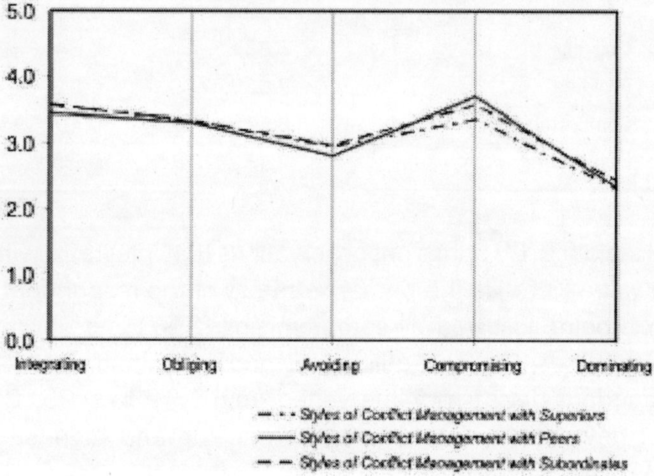

Fig. 5.9.1.4: Graphical Presentation of Styles of Conflict Management with Superiors/Peers/Subordinates (Grad. + B.L.I.Sc..)

Table 5.9.1.4 and Figure 5.9.1.4 makes clear that integrating method is found as primary strategy while dealing with superiors and subordinates. It is significant to note that compromising mode is preferred, while dealing with the peers.

Table reveals that conflict managing behaviour of respondents change with the superiors and peers. The back-up method is compromising, while dealing with superiors and subordinates and obliging while dealing with peers. The value of standard deviation calculated is found lowest in compromising while dealing with peers and highest in dominating, while dealing with subordinates. It is inferred from the table that integrating is the primary method for resolving conflict with superiors and subordinates and compromising, while dealing with peers.

5.9.2. Styles of Conflict Management (Post Grad.+ BLISc.)

The data collected from the library managers with this set of qualifications while resolving conflict with their superiors, peers and subordinates, has been analysed and presented in the paragraphs as follow

5.9.2.1. Styles of Conflict Management with Superiors

The data collected has been presented in Table 5.9.2.1.

Table 5.9.2.1: Styles of Conflict Management with Superiors

S. No.	*Conflict Management Styles*	*Mean Value*	*Standard Deviation*
1.	Integrating	3.47	0.99
2.	Obliging	3.32	1.02
3.	Avoiding	2.77	0.96
4.	Compromising	3.03	0.84
5.	Dominating	2.81	1.10

N = 51

Table 5.9.2.2 shows that respondents make use of integrating (3.47) method to the maximum extent, which is being followed by obliging (3.32) and compromising (3.03) methods. It is significant to note that avoiding (2.77) method is being utilized to the minimum extent and dominating (2.81) method is adopted less. The value of standard deviation varies from 0.84 to 1.10. It is inferred from the table that integrating method is highly applied followed by obliging and compromising.

5.9.2.2. *Styles of Conflict Management with Peers*

The data collected has been presented in Table 5.9.2.2.

Table 5.9.2.2 : Styles of Conflict Management with Peers

S. No.	*Conflict Management Styles*	*Mean Value*	*Standard Deviation*
1.	Integrating	3.53	1.13
2.	Obliging	3.03	1.01
3.	Avoiding	2.89	1.05
4.	Compromising	3.06	0.90
5.	Dominating	2.73	1.02

N = 51

Table 5.9.2.2 indicates that integrating (3.53) method has been assigned the highest priority followed by compromising (3.06) and obliging (3.03) methods. The priority assigned to the avoiding (2.89) and dominating (2.73) method is not significant as their value fall above "on a few occasions". The standard deviation's value is found less in compromising 0.90 and the more in integrating methods 1.13 of resolving conflict. It is concluded from the table that integrating is primary strategy adopted by the respondents followed by the compromising and avoiding.

5.9.2.3. *Styles of Conflict Management with Subordinates*

The data collected has been presented in Table 5.9.2.3.

Table 5.9.2.3 shows that integrating (3.58) method is mostly relied upon by the respondents, while dealing with the subordinates for resolving conflict followed by obliging (3.26) and compromising (3.08) methods. Avoiding (2.91) and dominating (2.81) methods are adopted least. Standard deviation calculated for the each method varies from 0.75 to 1.05. Findings of this table indicate that integrating method is utilized to the maximum extent followed by obliging.

Table 5.9.2.3: Styles of Conflict Management with Subordinates

S. No.	Conflict Management Styles	Mean Value	Standard Deviation
1.	Integrating	3.58	0.88
2.	Obliging	3.26	0.85
3.	Avoiding	2.91	1.05
4.	Compromising	3.08	0.75
5.	Dominating	2.81	0.96

N = 51

5.9.2.4. *Styles of Conflict Management with Superiors/ Peers/ Subordinates*

The data pertaining to library managers possessing Post Graduate degree with BLISc, while dealing with superiors/ peers/subordinates, has been analysed, compared, and presented in Table 5.9.2.4 and Figure 5.9.2.4.

Table 5.9.2.4 : Styles of Conflict Management with Superiors/ Peers/ Subordinates

S. No.	Conflict Management Styles	Superiors		Peers		Subordinates	
		Mean Value	Standard Deviation	Mean Value	Standard Deviation	Mean Value	Standard Deviation
1.	Integrating	3.47	0.99	3.53	1.13	3.58	0.88
2.	Obliging	3.32	1.02	3.03	1.01	3.26	0.85
3.	Avoiding	2.77	0.96	2.89	1.05	2.91	1.05
4.	Compromising	3.03	0.84	3.06	0.90	3.08	0.75
5.	Dominating	2.81	1.10	2.73	1.02	2.81	0.96

N = 51

Table 5.9.2.4 and Figure 5.9.2.4 present that integrating is the main method of resolving conflict irrespective of superiors, peers and subordinates which is being followed by obliging while dealing superiors and subordinates and compromising method while dealing with the peers. The value of standard deviation is found less in compromising method while dealing with

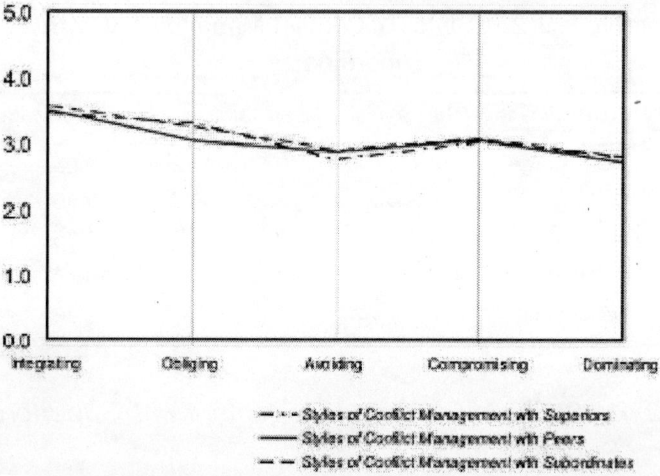

Fig. 5.9.2.4 : Graphical Presentation of Styles of Conflict Management with Superiors/ Peers/ Subordinates (Post Grad. + B.L.I.Sc..)

subordinates and more in integrating method while dealing with peers. This table brings-out a significant similarity of the styles of the respondents, while dealing with superiors, peers and subordinates. The primary style is found integrating method dealing with all the three groups.

5.9.3. Styles of Conflict Management (Post Grad. + M.L.I.Sc.).

The data collected from the library managers with this set of qualifications, while resolving conflict with their superiors, peers and subordinates, has been analysed and presented in the paragraphs as follow

5.9.3.1. Styles of Conflict Management with Superiors

The data collected has been presented in Table 5.9.3.1.

Table 5.9.3.1 reveals that integrating with mean value (3.53) is preferred most followed by obliging (3.16). It is significant to note that the other methods such as avoiding (2.68), compromising (2.73) and dominating (2.59) are reported to make use least. The standard deviation varies from 1.10 to

Table 5.9.3.1 : Styles of Conflict Management with Superiors

S. No.	*Conflict Management Styles*	*Mean Value*	*Standard Deviation*
1.	Integrating	3.53	1.35
2.	Obliging	3.16	1.22
3.	Avoiding	2.68	1.10
4.	Compromising	2.73	1.17
5.	Dominating	2.59	1.22

N = 64

1.35. The highest is found in integrating method and lowest in compromising. It is inferred from the table that most valued style is integrating followed by obliging.

5.9.3.2. *Styles of Conflict Management with Peers*

The data collected has been presented in Table 5.9.3.2.

Table 5.9.3.2 : Styles of Conflict Management with Peers

S.No.	*Conflict Management Styles*	*Mean Value*	*Standard Deviation*
1.	Integrating	3.41	1.42
2.	Obliging	3.08	1.22
3.	Avoiding	2.69	1.13
4.	Compromising	2.65	1.24
5.	Dominating	2.41	1.21

N = 64

Table 5.9.3.2 shows that respondents reported to make use to integrating method (3.41) most which is being followed by obliging method (3.08). Mean value of avoiding (2.69), compromising (2.65) and dominating methods (2.41) does not vary significantly. The respondents are making use of these methods least. Standard deviation is also found high in integrating method, which is preferred most. Findings of this table are that respondents prefer integrating method while dealing with peer followed by obliging.

5.9.3.3. Styles of Conflict Management with Subordinates

The data collected has been presented in Table 5.9.3.3.

Table 5.9.3.3 : Styles of Conflict Management with Subordinates

S. No.	Conflict Management Styles	Mean Value	Standard Deviation
1.	Integrating	3.67	0.86
2.	Obliging	3.21	0.90
3.	Avoiding	2.79	0.86
4.	Compromising	2.83	0.92
5.	Dominating	2.75	0.94

N = 64

Table 5.9.3.3 reveals that most prevalent method is integrating (3.67) followed by obliging (3.21) while dealing with the subordinate for resolving conflict. As more of the other methods avoiding (2.79), compromising (2.83) and dominating (2.75) emerged high as their mean value is below and do not vary significantly. They are in least used methods. There is also not significant variation as its value ranges from 0.86 to 0.94. Conclusion is drawn from the table that integrating is primary and obliging is the back-up for resolving conflict.

5.9.3.4. Styles of Conflict Management with Superiors/ Peers/ Subordinates

The data pertaining to library managers possessing Post Graduate degree with M.L.I.Sc, while dealing with superiors/ peers/subordinates, has been analysed, compared, and presented in Table 5.9.3.4 and Figure 5.9.3.4.

Table 5.9.3.4 and Figure 5.9.3.4 present a comparative picture of the styles, which indicates that integrating method is being utilized preferably than the other methods, which is being followed by obliging method dealing with superiors, peers and subordinates. It is significant that integrating method preferred by the respondents three groups and similarly is found in all

Table 5.9.3.4 : Styles of Conflict Management with Superiors/ Peers/ Subordinates

S. No.	*Conflict Management Styles*	*Superiors*		*Peers*		*Subordinates*	
		Mean Value	*Standard Deviation*	*Mean Value*	*Standard Deviation*	*Mean Value*	*Standard Deviation*
1.	Integrating	3.53	1.35	3.41	1.42	3.67	0.86
2.	Obliging	3.16	1.22	3.08	1.22	3.21	0.90
3.	Avoiding	2.68	1.10	2.69	1.13	2.79	0.86
4.	Compromising	2.73	1.17	2.65	1.24	2.83	0.92
5.	Dominating	2.59	1.22	2.41	1.21	2.75	0.94

N = 64

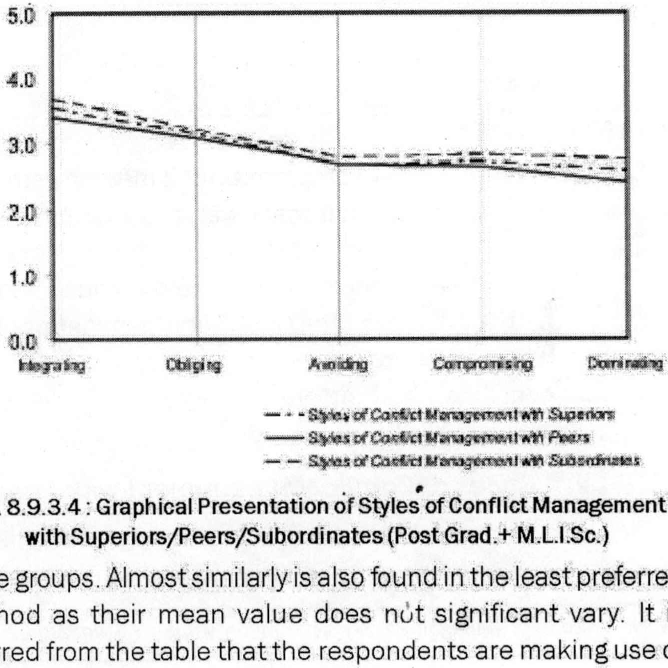

Fig. 8.9.3.4 : Graphical Presentation of Styles of Conflict Management with Superiors/Peers/Subordinates (Post Grad.+ M.L.I.Sc.)

three groups. Almost similarly is also found in the least preferred method as their mean value does not significant vary. It is inferred from the table that the respondents are making use of the integrating method followed by obliging.

5.9.4. Styles of Conflict Management (M.Phil./Ph.D. in A Subject other than L.I.S. + B.L.I.Sc./M.L.I.Sc)

The data collected from the library managers with this

set of qualifications, while resolving conflict with their superiors, peers and subordinates, has been analysed and presented in the paragraphs as follow

5.9.4.1. *Styles of Conflict Management with Superiors*

The data collected has been presented in Table 5.9.4.1.

Table 5.9.4.1 : Styles of Conflict Management with Superiors

S. No.	*Conflict Management Styles*	*Mean Value*	*Standard Deviation*
1.	Integrating	3.64	1.04
2.	Obliging	3.04	1.11
3.	Avoiding	2.84	1.16
4.	Compromising	3.04	0.95
5.	Dominating	2.58	1.33

N = 15

Table 5.9.4.1 shows that integrating method with mean value (3.64) is being applied most by the respondents with their superiors for resolving conflict followed by obliging (3.04) and compromising (3.04) as their mean value are equal. The least adopted methods are avoiding (2.84) and dominating (2.68). The deviation is less in compromising and high in obliging. It is therefore concluded that integrating method is being applied most followed by obliging and compromising.

5.9.4.2. *Styles of Conflict Management with Peers*

The data collected is being presented in Table 5.9.4.2.

Table 5.9.4.2: Styles of Conflict Management with Peers

S. No.	*Conflict Management Styles*	*Mean Value*	*Standard Deviation*
1.	Integrating	3.46	1.02
2.	Obliging	3.02	1.09
3.	Avoiding	2.88	1.16
4.	Compromising	3.00	1.03
5.	Dominating	2.48	1.28

N = 15

Table 5.9.4.2 reveals that integrating method with mean value (3.46) is reported most utilized method by the respondents while dealing with the peers. Obliging (3.02) and compromising method (3.00) are the other methods, which are the medium preferred strategies. Avoiding (2.88) and dominating (2.48) methods are least utilized by the respondents. The standard deviation is found less in integrating method and high in dominating method. It is inferred from the table that integrating mode for resolving conflict is preferred to the maximum extent followed by obliging and compromising.

5.9.4.3. Styles of Conflict Management with Subordinates

The data collected is being presented in Table 5.9.4.3.

Table 5.9.4.3 : Styles of Conflict Management with Subordinates

S. No.	*Conflict Management Styles*	*Mean Value*	*Standard Deviation*
1.	Integrating	3.51	0.95
2.	Obliging	2.97	1.02
3.	Avoiding	3.02	1.09
4.	Compromising	2.88	0.83
5.	Dominating	2.66	1.20

N = 15

Table 5.9.4.3 indicates that integrating method with mean value (3.51) is being utilized to the maximum extent, which is followed by avoiding (3.02) and obliging (2.97). Compromising (2.88) and dominating method (2.66) have been assigned lowest priority. Standard deviation varies 0.83 to 1.20, which shows a minimum deviation in compromising and maximum deviation in dominating. Finding is that integrating mode is highly preferred followed by avoiding.

5.9.4.4. Styles of Conflict Management with Superiors/ Peers/ Subordinates

The data pertaining to library managers possessing M.Phil./Ph.D. in a subject other than L.I.S. with B.L.I.Sc./M.L.I.Sc, while dealing with superiors/ peers/subordinates, has been analysed, compared, and presented in Table 5.9.4.4 and Figure 5.9.4.4.

Table 5.9.4.4 : Styles of Conflict Management with Superiors/ Peers/ Subordinates

S. No.	*Conflict Management Styles*	*Superiors*		*Peers*		*Subordinates*	
		Mean Value	*Standard Deviation*	*Mean Value*	*Standard Deviation*	*Mean Value*	*Standard Deviation*
1.	Integrating	3.64	1.04	3.46	1.02	3.51	0.95
2.	Obliging	3.04	1.11	3.02	1.09	2.97	1.02
3.	Avoiding	2.84	1.16	2.88	1.16	3.02	1.09
4.	Compromising	3.04	0.95	3.00	1.03	2.88	0.83
5.	Dominating	2.68	1.33	2.48	1.28	2.66	1.20

N = 15

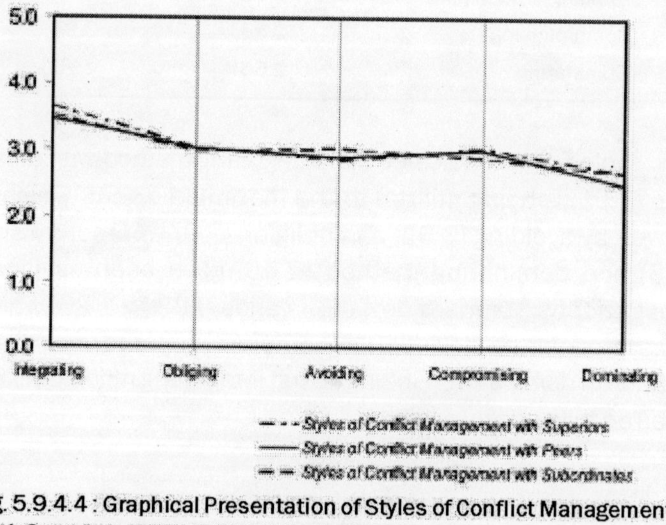

Fig. 5.9.4.4 : Graphical Presentation of Styles of Conflict Management with Superiors/Peers/Subordinates (M.Phil./Ph.D. other than L.I.S. + B.L.I.Sc./.M.L.I.Sc.)

Table 5.9.4.4 and Figure 5.9.4.4 makes clear the emerging pattern, that is, integrating method, in all the three groups, followed by obliging method and compromising method, while dealing with superiors and peers, and obliging method, while dealing with subordinates, are most preferred. The value of standard deviation varies from 0.83 to 1.28. The table reveals a significant homogeneity in the choice of conflict resolutions that integrating method is most preferred strategy, while dealing with superiors, peers and subordinates.

5.9.5. Styles of Conflict Management (M.Phil./Ph.D. in L.I.Sc. + Grad. /Post Grad.)

The data collected from the library managers with this set of qualifications, while resolving conflict with their superiors, peers and subordinates, has been analysed and presented in the paragraphs as follow

5.9.5.1. Styles of Conflict Management with Superiors

The data collected has been presented in Table 5.9.5.1.

Table 5.9.5.1: Styles of Conflict Management with Superiors

S. No.	*Conflict Management Styles*	*Mean Value*	*Standard Deviation*
1.	Integrating	2.71	1.82
2.	Obliging	2.15	1.59
3.	Avoiding	1.93	1.47
4.	Compromising	1.97	1.37
5.	Dominating	2.37	1.77

N = 15

Table 5.9.5.1 indicates that integrating method with mean value (2.71) is preferred high followed by dominating (2.37) but their mean value is less than 3, which is "some times". Respondents preferred avoiding (1.93) and compromising (1.97) least. The value of standard deviation is found high in dominating method and low in avoiding method. It is inferred from the table that integrating method is preferred more than any other method.

5.9.5.2. *Styles of Conflict Management with Peers*

The data collected has been presented in Table 5.9.5.2.

Table 5.9.5.2: Styles of Conflict Management with Peers

S. No.	*Conflict Management Styles*	*Mean Value*	*Standard Deviation*
1.	Integrating	2.11	1.92
2.	Obliging	1.73	1.62
3.	Avoiding	1.82	1.71
4.	Compromising	1.68	1.54
5.	Dominating	1.97	1.88

N = 15

Table 5.9.5.2 indicates that integrating method with mean value (2.11) is being utilized more than the others. The mean value of each method shows a significant revelation that none of the other methods is used significantly except integrating which also possesses less value. The standard deviation is found high more than 1. Conclusion is drawn from the table that respondents are making use of integrating method.

5.9.5.3. *Styles of Conflict Management with Subordinates*

The data collected is being presented in Table 5.9.5.3.

Table 5.9.5.3 : Styles of Conflict Management with Subordinates

S.No.	*Conflict Management Styles*	*Mean Value*	*Standard Deviation*
1.	Integrating	3.46	0.92
2.	Obliging	2.84	1.07
3.	Avoiding	2.73	1.07
4.	Compromising	2.73	1.00
5.	Dominating	3.37	0.95

N = 15

Table 5.9.5.3 reveals that integrating with mean value (3.4.6) is the foremost choice of the respondents, while dealing with the subordinates followed by dominating (3.37) and obliging (2.84). Avoiding (2.73) and compromising (2.73) are equal in numbers, which are preferred least. Standard deviation ranges from 0.94 to 1.07. Findings of this table are that integrating method is primary method and backup method is dominating.

5.9.5.4. Styles of Conflict Management with Superiors/ Peers/ Subordinates

The data pertaining to library managers possessing M.Phi.l/Ph.D. in L.I.S. with Graduation/Post Graduation, while dealing with superiors/ peers/subordinates, has been analysed, compared, and presented in Table 5.9.5.4 and Figure 5.9.5.4.

Table 5.9.5.4 : Styles of Conflict Management with Superiors/ Peers/ Subordinates

S. No.	*Conflict Management Styles*	*Superiors*		*Peers*		*Subordinates*	
		Mean Value	*Standard Deviation*	*Mean Value*	*Standard Deviation*	*Mean Value*	*Standard Deviation*
1.	Integrating	2.71	1.82	2.11	1.92	3.46	0.92
2.	Obliging	2.15	1.59	1.73	1.62	2.84	1.07
3.	Avoiding	1.93	1.47	1.82	1.71	2.73	1.07
4.	Compromising	1.97	1.37	1.68	1.54	2.73	1.00
5.	Dominating	2.37	1.77	1.97	1.88	3.37	0.95

N = 15

Table 5.9.5.4 and Figure 5.9.5.4 makes clear that integrating method is preferred over other methods, while dealing with the superiors, peers and subordinates. However, its mean value is found less than 3, which is "some time" dealing with superiors and peers and more than 3, while dealing with subordinates. The standard deviation is 0.95 and more than 1, which is 1.92. Conclusion is drawn from the table that similarity is found in adopting the methods for resolving conflict. It is found that integrating method is preferred in all three groups, which is followed by dominating method while dealing with superiors, and subordinates and avoiding, while dealing with peers.

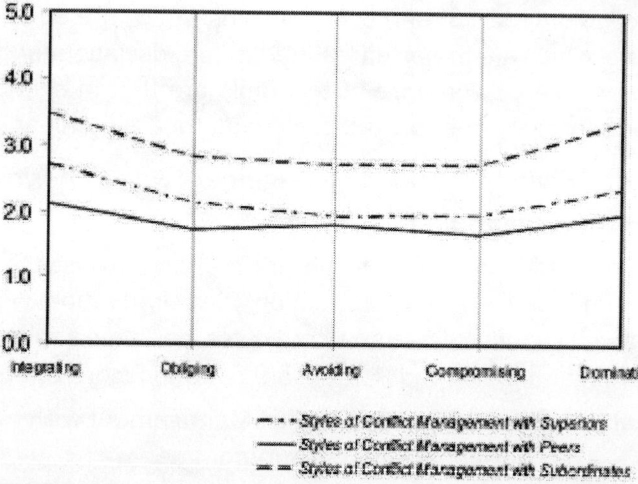

Fig. 5.9.5.4 : Graphical Presentation of Styles of Conflict Management with Superiors/Peers/Subordinates (M.Phil./Ph.D. in L.I.S. + Grad./Post Grad.)

5.10. STYLES OF CONFLICT MANAGEMENT: SUMMARIZED

So far in the preceding paragraphs, the various styles of conflict management by library managers in university libraries in Delhi, their behaviour with superiors, peers, and subordinates, have been studied by working out their mean value and standard deviation, individually and collectively. There is a need to study the entire data in a summary form, so that the picture 'At A Glance' may be viewed, as presented and discussed in the paragraphs as follow.

5.10.1. Styles of Conflict Management with Superiors, Peers And Subordinates: Summarized

The summary of the entire data, studied earlier is being further analysed and the same is presented and discussed in the paragraphs as follow.

5.10.1.1. Styles of Conflict Management with Superiors

The relevant data is presented in Table 5.10.1.1.

Table 5.10.1.1 : Styles of Conflict Management with Superiors

S. No.	Conflict Management Styles	Mean Value	Standard Deviation
1.	Integrating	3.43	1.22
2.	Obliging	3.14	1.17
3.	Avoiding	2.66	1.08
4.	Compromising	2.88	1.08
5.	Dominating	2.58	1.22

N = 168

Table 5.10.1.1 indicates that highest priority has been given to integrating with mean value (3.43), followed by obliging (3.14). The respondents are relying upon compromising (2.88) and dominating (2.58) are medium and least respectively. Further analysis of this table indicates that standard deviation calculated is lower 1.08 in case of avoiding and compromising and higher 1.22 in integrating and dominating. It is inferred from table that integrating style is the primary styles of the over all respondents of the university libraries followed by obliging mode.

5.10.1.2 Styles of Conflict Management with Peers

The relevant data is presented in Table 5.10.1.2

Table 5.10.1.2 : Styles of Conflict Management with Peers

S. No.	Conflict Management Styles	Mean Value	Standard Deviation
1.	Integrating	3.30	1.35
2.	Obliging	2.96	1.21
3.	Avoiding	2.67	1.17
4.	Compromising	2.85	1.19
5.	Dominating	2.44	1.21

N = 168

Table 5.10.1.2 reveals that integrating method with mean value (3.30) is being utilized by the respondents frequently, as against the dominating (2.44), which have been given the least priority. Respondents also make use of styles such as obliging

(2.96) and compromising (2.85). The lowest standard deviation 1.17 is found in avoiding and highest 1.35 in integrating. Conclusion is drawn from the table that respondents are making use of integrating most followed by obliging.

5.10.1.3. *Styles of Conflict Management with Subordinates*

The relevant data is being presented in Table 5.10.1.3.

Table 5.10.1.3: Styles of Conflict Management with Subordinates

S. No.	*Conflict Management Styles*	*Mean Value*	*Standard Deviation*
1.	Integrating	3.59	0.85
2.	Obliging	3.21	0.87
3.	Avoiding	2.87	0.90
4.	Compromising	3.00	0.85
5.	Dominating	2.76	0.99

N = 179

Table 5.10.1.3 indicates that preference of integrating style with mean value (3.59), which is adopted by the respondents followed by obliging (3.21) and compromising (3.00). Dominating (2.76) is being utilized the least. The standard deviation also shows lower value 0.85 in integrating as much as in compromising. But the highest value is found in dominating 1.22. It is inferred from the table that integrating is the primary style followed by obliging and compromising.

5.10.1.4. *Styles of Conflict Management with Superiors/Peers/ Subordinates*

The data (in a summary form) pertaining to library managers' strategies of conflict management with their superiors/ peers/ subordinates is being presented in Table 5.10.1.4 and Figure 5.10.1.4.

Table 5.10.1.4 : Styles of Conflict Management with Superiors/Peers/ Subordinates

S. No.	*Conflict Management Styles*	*Superiors*		*Peers*		*Subordinates*	
		Mean Value	*Standard Deviation*	*Mean Value*	*Standard Deviation*	*Mean Value*	*Standard Deviation*
1.	Integrating	3.43	1.22	3.30	1.35	3.59	0.85
2.	Obliging	3.14	1.17	2.96	1.21	3.21	0.87
3.	Avoiding	2.66	1.08	2.67	1.17	2.87	0.90
4.	Compromising	2.88	1.08	2.85	1.19	3.00	0.85
5.	Dominating	2.58	1.22	2.44	1.21	2.76	0.99

N = 179

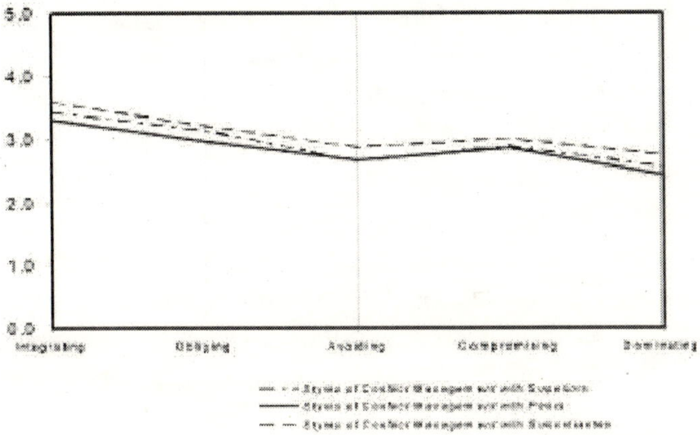

Fig. 5.10.1.4 : Graphical Presentation of Styles of Conflict Management With Superiors/Peers/Subordinates (Summary)

Table 5.10.1.4 and Figure 5.10.1.4 indicate that there is uniformity in adopting styles with superiors, peers and subordinates. The respondents prefer integrating (3.43), (3.30) and (3.59) followed by obliging (3.14), (2.96), (3.21) and compromising (2.88), (2.85) and (3.00) dealing with the superiors, peers and subordinates. Further analysis also shows similarity in adopting least style i.e. dominating (2.58), (2.44) and (2.76) while dealing with the superiors, peers and subordinates respectively. Standard deviation calculated for each specific method is found less than 1, while dealing with subordinates and more than 1, while dealing with superiors and peers. Conclusion is drawn from the table that there is uniformity found in styles of conflict management. Integrating is preferred more followed by obliging and compromising while dealing with superiors, peers and subordinates.

The present analysis indicates that among the styles of conflict management, library professionals utilized integrating the most followed by obliging for resolving conflict with superiors. The respondents have viewed integrating as prevalent strategy, followed by obliging and compromising for managing conflict with peers. It may be further noted that integrating method was preferred by the library professionals for dissolving conflict, and followed by obliging method, with subordinates. Thus, there is uniformity in pattern, while dealing with superiors, peers and subordinates. Conflict management styles of the library professionals is characterized by predominant use of integrating method, followed by obliging and compromising methods, while the least preferred method is dominating with superiors, peers and subordinates.

The results of earlier studies, made by other researchers (namely, Rahim, Das, Bhowon and many others), are more or less similar with the present analysis. One may, therefore, infer on the basis of the present study that integrating mode is preferred one, while dominating mode is the least used style of managing conflict with the superiors and subordinates. It has been observed that there are some changes in the behaviour of library managers with superiors and subordinates. However, in present analysis, it has revealed that the library professionals have observed uniformity in the styles of conflict management with superiors, peers and subordinates. They valued democratic and human relations aspects of the management in university libraries in Delhi.

5.11. INTER-CORRELATIONS AMONG FIVE CONFLICT MANAGEMENT STYLES WITH SUPERIORS/PEERS/ SUBORDINATES

The results of the study of inter-correlation among five conflict management styles utilized by the respondents with the superiors, peers and subordinates in university libraries in Delhi have been given in a summary form in Table 5.11

In Table 5.11, the upper triangle indicates conflict management styles of the respondents with superiors; middle triangle belongs to conflict management styles with peers, while the lower triangle indicates conflict management styles with subordinates. In the upper triangle inter-correlations among the five methods of conflict resolution used by respondents with superiors varies from 0.23 to 0.78. It shows that there is a positive correlation between integrating and obliging (0.78) found significant while insignificant between avoiding and compromising (0.23). In the middle triangle, inter-correlation among conflict resolution methods with peers ranges from 0.35 to 0.82. It shows positive correlation and having higher degree of correlation between integrating and obliging method (0.82), avoiding and compromising (0.74), and the lowest degree of correlation between compromising and dominating (0.35). In the lower triangle there is positive as well as negative relationship. Positive correlation varies from 0.22 to 0.48 and negative from -0.05 to -0.24. It is evident from Table 5.11 that neither positive nor negative correlation found significant, except the relationship between integrating and obliging (0.48), which is having moderate degree of positive relationship. It is inferred that in all the three triangles, there is significant correlation between integrating and obliging methods, while dealing with superiors, peers and subordinates.

8.12. CONCLUSION

The analysis and study carried in the preceding paragraphs makes clear that there are some differences in

Table 5.11 : Inter-correlations among five Styles of Conflict Management with Superiors, Peers and Subordinates

Styles of Conflict Management with	*1*	*2*	*3*	*4*	*5*	*6*	*7*	*8*	*9*	*10*	*11*	*12*	*13*	*14*	*15*
Superiors															
1. Integrating		0.78**	0.39**	0.64**	0.69**										
2. Obliging			0.60**	0.67**	0.39**										
3. Avoiding				0.23**	0.32**										
4. Compromising					0.23**										
5. Dominating															
Peers															
1. Integrating							0.82**	0.69**	0.68**	0.48**					
2. Obliging								0.67**	0.74**	0.47**					
3. Avoiding									0.65**	0.45**					
4. Compromising										0.35**					
5. Dominating															
Subordinates															
1. Integrating												0.48**	0.24**	0.22**	-0.06
2. Obliging													0.29**	0.41**	-0.05
3. Avoiding														0.29**	-0.05
4. Compromising															-0.05
5. Dominating															

** Correlation is significant at 0.01 level *Correlation is significant at 0.05 level N = 179

behaviour of the library managers on the basis of designations, across the hierarchy, library wise, sex wise, age wise, and qualifications wise, while dealing with superiors, peers and subordinates in university libraries in Delhi. It has been found in the over all styles of conflict management that respondents were making use of integrating method at the top priority, followed by obliging and compromising methods and relied least upon the dominating method while dealing with superiors, peers and subordinates.

6

Conclusions

The Findings/Observations/Comments, emerged during the course of this study, have been summarized under the main headings given as follows.

* Issues of Conflict in University Libraries
* Causes / Sources of Conflict in University Libraries
* Styles of Conflict Management in University Libraries
* Some Observations

6.1. ISSUES OF CONFLICT IN UNIVERSITY LIBRARIES

Findings relating to conflict issues are given in brief, as follows.

It is inferred that the 'job objectives' is an issue of the respondents of DULS, JNUL, ZHL, IARIL, HMSCL, wherein these are the older and bigger university libraries being studied

Conclusion is drawn that respondents from all the libraries, except JNUL, 'agree' that conflict over role is a conflict issue.

All the respondents are of the view that planning of activities is a conflict issue with their superiors, peers and subordinates.

One can draw the conclusion that respondents of all the libraries, except IARIL, have perceived that 'distribution of authority' is an issue of conflict,

The reward criteria is not a conflict issue of respondents of DULS, JNUL, IARIL, and HMSCL, while the respondents of ZHL, TERIL and Other Libraries, the 'Reward Criteria' has been reported as an issue of conflict while dealing with superiors, peers and subordinates.

The punishment criteria is not a conflict issue in DULS, JNUL, HMSCL, and Other Libraries, while ZHL professionals have opined that this is an issue of conflict. It is inferred that participation in decision-making is a conflict issue of the respondents.

Library professionals of all the university libraries 'agree' that participation in decision-making is a conflict issue while dealing with superiors, peers, and subordinates.

It is concluded that library policies and procedures is a conflict issue among the respondents of JNUL, ZHL and Other Libraries, while the same is not a conflict issue for respondents of DULS, IARIL and HMSCL.

Majority of the respondents from all the libraries have expressed their views as 'agree' in contrast to 'disagree'. It is inferred that promotion is a conflict issue amongst the respondents of all the libraries, except IARIL.

Provision and sanction of leave of absence to the employees is a natural requirement. Thus, availing leave creates problem before the supervisory staff, the problem of shortage of hands on a given moment. Sometimes 'leave' is used by the employee as a tool for irritating and disturbing the staff at the top. It is concluded that respondents of DULS, JNUL and HMSCL viewed that sanction of leave is not an issue of conflict, while ZHL and TERIL respondents have reported that they hold 'sanction of leave' as a conflict issue with their superiors, peers and subordinates.

Supervisors allot work to their subordinates fixing some deadlines. Sometimes, subordinates do not perform their work in time. It is observed that respondents of IARIL and HMSCL opined in equal numbers as 'agree' and 'disagree' respectively. It is inferred that 'not meeting deadlines' is not a conflict issue of the respondents with their superiors, peers and subordinates.

Workers' arriving late on the duty in the libraries is not a good habit and develops conflict. It is inferred that arriving late is a conflict issue of the respondents of all the libraries, except IARIL and Other Libraries.

Leaving early from the place of duty develops conflict among co-workers. It is concluded that 'leaving early' is a conflict issue of the respondents of DULS, JNUL, ZHL and TERIL while this is not a conflict issue for the respondents of IARIL, HMSCL and Other Libraries.

Misinterpretation of superiors' orders by the workers in library may develop conflict. It is inferred that 'misinterpretation of orders' is not a conflict issue of the respondents of DULS, JNUL, HMSCL, and Other Libraries, while this is a conflict issue of the respondents of ZHL, IARIL and TERIL.

For doing a good work efficiently, healthy working environment is needed. The insufficient physical conditions of work waste time, energy and skill of the workers, and may develops conflict. Conclusion is drawn that working environment is a conflict issue of the respondents of the DULS, JNUL, ZHL, TERIL and Other Libraries, except IARIL and HMCL.

Every worker develops his/her own personal habits. While working together, different habits of different persons may develop conflict situations.

Personal habits' is not a conflict issue amongst the respondents of all the libraries except TERIL, with their superiors, peers and subordinates.

The conflict 'over job objectives', conflict over 'role', 'planning of activities', 'distribution of authority', 'reward criteria', 'participation in decision making process', 'library policies and procedures', 'promotion', 'arriving late and 'working environment' are the conflict issues with the superiors, peers and subordinates. However, some of the issues like, 'sanction of leave', 'not meeting deadlines', 'leaving early', 'misinterpretation of orders' and 'personal habits' are not the substantive conflict issues of the respondents of the libraries, being studied.

6.2. CAUSES OF CONFLICT IN UNIVERSITY LIBRARIES

Findings pertaining to causes of conflict in university libraries, are being put together, as follows.

According to Coser, conflict occurs between individuals, groups and between individuals and groups. It may occur due to factors such as status, power and scarce resources but there are some other potent factors which have not been mentioned. The definition seems to have been drawn in social context.

Conflict is breakdown in the standard mechanism of decision making so that an individual or group experiences difficulty in selecting an action alternative.

Conflict is described as (1) antecedent conditions (for example scarcity of resources, policy giving rise to conflictual behavior, (2) affective states (e.g., stress; hostility, anxiety, etc.) of the individual involved, (3) cognitive states of individuals (the perception of awareness of conflictual situations), and (4) conflictual behavior, ranging from passive resistance to overt aggression.

In an organization when individuals or work groups have different goals, these goals may be incompatible and, hence, may lead to conflict. When one party's goal achievement is perceived as threatening to another's, the resulting conflict, likely to engender win-lose competition.

Performance appraisal can be a major cause of individual conflict within an organization. No employee wants that his or her doing poor job, is put on record.

Highly specialized job can lead to conflict because other employees know little about the tasks they are performing.

One's ability to trust each other has great impact on one's working life. When a person works in an organization, he is supposed to have trust on other colleagues. The more strongly people suspect that another party is out to get them, and likely to act without their own best interest in mind, the more likely they are to have a relationship with that party riddled with conflict Distrust may also build up due to misunderstanding among the employees.

We live in an era of technology, where information technology plays an important role in the libraries. Introduction of technology in the library has the potential to cause conflict in many ways. It may divide staff into those who are comfortable with the technology and those who are not.

In libraries, participation in professional meetings such as group discussions, workshops, seminars and conferences is one of the causes of interpersonal conflict.

In many libraries, especially in university libraries in India, a sizeable number of posts of university librarians, deputy librarians, assistant librarians and documentation officers etc., are lying vacant for long periods, but, posts of professional assistants and semi professional assistant are filled up, because, these are converted into promotional posts. It generates conflict among the library staff.

Due to financial crunch, the resources in the university libraries have been considerably squeezed. It is inferred that competition over scarce resources has been perceived as a cause for conflict amongst the respondents of DULS, JNUL, ZHL, HMSCL, and Other Libraries except the IARIL and TERIL.

Jurisdiction ambiguity may cause conflict. The respondents from all the libraries, except Other Libraries, have reported their views as 'agree' with this cause of conflict.

Different Perceptions of workers may cause interpersonal conflict. Conclusion is drawn from the data so analysed that 'different perceptions' are not endorsed as a cause of conflict of the respondents of DULS, IARIL, HMSCL, while the respondents of JNUL, ZHL, TERIL and Other Libraries have seen the 'different perceptions' as a cause of interpersonal conflict.

Personalised differences or the bias created among the respondents, may cause conflict. It is inferred that 'personal differences' have not been found as a cause for conflict among the library professionals of DULS, HMSCL, TERIL and Other Libraries, and this reason of conflict, has been perceived by the respondents of JNUL and ZHL.

It is inferred that differences in value was not perceived as a cause of conflict by the respondents of DULS, IARIL, HMSCL, while respondents o JNUL, ZHL, TERIL, and Other Libraries perceived it as a cause of conflict.

Communication plays an important role in maintaining good relations among workers in any organization. It is concluded that communication barrier is one cause of conflict in all the libraries, except in TERIL.

Interdependence among members of a group of workers in an organization is essential element of team -work. However, it may cause conflict among them. It is observed that respondents from all the libraries are 'agree' that 'interdependence' is a cause of interpersonal conflict of the respondents with superiors, peers and subordinates. Similar view is found in the over all responses, the majority responded as 'agree'.

The goals and objectives of different workers may differ from each other in an organization. The data reveals that respondents from all the libraries, except 'Other Libraries', have perceived the 'goal differences' as a cause of interpersonal conflict with superiors, peers and subordinates.

Performance appraisal is an essential element in administration in an organization. However, the act may become a cause of conflict among the workers, if it is not handled carefully. It is inferred that 'performance appraisal' is perceived as a cause for conflict.

It has been observed that mutual trust among workers results into better work environment. Distrust of any kind may develop conflict. It is concluded that the respondents did not perceive distrust as a cause of conflict in all the libraries, except ZHL. One may conclude that the larger number of respondents are in disagreement and are of the view that distrust among workers is not the cause of conflict among them.

Rapid changes and up-grading in technology adopted by the libraries, may cause conflict. It is concluded that 'technological changes' form a cause of conflict of the respondents with superiors, peers and subordinates, except in IARIL and TERIL.

Professional meetings offer an opportunity to the workers to understand various professional issues and the latest know-how. But, the opportunity provided and availed by them may cause conflict. Conclusion is drawn that 'participation in professional meetings' is perceived as a cause of interpersonal conflict amongst the respondents with superiors, peers and subordinates.

A larger number of respondents are "strongly agree" and "agree" with the causes of conflict with their superiors, peers and subordinates, such as,' competition over scarce resources', 'Jurisdiction ambiguity', 'Different Perceptions', 'communication barriers', 'interdependence', 'goal differences', 'performance appraisal', 'differences in expertise', 'technical changes', 'participation in professional meetings', and 'vacant posts'; while respondents opined as 'disagree' with such causes as 'personal differences', 'differences in value', and 'distrust'.

It may be observed that in the case of interpersonal conflict, (i) 'participation in professional meetings', and (ii) 'vacant posts', the higher percentage of over all the respondents are 'strongly agree' and 'agree'.

Further, under 'others, please specify', three respondents

from DULS have specified the 'differences in opinions' as a cause of conflict, while two respondents from JNUL have mentioned that 'hierarchical differences in status' is also one of the causes of conflict with the superiors, peers and subordinates.

Library professionals of university libraries in Delhi were found to have better understanding with their superiors, peers and subordinates on value, trust and personal differences while, competition over scarce resources, jurisdiction ambiguity, perceptions, communication barrier, interdependence, goal difference, performance appraisal, difference in expertise, technological changes, participation in professional meetings and vacant posts were perceived as a reason for conflict with superiors, peers and subordinates.

6.3. STYLES OF CONFLICT MANAGEMENT IN UNIVERSITY LIBRARIES

Every university library, in one form or the other, has conflict among its staff members over role, limited resources, personalities etc. Conflict is a reality in university libraries. It appears that there has been no such study conducted with regard to styles of conflict management of library professionals in India. Hence the present study is an effort to examine the factors that influence choice of conflict management and also to identity the most prevalent and practiced styles of library professionals. The results of such a study are summarized as follows.

Librarians of university libraries utilized 'integrating' method as their top priority, followed by 'dominating' for resolving conflict with subordinates.

No homogeneity is found in Deputy Librarians' behaviour to the extent that they preferred 'integrating' method while dealing with superiors, 'obliging' with peers, and 'dominating' with subordinates.

Uniformity was found in styles of conflict management of the Assistant Librarians, to the extent that they relied upon 'integrating' method, followed by 'obliging' and 'compromising' methods with their superiors, peers and subordinates.

There is an amount of similarity in applying conflict resolution modes by the Professional Assistants, to the extent that 'integrating' is most utilized method, followed by 'obliging' and 'compromising' while dealing with their superiors, peers and subordinates.

It has been observed that there are differences in the conflict management behaviour of library professionals across the hierarchy, such as, deputy librarians, assistant librarians and professional assistants, who rely upon integrating method for resolving conflict, dominating method followed by the deputy librarians, and obliging method by assistant librarians and professional assistants.

Deputy librarians preferred obliging mode followed by integrating mode, while assistant librarians and professional assistant were making use integrating mode to the maximum extent followed by obliging mode.

Librarians adopted integrating followed by dominating, deputy librarian valued style of dominating very high followed by integrating and assistant librarians and professional assistants adopted integrating to maximum extent followed by obliging, while dealing with subordinates.

Respondents of all university libraries relied upon integrating method followed by obliging and compromising in JNUL, except in ZHL, in which obliging was preferred most and followed by integrating mode.

Respondents of all the university libraries utilized integrating most with dominating as least, while dealing with peers.

Respondents of all the university libraries preferred integrating method, followed by obliging mode, except in JNUL who adopted compromising as prevalent method, and in TERIL in which obliging was utilized most followed by integrating, while dealing with subordinates.

Homogeneity was found in styles of conflict management in university libraries (other than libraries of deemed universities) in which integrating method preferred most followed by obliging and compromising. Avoiding and dominating were least operative methods with superiors, peers and subordinates.

Males and females tended to handle conflict similarly. In short, there was no gender effect on choice of conflict management as both professionals utilized integrating followed by obliging and compromising, while dealing with superiors, peers and subordinates.

Significant similarity of styles in both age groups revealed that respondents of both age groups adopted integrating for resolving conflict followed by obliging and compromising, while dominating was least preferred with superiors, peers and subordinates.

In the choice of conflict management styles, on the basis of education of the respondents, it was found that library professional possessing graduation with B.L.I.Sc.. preferred integrating method with superiors, peers and subordinates followed by compromising with superiors and obliging with peers and subordinates.

Respondents possessing post-graduation with B.L.I.Sc.. and its equivalent utilized integrating as primary method with superiors, peers and subordinates followed by obliging with superiors and subordinates and compromising with peers.

Uniformity was found in the choice of conflict management styles of the respondents' having post-graduation with M.L.I.Sc. They relied upon integrating followed by obliging and dominating least adopted method, while dealing with superiors, peers and subordinates.

Respondents possessing M.Phil./Ph.D. (other than library

and information science) with B.L.I.Sc../M.L.I.Sc. and their equivalent preferred integrating as primary style with superiors, peers and subordinates, followed by obliging with superiors, peers and avoiding with subordinates.

Respondents having M.Phil./Ph.D. (Library and Information Science) with graduation/Post graduation applied integrating behaviour for resolving conflict most, followed by dominating with superiors, peers and subordinates.

The result of inter-correlations among five conflict management styles revealed that there is positive as well as negative relationship between the styles of conflict resolution but significant relationship was found between integrating and obliging with the superiors, peers and subordinates.

The study indicated that styles of conflict management did not significantly vary while dealing with superiors, peers and subordinates. Integrating and obliging were found most operative, compromising and avoiding emerged as medium preferred and dominating adopted least, while dealing with superiors, peers and subordinates. It further indicated that conflict resolution behaviour of library professionals in the university libraries characterized by the immense utilization of integrating, obliging and compromising with relative absence of avoiding and dominating behaviour. Thus library professionals adopted more democratic, rationale and human approaches towards their superiors, peers and subordinates.

6.4. SOME OBSERVATIONS

The present study focused on the significant conflict issues related to superiors, peers and subordinates, and its management in university libraries in Delhi. It is much relevant to have studied the managerial behaviour of the library professionals and their management of conflict situations in their libraries. As per the findings of the study, the most effective behaviour for resolving conflict was integrating, which is followed by obliging and compromising modes. The least preferred method is dominating. It is felt that there is much scope for evaluating the various styles of conflict management in the context of socio-psycho variables in different types of libraries at national, regional, state and local levels in India. For this purpose, the services of a properly qualified Library Management Consultant may be deployed. Based on the analysis and evaluation of the existing facts/situations, the present researcher has formulated certain suggestions/ recommendations for use of all concerned. These are submitted as follows.

During the course of study, some more observations were made which have concern for the library management or the library authority. For enabling the library management to play its role in yet better form and to help the library management improve, some suggestions/recommendations are submitted for consideration by all concerned, such as follows.

Library management may encourage library professionals in the process of decision-making.

Wherever and whenever a situation demands, the library authority need to deploy the services and the expertise of Library Professional Management Consultant, who can play the role of a system analyst, advisor, man power provider, and an auditor in the better and more effective library administration.

The library authority need to provide and implement the maximum possible channels and opportunities for human resource development of library personnel.

A training to deal with the conflict be provided to the library professionals.

Researchers and observers have noted increasing levels of stress and conflict in the workplace, probably due to peculiarities of human behaviour and rapid pace of changes. In view of the innovations, and most of them derived from the Laws of Library Science (especially, the Fifth Law "**Library is a Growing Organism**", taking place in libraries and library services, it has become imperative that the library managers step forward in coping with the resultant stress and conflict. To manage changes effectively, one needs to differentiate between '*change*' and '*transition*', and to be aware of the process, the library staff members are experiencing.

There are described five styles of conflict management. The Integrating Style has been considered the best and most suitable for conflict management in university libraries. This style assures both, the persons in power, and the persons in opposition to make their best common achievements. By obliging method, one party plays down the differences and emphasizes the commonalities, and the other party is obliged. By compromising, neither side gets its best. By avoiding, one party tends to deny and avoid the problems of the other party, hence, the problems remain unsolved. By dominating, one party gains without being considerate for the other party, hence, the conflict mounts to new heights.

The conflict management is complex and some time hard to achieve the best results from the existing conflict. A greater understanding of the behavioural skills associated with it can have a bottom line impact on organizational productivity and performance. This fact leads to three important implications for management, such as,

There is no one best conflict resolution technique that mangers can use in every situation.

Managers need to understand that some conflict that affects organizational performance needs their immediate intervention to resolve potentially dangerous issues, and

Managers need also to recognize that organizational development (OD) programmes can train and educate both managers and subordinate in using such fruitful resolution techniques are collaboration, and these can lead to a more cooperative productive atmosphere over the long run.

Accepting that research and development are continuous

process and no research can claim as the last word, certain areas for researchers in the different type of libraries at national, regional, state levels in future, have been identified. These are submitted for consideration of all concerned, as follows.

* Conflict management styles and their impact on library effectiveness.
* Perceived library climate and managing conflict.
* Perceived power and managing interpersonal conflict in libraries.
* Cultural impact on styles of conflict management in libraries.
* Library professionals styles for managing conflict and their functional and dysfunctional sides.
* Conflict management styles and affect on teams in the libraries.
* Contingency approach to conflict management in libraries.
* Situational variables affecting the choice of conflict management styles and its potential consequences.

It is further concluded that conflict 'over job objectives', conflict over 'role', 'planning of activities', 'distribution of authority', 'reward criteria', 'participation in decision making process', 'library policies and procedures', 'promotion', 'arriving late and 'working environment' are the conflict issues with the superiors, peers and subordinates. However, some of the issues like, 'sanction of leave', 'not meeting deadlines', 'leaving early', 'misinterpretation of orders' and 'personal habits' are not the substantive conflict issues of the respondents of the libraries, being studied.

Conclusion is drawn that 'competition over scarce resources', 'jurisdiction ambiguity', 'perceptions', 'communication barriers', 'interdependence', 'goal differences', 'performance appraisal', 'difference in expertise', 'technological changes', 'participation in professional meetings', and 'vacant posts' are the major source of conflict by the respondents with their superiors, peers and subordinates in the university libraries being studied.

The Library professionals of university libraries were found to have better understanding with their superiors, peers and subordinates on value, trust and personal differences while, competition over scarce resources, jurisdiction ambiguity, perceptions, communication barrier, interdependence, goal difference, performance appraisal, difference in expertise, technological changes, participation in professional meetings and vacant posts were perceived as a reason for conflict with superiors, peers and subordinates.

The analysis and study carried in the preceding paragraphs makes clear that there are some differences in behaviour of the library managers on the basis of designations, across the hierarchy, library wise, sex wise, age wise, and qualifications wise, while dealing with superiors, peers and subordinates in university libraries. It has been found in the over all styles of conflict management that respondents were making use of integrating method at the top priority, followed by obliging and compromising methods and relied least upon the dominating method while dealing with superiors, peers and subordinates.

Bibliography

DOCUMENTS CONSULTED

1 ABBAS (S M) Managing Conflict in Central University libraries in Delhi. Library Herald, 46, 5, 2008; 130-37.

2 ADLER (Nancy J). International dimensions of organizational behavior. Ed 2. 1991. PWS-Kent; Boston. p 179-217.

3 ALESSANDRA (AJ) and HUNSAKER (PL). Communicating at work. 1993. Simon & Schuster; New York.

4 ALI (Syed Hashim). Conflict management. University News. 25, 43; 1987; 1-6.

5 ALLAWAY (SM). Conflict in Camden. Librarian's Christian Fellowship Newsletter. 70; 1998; 25-27.

6 ALLRED (Carol B). Anatomy of conflict : Some thought on managing staff conflict. Law Library Journal. 79, 1; 1987; 7-32.

7 ALLVESSON (M). Communication power and organization. 1996. Waters D. DeGruyter; New York.

8 AMASON (AC) and others. Conflict : Important dimension in successful management teams. Organizational Dynamics. 24, 1995; 25-30.

9 ANAND (JK). Role of professional assistant in a college library with special reference to Delhi university colleges. ILA Bulletin. 20, 1-2; 1984; 54-77.

10 ANCONA (DG). Outward bound : Strategies for team survival in an organization. Academy of Management

Journal. 33, 2; 1990; 334-56.

11 ANDERSON (Alan H) and KYPRIANOU (Anna). Result oriented organizational behaviour. 1998. Beacon Books; New Delhi. p124-31.

12 ARGYRIS (C). Integrating the individual and organization. 1964. John Wiley; New York.

13 ARNOLD (Hugh J) and FELDMAN (Daniel C). Organizational behavior. 1985. McGraw Hill; New York. p 209-33.

14 ARYA (PP) and YESH PAL, Eds. Research methodology in management : Theory and case studies. 2002. Deep & Deep; New Delhi.

15 ASSAEL (Henry). Constructive role of interorganizational conflict. Administrative Science Quarterly. 14, 4; 1969; 573-82.

16 ASSAEL (Henry). Political role of trade associations in distributive conflict resolution. Journal of Marketing. 32, 1; 1968; 21-28.

17 ASSOCIATION OF INDIAN UNIVERSITIES (New Delhi). University Institutions in India. 2002. p 34.

18 ASSOCIATION OF INDIAN UNIVERSITIES (New Delhi). University Handbook. Ed 29.2002. p 1217.

19 BALDRIDGE (VJ). Power and conflict in the university : Research in the sociology of complex organization. 1971. Willey; New York.

20 BARKER (Jeffrey) and others. Conflict approach of effective and ineffective project managers: Field study in matrix organization. Journal of Management Studies. 25, 2; 1988; 167-78.

21 BARNARD (Chester I). Functions of the executive. 1938. Harvard University Press; Cambridge.

22 BARON (RA). Positive effects of conflict : A cognitive perspective. Employee Responsibilities and Rights Journal. 4, 1; 1991; 25-35.

23 BARSADE (Sigal G) and others. To your heart's content : A model of affective diversity in top management teams. Administrative Science Quarterly. 45, 4; 2000; 802-36.

24 BAUER (CK). Managing management. Special Libraries. 71, 4; 1980; 204-16.

25 BAZERMAN (Max H). Judgement in managerial decision making. Ed 3. 1994. Wiley; New York.

26 BEALS (Alan R) and SIEGEL (Bernard J). Divisiveness and social conflict : An anthropological approach. 1966. Stanford University Press; Standford.

27 BENEDICT (Marjore). Librarians satisfaction with faculty status. College & Research Libraries. 52, 6; 1991; 538-48.

28 BERG (Thomas L). Designing the distribution system, marketing management and administrative action, ed by Stuart H Britt and Harper W. Boyd Jr. 1963. McGraw Hill; New York. p 400-08.

29 BERNE (Eric). Games people play. 1964. Grove Press; New York.

30 BERNE (Eric). Transactional analysis in psychotherapy. 1961. Grove Press; New York.

31 BHATTA (Bhim Dev). Conflict management. Prashasan. 19, 2; 1988; 15-23.

32 BHOWON (Uma). Perceived organizational climate and interpersonal handling strategies. Indian Journal of Industrial Relations. 35, 1; 1999; 43-51.

33 BHOWON (Uma). Perceived power and interpersonal handling strategies. Indian Journal of Industrial Relations. 34, 2; 1998; 183-92.

34 BIDDLE (Derek) and EVENDEN (Robin). Human aspects of management. Ed 2. 2002. Jaico; Mumbai. p 107-19.

35 BISHOP (Olga B). Use of professional staff in libraries : A Review. 1973. Canadian Library Association; Ottawa.

36 BITTEL (Lester R). What every supervisor should know. Ed 5. 1990. Tata McGraw Hill; New Delhi. p 61-85.

37 BLAKE (Rebert R) and MOUTON (Jane S). Managerial grid. 1964. Gulf Publishing; Houston.

38 BLAKE (Robert R) and MOUTON (Jane S). New management grid. 1985. Jaico, Bombay. P 11.

39 BLAKE (RR) and others. Managing inter-group conflict in industry. 1964. Gulf Publishing; Houston.

40 BLANCHARD (K) and O' CONNOR (M). Managing by values. 1997. Berret-Kohler; San Francisco.

41 BORDER (John M) and SCHMITT (Eric). Conflicting versions of war. Hindustan Times. 30 Mar., 2003; 21, 1-3.

42 BOSTOCK (William W) and HAIG (Robin A). Management of conflict : Psychological organizational and cultural factors. Philippine Jouranl of Public Administration. 36, 2; 1992; 159-68.

43 BOULDING (K B). Preface to special issue. Journal of Conflict Management. 12; 1968; 409-11.

44 BOULDING (K E). Organization as a party to conflict. In THOMAS (T M) and Bennis (WG), Eds. Management of change and conflict. 1972. Penguin Books; London.

45 BOULDING (Kenneth). Conflict and defense. 1963. Harper & Row; New York.

46 BOWDEN (Russell). Professional responsibilities of librarians and information workers. IFLA Journal. 20, 2; 1994; 120-29.

47 BRETT (J M) and UKUMURA (T). Inter – and intracultural negotiation : U.S. and Japanese negotiations. Academy of Management Journal. 41, 5; 1998; 495-510.

48 BRETT (J M) and others. Breaking the bonds of reciprocity in negotiations. Academy of Management Journal. 33, 2; 1990; 410-24.

49 BRIEF (Arthur P). Managing job stress. 1981. Little-Brown; Boston.

50 BROWN (Charles T) and others. Communication conflict predisposition : Development of a theory and an instrument. Human Relations. 34, 12; 1981; 1103-17.

51 BROWN (David L) and CLARkSON (Andrew E). Conflict. In NICHOLSON (Nigel), Ed. Blackwell encyclopedia dictionary of organization behaviour. 1997. Blackwell; Cambridge. p 92-98.

52 BROWN (L D) and CLARKSON (A E). Conflict. In COPPER (C L) and ARGYRIS (C), Eds. Concise Blackwell encyclopedia of management. 1988. Blackwell; Oxford. p 105-07.

53 BROWN (L D). Managing conflict at organizational interface. 1983. Addison – Wesley; Massachusetts.

54 BUNDY (Mary Lee). Conflict in libraries. College & Research Libraries. 27, 4; 1966; 253-62.

55 BURKE (R F). Methods of resolving superior-subordinate conflict : The constructive use of subordinate differences and disagreements. Organizational Behavior and Human Performance. 5, 3; 1970; 393-411.

56 BURKE (R F). Methods of managing superior-subordinate conflict, their effectiveness and consequences. Canadian Journal of Behavioral Science. 2, 1; 1971; 124-35.

57 BURKE (R J). Methods of resolving interpersonal conflict. Personnel Administration. 32, 1; 1969; 48-55.

58 BURNS (Mary Anne) and CARTER (Jeabbetee). Collective bargaining and faculty status for librarians : West Chester state college. College & Research Libraries. 36, 2; 1975; 115-20.

59 BUSH (R A) and FLOGER (J P). Promise of mediation : Responding to conflict through empowerment and recognition. 1994. Jossey-Bass; San Francisco..

60 CAMPBELL (D J). Inter-personal unco-operation : some causes and cures. ASLIB Proceedings. 21, 12; 1969; 510-20.

61 CHAISON (Gary N) and PLOVNICK (Mark S). How concession and co-operation affect labour management relations. Personnel. 61, 6; 1984; 57-59.

62 CHALARAGASE (Pairot). Analytical study of the professional staff with regard to their cooperation and conflict among the professional staff in the selected university libraries in Thailand. 1997. Ph.D. thesis, Supervisor: Dr. S.R. Gupta, University of Delhi. (Unpublished.)

63 CHAN (M). Inter-group conflict and conflict management in R & D decisions of four aerospace companies. IEEE Transaction on Engineering Management. 36, 1; 1989; 95-104.

64 CHANIN (M). Empirical study of problem solving techniques and conflict behavior modes. 1980. Ph.D. Thesis; City University of New York. (Unpublished).

65 CHANIN (Michael N) and SCHNEER (Joy A). Study of the relationship between Jungian personality dimensions and conflict - handling behaviour. Human Relations. 37, 10; 1984; 863-79.

66 CHATTERJEE (M N). Conflict resolution begins at home. Times of India. 15 Jan., 2004; 16, 5-6.

67 CHEN (CC) and others. How can cooperation be fostered? The cultural effect of individualism – collectivism. Academy of Management Review. 23, 2; 1998; 285-304.

68 CHESLER (Mark A) and others. Power training : An alternative path to conflict management. California Management Review. 21, 2; 1978; 84-90.

69 CHHABRA (TN) and SURI (RK). Management process and perspectives. 2000. Kitab Mahal, New Delhi. P 535.

70 CHHOTEY LAL. Indian Agricultural Research Institute

Library. In GUPTA (B M), Ed. Handbook of libraries, archives and information centres in India. V 1. 1984-85. Information Industry Publications; Delhi. p 30.

71 CHOPRA (P N), Ed. Encyclopedia of India : Delhi. V 1. 1992 Rima; New Delhi. p 27.

72 CHOUDHARY (B R). Collection development policy in university libraries. Indian Journal of Information Library and Society. 1, 2; 1988; 129.

73 CHOUDHARY (Poonam). Study of the para-professional staff, their co-operation and conflict, in University Libraries in India: Based on survey of universities of Madhya Pradesh, Haryana and Delhi. 1993.Ph.D. Thesis; Supervisor: Dr. S.R.Gupta and Prof. S.M. Tripathi; Jiwaji University, Gwalior;(Unpublished).

74 CHUNG (Kae H) and MEGGINSON (Leon C). Organizational behavior. 1981. Harper & Row; New York. p 252.

75 CHURCHILL (Winston). World crisis : The aftermath. V 4. 1928. Butter Morth; London.

76 CIESLICK (DH). New status model for academic librarians. Journal of Librarianship. 8, 1; 1982; 76-81.

77 COCHARANE (John). Be a better supervisor with behavioural management. New Zealand Libraries. 45, 8; 1987; 177-79.

78 COLEMAN (James S). Community conflict. 1957. Free Press; New York. p 14.

79 CONLON (D E) and SULLIVAN (D P). Examining the actions of organizations in conflict : Evidence from the Delaware court of chancery. Academy of Management Journal. 42, 3; 1999; 319-29.

80 CONROY (Barbara) and SCHINDLER-JONES (Barbara). Improving communication in the library. 1986. Oryx; Phoenix. p 95.

81 COOK (Curties W) and HUNSAKER (Phillips L).

Management and organizational behavior. Ed 3. 2001. McGraw Hill; New York. p 372-409.

82 COOLEY (Chares H). Social Process. 1918. Scribner's Son; New York. p 39.

83 CORWIN (Ronald G). Pattern of organizational conflict. Administrative Science Quarterly. 14, 4; 1969; 507-20.

84 COSER (Lewis A). Conflict : Social aspect. In SILLS (DL), Ed. International encyclopedia of social sciences. V3. 1968. Crowell and Macmillan; New York. p 232-36.

85 COSER (Lewis A). Conflict. In SILLS (David L), Ed. International encyclopedia of social sciences. V3. 1968. Macmillan & Free Press; New York. p 232.

86 COSER (Lewis A). Functions of social conflict. 1956. Free Press; New York.

87 COSIER (R A) and DALTON (D R). Positive effects of conflict : A field experiment. International Journal of Conflict Management. 1, 1; 1990; 81-92.

88 COSIER (Richard A) and RUBLE (Thomas L). Research on conflict handling behavior : An experimental approach. Academy of Management Journal. 24, 4; 1981; 816-31.

89 COSTANTINO (CA) and Merchant (CS). Designing conflict management system. 1996. Jossey-Bass; San Francisco.

90 COVERMAN (S). Role overload, role conflict and stress : Addressing consequences of multiple role demands. Social Forces. 67, 4; 1989; 965-82.

91 COX (TH) and others. Effects of ethnic group cultural differences on cooperative behavior on a group task. Academy of Management Journal. 34, 4; 1991; 827-47.

92 CRETH (Shila D). Personnel issues for academic librarians : A review and perspective for future. College & Research Libraries. 50, 2; 1989; 144-52.

93 CYERT (R) and MARCH (J G). Behavioural theory of the firm. 1963. Prentice Hall; New Jersy.

94 CZANDER (W H). Psychodynamics of work and organizations : Theory and applications. 1993. Guilford; New York.

95 DAHRENDORF (Ralf). Class and class conflict in industrial society. 1959. Stanford University Press; Standford. p 135.

96 DALTON (M). Changing staff line relationship. Personnel Administrator 29, 2; 1966; 3-5.

97 DALTON (M). Conflict between staff and line managerial officers. American Sociological Review. 15, 3; 1950; 342-51.

98 DALTON (Melville). Men who manage. 1959. Wiley; New York.

99 DARLING (John R) and CLUFF (Dale E). Managing inter-personal conflict in university library. Library Administration and Management. 1, 1; 1987; 7-32.

100 DARR (Asaf). Conflict and conflict resolution in a cooperative : The case of the Niv Taxi station. Human Relations. 52, 3; 1999; 279-300.

101 DAS (G S). Conflict management styles of efficient branch managers : As perceived by others. ASCI Journal of Management. 17, 1; 1987; 31-38.

102 DAS (S L). Conflict : Basis of collective and constructive functioning. Indian Management. 21, 12; 1982; 21.

103 De LONG (David) and SEEMANN (Patricia). Confronting conceptual confusion and conflict in knowledge management. Organizational Dynamics. 29, 1; 2000; 33-44.

104 DELROCH (Marva I). Human resource management in technical services. Illinois Libraries. 69, 2; 1987; 112-26.

105 DERR (C Brooklyn). Managing organizational conflict : Collaboration, bargaining, and power approaches. California Management Review. 21, 2; 1978; 76-83.

106 DEUTSCH (M). Resolution of conflict. 1973. Yale University Press; Connecticut.

107 DOLLARD (John) and MILLER (Neal A). Personality and psychotherapy : An analysis in terms of learning, thinking and culture. 1950. McGraw Hill; New York.

108 EDWARDS (C) and WALTON (G). Change and conflict in the academic library. Library Management. 21, 1-2; 2000; 35-41.

109 EDWARDS (Ralph M). Management of libraries and professional functions of librarians. Library Quarterly. 45, 1; 1975; 150-59.

110 EGGLETON (Richard). Conflict in libraries revisited. Libri. 29, 1; 1979; 64-77.

111 ELANGOVAN (A R). Managerial third party dispute intervention : A perspective model of strategy selection. Academy of Management Review. 20, 4; 1995; 800-30.

112 EVAN (W M). Conflict and performance in R & D. organizations : Some preliminary findings. Industrial Management Review. 7, 1; 1965; 37-46.

113 EVANS (G Edward). Management techniques for librarians. Ed 2. 1983. Academic Press; New York.

114 FENSTERHEIM (H) and BAER (J). Don't say yes when you want to say no. 1975. David McKay; New York.

115 FERRARO (Vincent L) and ADAMS (Sheila A). Interdepartmental conflict : Practical ways to prevent and reduce it. Personnel. 61, 4; 1984; 12-23.

116 FILLEY (A C). Some normative issues in conflict management. California Management Review. 21, 2; 1978; 61-66.

117 FILLEY (Alan C). Interpersonal conflict resolution. 1975. Foresman; Glenview.

118 FINK (C F). Some conceptual difficulties in the theory of social conflict. Journal of Conflict Resolution. 12, 4; 1968;

412-60.

119 FISHER (R) and others. Getting to Yes. Ed 2. 1991. Houghton Mifflin; New York.

120 FISHER (R). Getting ready to negotiate : The getting to yes workbook. 1995. Viking Penguin; New York.

121 FISHER (W) and KOUE (Glen). Conflict management. Library Administration and Management. 5, 3; 1991; 145-50.

122 FLIPPO (Edwin). Personnel management. 1988. McGraw Hill; New York. p 479.

123 FOERSTEL (H). Conflict and compromise over homosexual literature. Emergency Librarian. 22, 2; 1994; 28-30.

124 FOLLETT (Mary Parker). Creative experience. 1951. Peter Smith; New York.

125 FORD (Rebecca) and JOHNSON (Cathryn). Perception of power : dependence and legitimacy in conflict. Social Psychology Quarterly. 61, 1; 1998; 16-32.

126 FOX (A). Coming to terms with conflict. Personnel Management. 14, 1; 1972; 20-23.

127 FREDERICKSON (H George). Role occupancy and attitudes towards labor relation in government. Administrative Science Quarterly. 14, 4; 1969; 595-606.

128 FRENCH (Wendell L). Human resource management. 1997. All India Publishers & Distributors; Chennai. p 119.

129 FREUD (Sigmund). General introduction to psychoanalysis. 1920. Boni and Liveright; New York.

130 FRITZ (S) and Others. Case study in conflict management : He said she said... 'interpresonal skill for leadership. 1999. Prentice Hall; New Jersy. p 208-09.

131 GANDEZ (Jeffrey) and MURRAY (Victor V). Experience of workplace politics. Academy of Management Journal. 23, 2; 1980; 244.

132 GATES (Jean Key). Introduction to librarianship. 1968. McGraw Hill; New York.

133 GEORGE (S L). Out of theory into practice supervising library employees. Journal of Academic Librarianship. 19, 3; 1993; 154-57.

134 GIBLADI (Joseph). M L A handbook for writers of research papers. Ed 5. 2000. Affiliated East – West Press; New Delhi.

135 GLASL (F). Process of conflict escalation and the role of third parties. In BOMERS (D J B) and FTERSON (R), Eds. Conflict management and Industrial Relations. 1982. Kluwer – Nijhoff; Boston. p 119-40.

136 GOEL (S L) and RAJNEESH (Shalini). Management techniques : Principles and practices. 2001. Deep & Deep; New Delhi. p 426-35.

137 GOIL (N K). Conflict between objectives and contents : Need for enlargement and adjustment of the scheme of papers for Master of Library Science. Library Herald. 9, 4; 1967; 313-20.

138 GOULDNER (Alvin). Organizational tensions. In MESTON (Robert), Ed. Sociology Today. 1959. Basic Books; New York. 400-28.

139 GREENBERG (Jerald) and BARON (Robert A). Behaviour in organizations : Understanding & managing the human side of work. Ed 5. 2000. Prentice Hall of India; New Delhi. p 412-50.

140 GREENHALGH (L). Managing conflict. In LEWICKI (F J) and others, Eds. Negotiation. Ed 3. 1999. McGraw Hill; Boston. p 6-13.

141 GUETZKOW (Harold) and GYR (John). Analysis of conflict in decision making groups. Human Relations. 7, 3; 1954; 361-81.

142 GUPTA (S R) and BABBAR (Parveen). Need and provision

of professional library management consultancy. Journal of Library and Information Science. 27, 2; 2002; 142-51.

143 GUPTA (S R). Institute of chartered librarian: A conceptual framework. Journal of Library and information Science. 17, 2; 192; 43-57.

144 GUPTA (S R). Management of library collection of professional colleges in India. 1988. Ph.D. Thesis; Supervisor: Prof. P.N. Kaula, Banaras Hindu University. (Unpublished).

145 GUPTA (S R). Discussion on 6/7/2007.

146 GUPTA (Santosh). Research methodology and statistical techniques. 1993. Deep & Deep; New Delhi.

147 HALL (J) and WILLIAM (M S). Comparison of decision making performance in established and adhoc groups. Journal of Personality and Social Psychology. 3, 2; 1966; 214-22.

148 HALL (J). Conflict management survey : A survey on one's characteristic reaction to and handling conflicts between himself and others. 1969. Telecometrics International; Taxas.

149 HALL (Richard H). Organizations: Structures, processes and outcomes. 1998. Prentice Hall of India; New Delhi. p 492-95.

150 HARKAVY (Michael), Ed. New Webster's international encyclopedia : The new illustrated home reference guide . 1994. Trident Press International; Florida. p 299.

151 HARRIMAN (PL), Ed. Handbook of psychological terms. 1965. Asam; Totawa. p 27.

152 HELLRIEGEL (Don) and others. Organizational behavior. Ed 9. 2000. South-Western; Mason. p 292-320.

153 HODGE (J E). Stress in the library. Library Association Record. 92, 10; 1990; 751-53.

154 HORENSTEIN (B). Job satisfaction among academic

librarians: Examination of the relationship between satisfaction, faculty status and participation. College & Research Libraries. 54, 3; 1993; 55-69.

155 HOWATT (Gary) and LONDON (Manuel). Attribution of conflict management strategies in superior-subordinate dyad. Journal of Applied Psychology. 65, 2; 1980; 172-75.

156 HUDSON (M P). Conflict and stress in time of change. Library Management. 20, 1 & 2; 1999; 35-38.

157 INDIA, INFORMATION AND BROADCASTING (Ministry of...) PUBLICATIONS (Division). India 2003: A reference annual. 2003. p 824.

158 INDIAN AGRICULTURAL RESEARCH INSTITUTE. Annual report 2001-2002. 2002. IARI; New Delhi. p 162.

159 INDIAN INSTITUTE OF FOREIGN TRADE. Annual report 2001-02. 2002. IIFT; New Delhi. p 25.

160 INDIAN STANDARDS INSTITUTE, New Delhi. IS:2381 – 1978.

161 JAMIESON (D W) and THOMAS (K W). Power and conflict in the student-teacher relationship. Journal of Applied Behavioral Science. 10; 1974; 321-26.

162 JANIS (Irving L). Group think : psychological studies of policy decisions and fiascoes. Ed 2. 1982. Houghton Mifflin; Boston.

163 JANSSEN (B). Conflict in Hoevelaken : Library committee steps down after a disagreement with the town council. Bibliotheek Blad. 3, 6; 1999; 12-14.

164 JAWAHARLAL NEHRU UNIVERSITY. Library guide 1993-94. 1994. JNU; New Delhi. p 1.

165 JEHN (K A) and others. Why differences make a difference : Field study of diversity, conflict, and performance in workgroups. Administrative Science Quarterly. 44, 3-4; 1999; 741-63.

166 JEHN (K A). Multi-method examination of the benefits and detriment of inter-group conflict. Administrative Science Quarterly. 40, 2; 1995; 256-85.

167 JEHN (K). Enhancing effectiveness : Investigation of advantages and disadvantages of value, based inter-group conflict. International Journal of Conflict Management. 4, 2; 1994; 223-38.

168 JEHN (KA). Qualitative analysis of conflict in organizational groups. Administrative Science Quarterly. 42, 3; 1997; 530-57.

169 JOHNSON (D W). Reaching out : interpersonal effectiveness and self actualization. 1967. Allyn and Bacon; Boston. p 205-07.

170 JONES (Gareth R). Organizational theory : Text and cases. 2000. Addison Wesley; New York. 550-63.

171 JONES (Ken H). Conflict and change in library organization : people, power and service. 1984. Clive Bingley; London.

172 JONES (Noragh) and JORDAN (Peter). Staff management in library and information work. Ed 2. 1987. Gower Publishing; Brookfield.

173 JONES (Robert E) and MELCHER (Bonita H). Personality and preference for modes of conflict resolution. Human Relations. 35, 8; 1982; 649-58.

174 KABANOFF (B). Equity, equality, power and conflict. Academy of Management Review. 16, 2; 1991; 416-41.

175 KABANOFF (Boris). Predictive validity of the mode conflict instrument. Journal of Applied Psychology. 72, 1; 1987; 160-63.

176 KAHN (R L) and others. Occupational stress: Studies in role conflict and ambiguity. 1964. John Wiley; New York.

177 KAHN (R L). Role conflict and role ambiguity in organizations. Personnel Administrator. 9, 1; 1964; 8-13.

178 KANTER (R M). Men and women of the corporation. 1977.

Colophon; New York.

179 KATHMAN (Jane McGurn) and KATHMAN (Michael D). Conflict management in the academic library. Journal of Academic Librarianship. 16, 3; 1990; 145-49.

180 KATHMAN (Jane McGurn) and KATHMAN (Michael D). Conflict management in libraries. In Allen (Kent), Ed. Encyclopedia of library and information science. V 51. 1993. Marcel Dekker; New York. p 190-94.

181 KATZ (Daniel) and KAHN (Robert L). Social psychology of organization. 1966. John Wiley; New York.

182 KATZ (R L). Skill of effective administrator. Harvard Business Review. 52, 5; 1974; 90-110.

183 KAZDIN (Alan E), Ed. Encyclopedia of psychology. V 2. 2000. American Psychological Association, Washington. p 261.

184 KELLY (J). Organization behavior. 1974. Richard D. Irwin; Burr Ridge. p 543.

185 KELLY (Joe). Making conflict work for you. Harvard Business Review. 48; 1970; 104.

186 KEMERY (Edward R) and others. Outcomes of role stress : Multi sample constructive replication. Academy of Management Journal. 28, 2; 1985; 363-75.

187 KEMP (Janice C). Primer on conflict management. Library Management Quarterly. 12, 4; 1989; 20-25.

188 KILMANN (Ralph H) and THOMAS (Kenneth W). Developing forced choice measure of conflict handling behavior: The 'Mode' instrument. Educational and psychological Measurement. 37; 1977; 309-25.

189 KING (Dennis). Three cheers for conflicts. Personnel. 58, 1; 1981; 13-22.

190 KOLB (D M) and BARTUNEK (J M), Eds. Hidden conflicts in organizations. 1992. Sage; Thousand Oaks.

191 KOLB (D) and PUTNAM (L). Multiple faces of conflict in organizations. Journal of Organizational Behavior . 13, 3; 1992; 311-24.

192 KOTHARI (C R). Research methodology : Methods and techniques. Ed 2. 2001. Vishwa; New Delhi. p 124.

193 KOTLER (J). Beyond blame: A new way of resolving conflicts in relationship. 1994. Jossey-Bass; San Francisco.

194 KOZAN (M K). Cultural influence on styles of handling interpersonal conflict : Comparison among Jordanian, Turkish, and U.S. managers. Human Relations. 42, 9; 1989; 787-99.

195 KREITNER (Robert) and KINICKI (Angelo). Organization behavior. 2000. McGraw Hill; Boston. p 444-74.

196 KRISHAN KUMAR. Research methods in library and information science. 1992. Har-Anand; New Delhi. p 121.

197 KUMAR (E. Sendil) and PANDEY (S). Organizational conflict, role conflict and correlates : Empirical study. Indian Journal of Social Work. 55, 2; 1994; 201-09.

198 KUMAR (R). Cognition and decision making in negotiations : Conceptual integration. In RAHIM (M A), Ed. Managing conflict : An integrative approach. 1989. Praeger; New York. p 185-94.

199 LABIANCA (Giuseppe) and others. Social networks and perceptions of inter-group conflict : Role of negative relationships and third parties. Academy of Management Journal. 41, 1; 1998; 55-67.

200 LABIG (C E). Preventing violence in the workplace. 1995. AMACOM; New York.

201 LAHIRI (R). Human side of the library : The study of the theory and literature. Annals of Library Science and Documentation. 34, 2; 1989; 41-51.

202 LAMMERS (Cornelis J). Strikes and mutinies : Comparative study of organizational conflict between rules and ruled.

Administrative Science Quarterly. 14, 4; 1969; 558-72.

203 LAWRENCE (P R) and LORSCH (J W). Organization and environment. 1967. Irwin – Dorsey; Burr Ridge.

204 LEE (Susan A). Conflict and ambiguity in the role of the academic library director. College & Research Libraries. 38, 5; 1977; 396-404.

205 LEVINE (Robert A). Anthropology and study of conflict : An Introduction. Journal of Conflict Resolution. 5, 1; 1961; 3-15.

206 LEWIN (Kurt). Dynamic theory of personality : Selected papers. 1935. McGraw Hill; New York. p 87.

207 LIKERT (R) and LIKERT (J. Gibson). New ways of managing conflict. 1976. McGraw Hill; New York.

208 LIKERT (R). New patterns of management. 1961. McGraw Hill; New York.

209 LINDSEY (Jonathan A). Using negotiation theory, conflict management and assertive theory in performance evaluation. Library Administration and Management. 4; 1990; 195-200.

210 LITTERER (Joseph A). Conflict in organization : A re-examination. Academy of Management Journal. 9, 3; 1966; 178-86.

211 LOBEL (SA) and McLEOD (PL). Effect of ethnic group cultural differences on cooperative behavior on a group tasks. Academy of Management Journal. 34, 4; 1991; 827-47.

212 LOCKE (EA) and others. Effect of individual goal conflict on performance. Journal of Management. 20, 1; 1994; 67-91.

213 LONDON (M) and HOWAT (G). Relationship between commitment and conflict resolution behavior. Journal of Vocational Behavior. 13, 1; 1978; 1-14.

214 LOUIS (Meryl Reis). How individuals conceptualize

conflict? Identification of steps in the process and the role of personal/developmental factors. Human Relations. 30, 5; 1977; 451-67.

215 LUX (Claudia). Managing libraries staff from a different cultural background: The East-West conflict in Berlin. IFLA Journal. 26, 1; 2000; 21-24.

216 MAGID (Alvin). Dimensions of administrative role and conflict resolution among local officials in Northern Nigeria. Administrative Science Quarterly. 12, 2; 1967; 321-31.

217 MAIER (N R F). Problem solving discussions and conferences : Leadership methods and skills. 1963. McGraw Hill; New York.

218 MAMGAIN (Asheesh). Conflict : Peace or play! Mothers in Nizamuddin East want their kids to play, but parks offer little scope to do so. Hindustan Times, HT South Delhi Live. 17 Oct., 2002; 1, 5-6.

219 MARCH (James G) and SIMON (Herbert A). Organization. 1958. John Wiley; New York.

220 MARCIC (Dorothy) and others. Organizational behavior : Experiences and cases. Ed 6. 2001. South-West; Mason. p121-35.

221 MAREK (J). Battle of strategies. In LAWERENCE (J R), Ed. Operational research and social sciences. 1966. Tavisteek; London. p 64.

222 MARTINS (L. Luis) and others. Moderators of the relationship between work-family conflict and career satisfaction. Academy of Management Journal. 45, 2; 2002; 399-409.

223 MARTOCCHIO (J J) and JUDGE (T A). When we don't see eye to eye : Discrepancies between supervisors and subordinates in absence disciplinary decisions. Journal of Management. 21, 2; 1995; 251-78.

224 MASON (R O). Dialectical approach to strategic planning. Management Science. 15, 3; 1969; 403-13.

225 MATHEW (R M). Effective human relations : Key for successful university library management. Herald of Library Science. 21, 3-4; 1982; 223-26.

226 MATHUR (H B) and SAYEED (Omer Bin). Application of conflict management strategic as perceived by the manager for himself and for his superior : Comparison. Indian Journal of Social Work. 41, 2-3; 1980; 163-68.

227 MATHUR (H B) and SAYEED (Omer Bin). Conflict management in organizations : Development of a model. Indian Journal of Social Work. 44, 2; 1983; 175-83.

228 MAYO (Elton). Social problems of an industrial civilization. 1945. Harvard Graduate School of Business Administration; Boston.

229 McGREGOR (D M). Professional manager. 1967. McGraw Hill; New York.

230 MERCHANT (Maurice P). Faculty – library conflict. Library Journal. 94, 15; 1969; 286-89.

231 MEYER (J P) and others. Evaluating the management of interpersonal conflict in organisations : A factor – analytic study of outcome criteria. Candain Journal of Administrative Sciences. 14, 1; 1997; 1-13.

232 MILES (R H). Macro organizational behavior. 1980. Good Year; San Francisco.

233 MILES (R H). Role requirements as source of organizational stress. Journal of Applied Psychology. 61, 2; 1976; 172.

234 MILLER (M T). Conflict management in organisations. Argus. 24, 3; 1995; 37-44.

235 MILLER (Neal E). Experimental study of conflict, personality and clinical disorder : A handbook based on experimental and clinical research. 1944. Ronald; New

York. p 431-65.

236 MILLS (Joan) and others. Conflict handling and personality dimensions of project-management personnel. Psychological Reports. 57; 1985; 1135-43.

237 MISHRA (Prashant) and DHAR (Upinder). Liveraging functional conflict. Indian Journal of Industrial Relations. 38, 1; 2002; 113-19.

238 MISHRA (Prashant) and others. Restrategising the management of conflict: An empirical study. Indian Journal Industrial Relations. 35, 2; 1999; 160-74.

239 MITROF (I I). and MASON (R O). Metaphysic of policy and planning : A reply to Cosier. Academy of Management Review. 6, 4; 1981; 649-51.

240 MOORE (C W). Mediation process : Practical strategies for resolving conflict. 1996. Jessey Bass; San Francisco.

241 MORRIS (Michach W) and others. Conflict management styles : Accounting for cross-national differences. Journal of International Business Studies. 29, 4; 1998; 729-48.

242 MURRAY (Edward J). Conflict : Psychological aspect. In SILLS (David L), Ed. International encyclopedia of social sciences. V 3. 1968. Macmillan & Free Press; New York. p 220.

243 NAIR (R Gangadharan). Relevance of conflict management in managing higher educational systems. Management in Government. 21, 4; 1990; 193-98.

244 NARSIMAH RAO (P V) . Post-cold war world. Hindu. 22 Mar., 2004; 10, 3-7.

245 NATIONAL MUSEUM INSTITUTE OF HISTORY OF ART, CONSERVATION AND MUSEOLOGY. Annual report 2001-02. 2002. National Museum; New Delhi. p 47.

246 NELSON (Debra L) and QUICK (James Campbell). Organizational behavior : Foundations, realities, and challenges. Ed 3. 2003. South-Western College; Mason.

p 421-57.

247 NELSON (Reed E). Strength of strong ties : Social networks and intergroup conflict in organizations. Academy of Management Journal. 32, 2; 1989; 377-401.

248 NEWMAN (W H) and WARREN (E K). Process of management. 1979. Prentice Hall; New Delhi. p 174.

249 NEWSTORM (John W). Leveraging management development through transfer of training strategies. Journal of Management Development. 5, 4; 1986; 33-45.

250 NEWSTROM (John W) and DAVIS (Keith). Organizational behavior: Human behaviour at work. Ed 10. 2001. Tata McGraw Hill; New Delhi. p 312-20.

251 NORTHCRAFT (Gregory B) and NEALE (Margaret A). Organization behavior. 1990. Dryden; Chicago. p 247-48.

252 OATES (David). Way to change managerial behavior. International Management. 28, 4; 1973; 54-58.

253 OPPENHEIM (A N). Questionnaire design and attitude management. 1966. Basic Books; New York. p 1.

254 PALEN (John J). Belief in government control and displace workers. Administrative Science Quarterly. 14, 4; 1969; 584-93.

255 PAREEK (Udai). Managing conflict and collaboration.1982. Oxford and IBH Publishing; New Delhi.

256 PARK (Robert E). Social foundation of war. American Journal of Sociology. 46, 4; 1941; 551.

257 PARKER (Christopher P) and others. Perceptions of organizational politics: An investigation of antecedents and consequences. Journal of Management. 21, 5; 1995; 891-912.

258 PARSONS (Talcot). Social system. 1951. Free Press; New York.

259 PARTHASARTHY (Kokila) and SINGH (P). Strategies for

conflict management : An Indian experience. Indian Management. 23, 7; 1984; 13-22.

260 PAUL (R J) and SCHOOLER (R D). Analysis of performance standards and generation conflict in academia. Academy of Management Journal. 13, 2; 1970; 212-16.

261 PAVLOV (I P). Conditioned reflexes, tr. by G V Anrep. 1927. Oxford University Press; London.

262 PEARSALL (July), Ed. Concise Oxford dictionary. 2001. Ed 1. Oxford University Press; New Delhi.

263 PELLED (L H) and others. Exploring the black box : An analysis of work group diversity, conflict and performance. Administrative Science Quarterly. 44, 1; 1999; 1-28.

264 PELZ (D C) and ANDREWS (F). Scientists in organizations. 1966. John Wiley; New York.

265 PELZ (D). Creative tensions in the research and development climate Science. 157, 3785; 1967; 160-65.

266 PETERSON (M F) and others. Role conflict ambiguity and overload : A 21 nations study. Academy of Management Journal. 38, 2; 1995; 429-52.

267 PETTAS (William) and GILLILAND (Steven L). Conflict in the large academic library : Friend or foe? Journal of Academic Librarianship. 18, 1; 1992; 24-29.

268 PHILLIPS (Eleanor) and CHESTON (Ric). Conflict resolution : What works. California Management Review. 21, 4; 1979; 76-83.

269 PHILLIPS (Estelle M) and PUGH (D S). How to get Ph.D. : A hand-book for students and their supervisors. 1993. UBS; New Delhi.

270 PINKLEY (R L). and NORTHCRAFT (G B). Cognitive interpretations of conflict : Implications for dispute processes and outcomes. Academy of Management Journal. 37, 1; 1994; 193-205.

271 PINKLEY (Robin L). Dimensions of conflict frame :

Disputant interpretations of conflict. Journal of Applied psychology. 75, 2; 1990; 117-26.

272 PONDY (Louis R). Varieties of organizational conflict. Administrative Science Quarterly. 14, 4; 1969; 499-505.

273 PONDY (Louis R). Organizational conflict : Concepts and models. Administrative Science Quarterly. 12, 2; 1967; 296-320.

274 PRASAD (Lallan) and BANNERJEE (A M). Management of human resources. 1990. Sterling; New Delhi. p 56.

275 PRICE (Charley A). What professional librarians expect from administrators : One librarian's view. College & Research Libraries. 48, 5; 1987; 408-12.

276 PRIEM (R L) and others. Structured conflict and consensus outcomes in group decision making. Journal of Management. 21, 4; 1995; 691-710.

277 PRIEM (Richard) and PRICE (Kenneth). Process and outcome expectations for the dialectical inquiry, devil's advocacy, consensus, techniques of strategic decision making. Group and Organization Studies. 16, 2; 1991; 206-25.

278 PROCTER (Paul), Ed. Cambridge international dictionary of English. 1996. Cambridge University Press; Cambridge.

279 PRUITT (DG) and RUBIN (J Z). Social conflict : Escalation, stalemate, settlement. 1986. Random House; New York.

280 PRYTCHESCH (Ray), Com. Harrrod's librarians glossary and reference book. 1987. Gower; Hants. p 821.

281 QUINN (Robert E) and others. Becoming a master manager. 1990. Wiley; New York. p 289-94.

282 QUINN (Robert E). Beyond rational management : Mastering the paradoxes and competing demand of high performance. 1988. Jossey-Bass; San Francisco.

283 RADHAKRISHNAN (S). Delhi University Library : The opening of the new library. 1938. University Press, Delhi.

p 1 (mimeographed)

284 RAHIM (A). Management of intraorganizational conflicts : A laboratory study with organisational design. Management International Review. 19, 1; 1979; 97-106.

285 RAHIM (A). Some contingencies affecting interpersonal conflict in academics : A multivariate study. Management International Review. 20, 2; 1980; 117-21.

286 RAHIM (M A) and BLUM (A A), Eds. Global perspective on organizational conflict.1995. Praeger; Connecticut.

287 RAHIM (M A) and BONOMA (T V). Managing organizational conflict : A model for diagnosis and intervention. Psychological Reports. 44; 1979; 1323-44.

288 RAHIM (M A) and BUNTZMAN (G F). Supervisory power bases and styles of handling conflict with subordinates and subordinates compliance and satisfaction. Journal of Psychology. 123; 1988; 195-210.

289 RAHIM (M A). Organizational conflict inventory i & ii : Professional manual. 1983. Consulting Psychologists Press; Palo Alto.

290 RAHIM (M A). and MAGNER (N R). Confirmatory factor analysis of the style of handling interpersonal conflict : First order factor model and its invariance across groups. Journal of Applied Psychology. 80, 1; 1995; 122-32.

291 RAHIM (M A). Managing conflict in organisations. Ed 2. 1992. Praeger; New York.

292 RAHIM (M A). Measure of styles of handling interpersonal conflict. Academy of Management Journal. 26, 2; 1983; 365-76.

293 RAHIM (M Afzalur), Ed. Managing conflict : An inter-disciplinary approach. 1989. Praeger; New York.

294 RAHIM (M Afzalur). Measurement of organizational conflict. Journal of General psychology. 109; 1983; 189-99.

295 RAHIM (M Afzalur). Strategy for managing conflict in complex organizations. Human Relations. 38, 1; 1985; 81-89.

296 RAJYALAKSHIMI (D). Managing human relation in libraries and information centres. Library Herald. 30, 1-2; 1994; 46-59.

297 RAKESH PRASAD and others. Role of IARI Library in development of agriculture. National seminar on role of books in development of Chhatisgarh, 2003. Indira Gandhi Krishi Vishwavidyalaya, Raipur. 2003. p 6.

298 RANGANATHAN (S R) and BHATTACHARYA (G). Conflict of authorship : Person vs corporate body. Library Science with a Slant Documentation. 6, 2; 1969; 116-29.

299 RANGANATHAN (S R) and BHATTACHARYA (G). Conflict of authorship : Person vs person. Library Science with a Slant to Documentation. 6, 1; 1969; 39-51.

300 RANGANATHAN (S R) and BHATTACHARYA (G). Conflict of authorship : Corporate body vs corporate body. Library Science with a Slant to Documentation. 7, 2; 1970; 115-78.

301 RANGANATHAN (S R). Library administration. Ed 2. 1989. Sarda Ranganathan Endowment for Library Science; Bangalore.

302 RAPOPORT (Anatol). Fights, games, and debate. 1960. University of Michigan Press; Anna Arbor. p11.

303 RAYWARD (W Boyd). Conflict, interdependence, mediocrity : Librarians and library educators. Library Journal. 108, 13; 1983; 1313-17.

304 RENWICK (P A). Effect of sex differences on the perceptions and management of superior-subordinate conflict : An exploratory study. Organizational Behavior and Human Performance. 19, 3; 1977; 403-15.

305 RENWICK (P A). Impact of topic and source of

disagreement on conflict management Organizational Behavior and Human Performance. 14, 3; 1975; 416-25.

306 RENWICK (P A). Perception and management of superior-subordinate conflict. Organizational Behavior and Human Performance. 13, 3; 1975; 444-56.

307 RIDGEWAY (Valentine F). Administration of manufacturer dealer system. Administrative Science Quarterly. 1, 4; 1957; 466-83.

308 RIZZO (John R) and others. Role conflict and ambiguity in complex organisations. Administrative Science Quarterly. 15, 1; 1970; 150-63.

309 RIZZO (John R). Management for librarians. 1980. Greenwood Press; Connecticut. p 216-25.

310 ROBBINS (S P) and HUNASAKER (P L). Training in interpersonal skills : Tips for managing people at work. Ed 2. 1996. Prentice Hall; New Jersey. p 244-45.

311 ROBBINS (S P). Conflict can be stimulating. International Management. 28, 9; 1973; 50-54.

312 ROBBINS (Stephen P). Essentials of organization behavior. Ed 5. 2001. Prentice Hall of India; New Delhi. p 169.

313 ROBBINS (Stephen P). Conflict management and conflict resolution are not synonymous terms. California Management Review. 21, 2; 1978; 67-75.

314 ROBBINS (Stephen P). Managing organizational conflict : A non-traditional approach. 1974. Prentice Hall; New Jersey.

315 ROBBINS (Stephen P). Organization theory: Structure, design and applications. Ed. 3. 2001. Prentice-Hall of India, New Delhi; 410-36

316 ROBBINS (Stephen P). Organizational behavior. Ed 9. 2001. Prentice Hall of India; New Delhi. p 382-411.

317 ROSS (Edward A). Principles of sociology. 1920. University of Chicago Press; Chicago. p 199.

318 ROUT (R K). Managerial revolution and university libraries. University News. 30, 31; 1992; 139-44.

319 RUBIN (J A). and BROWN (B R). Psychology of bargaining and negotiation. 1975. Wiley; New York.

320 RUBLE (T L) and THOMAS (K W). Support of a two dimensional model of conflict behavior. Organizational Behavior and Human Performance. 16, 1; 1976; 143-55.

321 SAINI (M L). Delhi University library System. Library Hearld. 36, 2; 1998; 94.

322 SAMANTRA (Rabinarayan). Management of superior-subordinates conflict: An exploration. Indian Journal of Industrial Relations. 38, 4; 2003; 444-59.

323 SAMANTRA (Rabindrayan). Conflict management strategies and their impact on organizational effectiveness in Indian industry. 1999. Ph.D.Thessis; University of Delhi. (unpublished).

324 SANDHU (Sarbjit). Improving personal relations in libraries. Herald of Library Science. 17, 2-3; 1978; 142-46.

325 SANDOLE (D J D).. Conflict management and problem solving : Interpersonal to international application. 1987. Francis Pinter; London. p 17.

326 SARENSON (P W) and others. Gender, psychological type and conflict style preference. Management Communication Quarterly. 9, 1; 1995; 115-26.

327 SAYEED (Omer Bin). Conflict management styles : Relationship with leadership styles and moderating effect of esteem for co-worker. Indian Journal of Industrial Relations. 26, 1; 1990; 28-52.

328 SAYEED (Omer Bin). Management response to handling conflict situations: An appraisal of conflict management strategies. Decision. 19, 1; 1990; 1-18.

329 SCHEIN (D H). Organizational psychology. 1965. Prentice Hall; New Jersey. p 80-86.

330 SCHERMERHORN, Jr. (John R) and others. Organizational behavior. Ed 7. 2000. John Wiley; Singapore. p 374.

331 SCHMIDT (Stuart M) and KOCHAN (Thomas A). Conflict : Towards conceptual clarity. Administrative Science Quarterly. 17, 3; 1972; 359-68.

332 SCHMIDT (W H) and TANNENBAUM (R). Management of differences. Harvard Business Review. 38, 6; 1960; 107-15.

333 SCHMIDT (W H). Conflict : A powerful process for (Good or Bad) change. Management Review. 63, 12; 1974; 4-10.

334 SCHOCKLEY – ZOLABAK. Assessing the Hall's conflict management survey. Management Communication Quarterly. 1, 3; 1988; 302-20.

335 SCHVANEVELDT (Jay R). Understanding research methods. 1985. Longman; New York. p 103.

336 SCHWEPPER (Charley H). Relation between ethical conflict, organizational commitment and turnover intentions in sales force. Journal of Personal Selling & Sales Management. 19, 1; 1999; 43-49.

337 SESSA (Valerie I). Using perspective taking to manage conflict and affect in teams. Journal of Applied Behavioral Science. 32, 1; 1996. 101-15.

338 SHARMA (Lokesh). Organisation role stress, work environment and job involvement among library professionals in college and universities in Delhi. Library Herald. 31, 3-4; 1992-93; 163-66.

339 SHARMA (R A) and SAMANTRA (R). Conflict Management in an Indian firm : A case study. Decision. 21, 4; 1994; 235-49.

340 SHARMA (R A) and SAMANTRA (Rabinarayan). Conflict management in an Indian firm. Indian Journal Industrial Relations. 30, 4; 1995; 439-53.

341 SHARMA (Ravindra N). Librarian and administrative

conflicts. International Library Review. 32, 1; 1982; 41-53.

342 SHEPPARD (B H). Conflict research as schizophrenia : The many faces of organizational conflict. Journal of Organizational Behavior. 13, 3; 1992; 325-35.

343 SHERIF (M) and SHERIF (C W). Groups in harmony and tension. 1953. Harper; New York. p 229-95.

344 SHERIF (M). Experiments in group conflict and cooperation. In LEAVITT (H J) and PONDY (L R), Eds. Reading and managerial psychology. 1964. University of Chicago Press; Chicago. p 410.

345 SHERIF (M). Inter group conflict and cooperation. 1977. University Books Exchange; Okla.

346 SHERIF (Muzafer). In common predicament : Social psychology of intergroup conflict and cooperation. 1966. Houghton Mifflin; Boston. p 93.

347 SILLS (David L), Ed. International encyclopedia of social sciences. V 3. 1968. Macmillan & Free Press; New York. p 220.

348 SIMMEL (George). Conflict & the web of group affiliations. 1955. Free Press; New York.

349 SIMONS (T) and others. Making use of difference : Diversity, debate, and decision comprehensiveness in top management teams. Academy of Management Journal. 42, 4; 1999; 662-73.

350 SINGH – SENGUPTA (Sunita). Brighter aspect of conflict. Indian Journal of Industrial Relations. 33, 3; 1998; 329-48.

351 SINGH (Nirmal). Organizational behaviour: Concept theory and practice, managing people and organizations in the 21st century. 2001. Deep & Deep; New Delhi. p 399-417.

352 SINGH (P). and PARTHASARTHY (Kokila). Conflict management strategy: A scenario of avoidance. Abhigyan.

3, 2; 1985; 57-84.

353 SINGH (Ravi B P). Conflict and cooperation : Manager workers relationship. 1991. Anmol Publications; New Delhi.

354 SINGH (S K) and others, Eds. People of India : Delhi. V 20. 1996. Manohar; New Delhi. p 1.

355 SPANG (Lothar). Collective bargaining and university librarians : Wayne state university. College & Research Libraries. 36, 2; 1975; 106-14.

356 SRIVASTVA (S N) and VERMA (S C) . University libraries in India : Their organization and administration. 1980. Sterling; New Delhi. p 1.

357 STAMATIS (D H). Conflict you've got to accentuate the positive. Personnel. 64, 12; 1987; 47-50.

358 STEIN (Jess), Ed. Random's House dictionary of English language. 1970. Tulsi Shah Enterprises; Bombay.

359 STEINBERG (L). Winning with integrity. 1998. Villard; New York.

360 STENBERG (R J) and SORIANO (L J). Styles of conflict resolution. Journal of Personality and Social Psychology. 21, 1; 1984; 115-26.

361 STIMAC (Michele). Strategies for resolving conflict : Their functional and dysfunctional sides. Personnel. 59; 1982; 54-64.

362 STONER (James A) and others. Management. 1999. Prentice Hall of India; New Delhi. p 539.

363 STRICKLAND (Bonne), Ed. Gale encyclopedia of psychology. Ed 2. V2. 2000. Gale Group; New York. p 148.

364 SUMAN (H C). Anatomy of conflict and its management. Prashasnika. 35, 1; 1998; 13-17.

365 TATA ENERGY RESEARCH INSTITUTE. Annual report 2001-02. 2002. TERI; New Delhi. p 47.

366 TEDESCHI (J T). and others. Conflict power and game. 1973. Alden; Chicago.

367 THOMAS (K W) and KILMANN (R H). Thomas-Kilmann conflict mode instrument. 1974. Xicom; New York.

368 THOMAS (K W). Conflict handling modes : Towards more precise theory. Management Communication Quarterly. 1, 4; 1988; 430-36.

369 THOMAS (K W). Toward multidimensional values in teaching : The example of conflict behaviors. Academy of Management Review. 2, 3; 1977; 484-90.

370 THOMAS (K) and PONDY (L). Toward an intent model of conflict management among principal parties. Human Relations. 30, 12; 1977; 1089-1102.

371 THOMAS (Kenneth W) and others. Conflict and collaboration : Some concluding observations. California Management Review. 21, 2; 1978; 91-95.

372 THOMAS (Kenneth W) and SCHMIDT (Warren H). Survey of managerial interest with respect to conflict. Academy of Management Journal. 19, 2; 1976; 315-18.

373 THOMAS (Kenneth W). Conflict and conflict management. In DUNNETTE (M D), Ed. Handbook of Industrial and organizational psychology. 1976. Rand McNally; Chicago. p 889-935.

374 THOMPSON (J D). Organizations in action. 1967. McGraw Hill; New York. p 54-55.

375 THOMPSON (V). Modern organizations. 1961. Knopf; New York.

376 TINSLEY (C). Models of conflict resolution in Japanese, German, and American cultures. Journal of Applied Psychology. 83, 2; 1998; 316-23.

377 TJOSVOLD (D) and POON (M). Dealing with scarce resources : Open minded interaction for resolving budget conflicts. Group & Organizational Management. 23, 3;

1998; 237-55.

378 TJOSVOLD (D). Conflict positive organization. 1991. Addison Wesley; Massachusetts.

379 TJOSVOLD (D). Making conflict productive. Personnel Administrator. 29, 6; 1984; 121-30.

380 TJOSVOLD (Dean) and JOHNSON (David W). Productive conflict management perspective for organizations. 1983. Irvington Publishers; New York.

381 TJOSVOLD (Dean) and others. Managing conflict between departments to serve customers. Human Relations. 45, 10; 1992; 1049-50.

382 TURNER (Barry), Ed. Statesman's year book 2004 : The politics cultures and economics of the world. 2003. Palgrome Macmillan; Hampshire. p 888.

383 TYAGI (Archana). Organizational behaviour. 2000. Excell Books; New Delhi. p 105-26.

384 TYAGI (K G) and JOHRY (Nutan), Eds. Directory of social science libraries and information centres in India. 2001. National Social Science Documentation Centre; New Delhi.

385 TYSON (Shaun) and TACKSON (Tony). Essence of organisational behavior. 1997. Prentice Hall of India; New Delhi. p 49-54.

386 TYSON (Shaun) and YORK (Alfred). Essentials of HRM. Ed 4. 2001. Butterworkth Heinemann; New Delhi. p 282-87.

387 URY (W L) and others. Getting dispute resolved : Designing system to cut the cost of conflict. 1988. Jossey-Bass; San Francisco.

388 VAN de VLIERT (E) and De DREU (C). Optimising performance by stimulating conflict. International Journal of Conflict Management. 4, 2; 1994; 211-22.

389 VAN de VLIERT (E) and KABANOFF (Boris). Toward theory – based measures of conflict management. Academy of

Management Journal 33, 1; 1990; 199-209.

390 VAN de VLIERT (E) and PREIN (H CM). Difference in the meaning of forcing in the conflict management of actors and observers managing conflict : An interdisciplinary approach. 1989. Praeger; New York.

391 VAN VELSOR (Ellen) and LESLIE (Jeam Brittain). Why executives derail : Perspective across time and cultures. Academy of Management Executive. 9, 4; 1995; 62-72.

392 VARMA (Madhurendra K). Managing conflict at work. Growth. 27, 4; 2000; 7-16.

393 VISCUSI (W Kip) and CHESSON (Harrell). Hopes and fears : The conflicting effect of risk ambiguity. Theory and Decision. 47, 2; 1999; 153-78.

394 VOLKEMA (R J) and BERGMANN (T J). Conflict styles as indicators of behavioral patterns in inter-personal conflicts. Journal of Social Psychology. 135, 1; 1995; 5-15.

395 WALKER (G) and POPPO (L). Profit centers, single source suppliers and transaction costs. Administrative Science Quarterly. 36, 1; 1991; 66-87.

396 WALL (Victor) and NOLAN (Linda). Perceptions of inequality, satisfaction and conflict in task oriented groups. Human Relations. 39, 11; 1986; 1033-52.

397 WALL Jr. (J A) and CALLISTER (R R). Conflict and its management. Journal of Management. 21, 3; 1995; 515-58.

398 WALLACE (Harold R) and MASTERS (L Ann). Personal development for life and work. Ed 8. 2001. South-Western; Mason. p 115-37.

399 WALTON (R E) and MCKENSIE (R B). Behavioral theory of labor negotiations : An analysis of a social interaction system. 1965. McGraw Hill; New York.

400 WALTON (R E). Theory of conflict in lateral organizational

relationship. In LAWRENCE (J R), Ed. Operational research and social sciences. 1966. Tavisteek; London. p 409-28.

401 WALTON (Richard E) and DUTTON (John M). Management of interdepartmental conflict : A model and review. Administrative Science Quarterly. 14, 1; 1969; 73-84.

402 WALTON (Richard E) and others. Organizational context and inter-departmental conflict. Administrative Science Quarterly. 14, 4; 1969; 522-42.

403 WARNER (W Lloyd) and LOW (J O). Social system of modern factory. 1947. Yale University Press; New Haven.

404 WARREN (Donald I). Effects of power basis and peer groups on conformity in formal organization. Administrative Science Quarterly. 14, 4; 1969; 544-56.

405 WAYNE (Sandy J) and LIDEN (Robert C). Effects of impression management on performance ratings : A longitudinal study. Academy of Management Journal. 38, 1; 1995. 232-60.

406 WEAVER – MEYERS (Pat). Conflict resolution : A Case study about academic librarians and faculty status. College & Research Libraries. 63, 1; 2002; 25-34.

407 WEBBER (Ross A). Management : Basic elements of managing organization. 1979. Richard D Irwin; New York. p 453.

408 WEBER (Max). Max Weber on the methodology of social sciences, tr and ed by Edward A. Shils and H.A. Finch. 1949. Free Press; New York. p 26-27.

409 WEBESTER'S ENCYCLOPEDIC unabridged dictionary of the English language. 1994. Gramercy Books; New York.

410 WEIDER-HATFIELD (Deborah) and HATFIELD (John D). Supervisors' conflict management strategies and subordinate outcomes. Management Communication Quarterly. 10, 2; 1996; 189-208.

411 WEISS (Joseph W). Organizational behavior and change :

Managing diversity, cross cultural dynamics and ethics. Ed 2. 2001. Vikas; New Delhi. p 263-92.

412 WETLAUFER (S). Common sense and conflict : An interview with Disney's Michael Eisner. Harvard Business Review. 78, 1; 2000; 116.

413 WHETTEN (David A) and CAMERON (Kim S). Developing management skills. Ed 2. 1991. Harper Collins; New York. p 397-99.

414 WHITE (Carl M). Survey of University of Delhi Library. 1965. University of Delhi; Delhi. p 184.

415 WHITE (H S). Conflict between professional and organizational loyalty. Library Journal. 116, 9; 1991; 59-60.

416 WILKINSON (M A) and WILKINSON (J P). Plotting conflict. Library Administration and Management. 11, 4; 1997; 205-16.

417 WONDER (Bruce) and PETERSON (Richard B). Impact of different role senders on perceived person-role conflict and job satisfaction. Organization and Administrative Sciences. 8, 4; 1978; 159-70.

418 YOUNG (Heartsill), Ed. A L A glossary of library and information science 1983. American library Association; Chicago. p 236.

419 ZALD (Mayer). Power balance and staff conflict in correctional institutions. Administrative Science Quarterly. 7, 1; 1962; 22-49.

420 ZALEZNIK (Abraham). Power and politics in organizational life. Harvard Business Review. 48, 3; 1970; 47.

WEBLIOGRAPHY

1. http://operatix.emerald-library.com/pdfs/lm2367.pdf

2. http://www.crinfo.org/link_frame.cfm?linkto=http %3A%2F%2Fwww%2Emediationworks %2Ecom%

2F&reffrom=http%3A %2F%2Fwww%2Ecolorado%2Eedu %2Fconflict%2F

3. http://www.mapnp.org/library/intrpsnl/conflict.htm Parent url: *http://www.ilr.cornell.edu/alliance/*.
4. http://www.crinfo.org/link_frame.cfm?linkto
5. *http://www.coventry.ac.uk/acad/isl/forgive/images/aid.pdf* Parent url: *http://www.coventry.ac.uk/acad/isl/forgive/*
6. *http://www.isis-europe.org/isiseu/english/no16.html* Parent url: *http://www.isis-europe.org/*.
7. http://www.eiconsortium.org/ model_programs/interpersonal_conflict_ training_police.htm Questionnaire:: http://www.eiconsortium.org/ measures/wpi_ei.htm
8. http://www.neportal.org/northeastfiles/misc/icm.asp
9. http://www.6seconds.org/modules.php?name=News&file= article&sid=139
10. http://www.librarysupportstaff.com/conflictmngt.html
11. http://www.umanitoba.ca/coned/mdp/programs/amicdop.shtml
12. http://www.maxwell.syr.edu/parc/Annual%20Report%202001-2002/annual 01-02M%20applied_dispute_resolution_and_c.htm
13. http://ag.arizona.edu/fcr/fs/nowg/sc_cr_measures.html
14. http://www.worldwidelearn.com/business-course/conflict-management-training.htm
14. http://www.worldwidelearn.com/business-course/index.html
15. http://www.sbm.temple.edu/~geddes/lect20.html
16. http://www.worldwidelearn.com/business-course/conflict-management-training.htm

17. http://www.librarysupportstaff.com/conflictmngt.html #conflict

http://www.librarysupportstaff.com/probwmngt.html

18. http://appl003.lsu.edu/hrm/hrmtraining.nsf/$Content/Conflict+ Resolution?OpenDocument

19. http://wwwsoc.nii.ac.jp/jssp/index/kenkyu/summary1802e.html

20. http://www.swcollege.com/management/hellriegel/hellriegel_ob/ ch10/ch10.html

21. http://www.maccauvlei.co.za/Conflicthandling.htm

22. http://www.bus.okstate.edu/mgmt/degroot/conflict%20exam%20qs.html

23. http://www.amazon.com/exec/obidos/ASIN/007231253X/kamurj0b/102- 3526637-6280921

24. http://www.css.edu/users/dswenson/web/OB/personality.htm

25. http://www.css.edu/users/dswenson/web/OB/managerialstyle.html

26. http://www.usq.edu.au/unit-1997/fullspec/88067s1x.htm

27. http://www.hnnsweden.com/external/03jun15-007.htm

28. http://www.geocities.com/Athens/Forum/1650/qacollaborate.html

29. http://www.idiotsguides.com/Quick-30.

30. Guides/MG_Conflict_Workplace/file.htm

31. http://www.speakingaboutwork.com/communicate/conflict.htm

32. http://www.maccauvlei.co.za/Conflicthandling.htm

33. http://www.optimizelifenow.com/members/cc/modules.php? op=modload & name=Topics&file=index

34. http://www.wlc.info/pdf/mic.pdf

35. http://pubs.aged.tamu.edu/jae/pdf/Vol35/35-03-18.pdf
36. http://www.pennellseminars.com/situational_leadership_ case_studies.htm
37. http://www.info.com.ph/~tspeace/trans_32.htm
38. http://www.abetterworkplace.com/conflicts.html
39. http://www.catalysthrd.co.uk/Handling_Conflict_and_Aggression.htm
40. http://www.amazon.com/exec/obidos/search-handle-form/ref=dp_sr_00/ 102-3526637-6280921
41. http://www.amazon.com/exec/obidos/search-handle-form/102-3526637-6280921
42. http://enotalone.com/article/2689.html
43. http://www.legal-forms-kit.com/freelegaladvice/employment/5.html
44. http://sunzi.lib.hku.hk/hkuto/searchSubject.jsp?subj=Conflict%20 management
45. http://www.mediationworks.com/dmi/rsch/bibcr.htm
46. http://www.drbalternatives.com/articles/cc2.html
47. http://www.adm.uwaterloo.ca/bulletin/1999/may/12we.html
48. http://www.adm.uwaterloo.ca/bulletin/1999/may/12we.html
49. http://www.corp-psych-mgmt.com/conflict_resolution.htm
50. http://www.asmweb.org/apm/syllabi/files/OMSCElmer.pdf
51. http://www.bus.okstate.edu/mgmt/degroot/conflict%20exam%20qs.html
52. http://urban.csuohio.edu/~sanda/conflict.htm
53. http://www.ntl.org/training-public-courseinfo.asp?CourseCntrlNo=64

54. http://www.mcmaster.ca/mufa/handbook/confllib.htm
55. http://web.gmu.edu/departments/ICAR/
56. http://www.expat.or.id/business/conflictresolution.html
57. http://www.workforcelearning.com/case2.asp
58. http://www.seminarfinder.com/deluxe/seminar/50543.html
59. http://www.research.uiuc.edu/conflict2002.ppt
60. http://www.ualberta.ca/~unisecr/policy/35sec.pdf
61. http://www.buraphalinux.org/~twatchai/hotel/confrstr.html
62. http://internet.ggu.edu/university_library/confrstr.html
63. http://www.ualberta.ca/~unisecr/policy/sec35.html
64. http://www.umanitoba.ca/coned/mdp/pages/amcnidop.shtml
65. http://www.teamtrainingsolutions.com/PDFfiles/thomaskilmann.pdf
66. http://www.csuchico.edu/~wbergman/The%20Thomas-Kilmann%20Conflict%20Mode%20Instrument.ppt
67. http://www.au.af.mil/au/aul/school/sncoa/conflict.htm
68. http://translate.google.com/translate?hl=en&sl=it&u=http://www-psicologia.psibo.unibo.it/test/roci.htm&prev=/search%3Fq%3Drahim%2Borganizational%2Bconflict %2Binventory%2BII%26hl%3Den%26lr%3D%26ie%3DUTF-8
69. http://www.sciencesbookreview.com/Managing_Conflict_in_Organizations_Third_Edition_1567202624.html
70. http://www.computer.org/proceedings/hicss/ 0001/00017/00017036.PDF
71. http://www.iyoco.org/library3.htm
72. http://www.ling.gu.se/~jens/publications/docs051-075/066.pdf

73. http://p2001.health.org/ctw06/mod3pm.htm

74. http://www.peacemakers.ca/education/educationlinks.html.

75. http://www.hicss.hawaii.edu/HICSS36/HICSSpapers/CLUSR05. *pdf*

76. http://www.umsl.edu/~sauter/analysis/488_f01_papers/ Ohlendorf.htm#acr

78. http://www.umsl.edu/~sauter/analysis/488_f01_papers/ *Ohlendorf.htm#acr*

79. http://www.state.oh.us/cdr/schools/schresources.htm

80. http://www.ncsu.edu/cpsv/Acrobatfiles/Pre-Service%20Teacher%20Curriculum.pdf

81. http://hermescat.lib.cbs.dk/is/wwwuk/query-sh.asp?ccl=If%3DRahim,%20M.A.

82. http://www.ruf.rice.edu/~jgspaper/P_Currall00_ IJCM_Conflict.PDF

83. http://www.nationalmuseumofindia.com

84. http://library@iari.res.in

85. http://www.iift.edu

86. http:/www.teri.in.org/lib

87. http:/www.indiawatch.org.in/spa

88. http:/www.jamiahamdard.edu/facilities/library.htm

89. http:/www.jnu.ac.in/main.asp?sendval=library#services

90. http:/jmi.nic.in/zhl/zhlibrary.htm

91. http:/www.ignou.ac.in/division/library/system.html

92. http:/www.ggsipu.nic.in

93. http:/www.du.ac.in/libraries.htm

List of Abbreviations

A.M.	Ante Meridiem
BLISc	Bachelor of Library & Information Science
BSNL	Bharat Sanchar Nigam Ltd.
CALIBNET	Calcutta Library and Information Network
CD	Compact Disk
CD-ROM	Compact Disk Read Only Memory
CDS/ISI	Computarized Documentation Service/Integrated Set of Information System
Co	Company
DELNET	Developing Libraries Network
DSIDC	Delhi State Industrial Development Corporation
DULS	Delhi University Library System
E-book	Electronic Book
E-journal	Electronic Journal
E-mail	Electronic Mail
ERNET	Education and Research Network
GATT	General Agreement on Tariff and Trade
Grad.	Graduation
GSIU	Guru Govind Singh Indraprastha University
HMSCL	Hakim Mohd. Said Central Library
HTML	Hyper Text Markup Language
IARIL	Indian Agricultural Research Institute Library
IGNOUL	Indira Gandhi National Open University Library

IIFTL	Indian Institute of Foreign Trade Library
IIT	Indian Institute of Technology
ILA Bulletin	Indian Library Association Bulletin
INFLIBNET	Information and Library Network
JNUL	Jawaharlal Nehru University Library
LAN	Local Area Network
LIS	Library & Information Science
LISA	Library and Information Science Abstract
LPSRC	Dr. L.P. Sihare Resource Centre
Ltd.	Limited
M.Phil.	Master of Philosophy
MALIBNET	Madras Library and Information Network
MLISc	Master of Library & Information Science
MML	Dr. Mandan Mishra Library
MTNL	Mahanagar Telephone Nigam Ltd.
NIC	National Informatics Centre
NMIHACM	National Museum Institute of History of Art Conservation and Museology
OPAC	Online Public Access Catalogue
P	Page
P.M.	Post Meridiem
PC	Personal Computer
Ph.D.	Doctor of Philosophy
Post Grad.	Post Graduation
Pvt.	Private
RCLs	Regional Center Libraries
S.D.I.	Selective Dissemination of Information
SCLs	Study Center Libraries
SIRNET	Scientific and Industrial Research Network

SLBSSV	Shri Lal Bahadur Shastri Sanskrit Vidyapeeth
SPAL	School of Planning and Architecture Library
SPSS	Statistical Package for Social Sciences
TERIL	Tata Energy Research Institute Library
UGC	University Grants Commission
UIRC	University Information Resource Centre
UNCTAD	United Nation Commission on Trade and Development
UNESCO	United Nations Educational, Scientific and Cultural Organization
VCD	Video Compact Disk
VIC	Virtual Information Centre
VSNL	Videsh Sanchar Nigam Ltd.
WAN	Wide Area Network
WTO	World Trade Organization
ZHL	Dr. Zakir Husain Library

Author Index

Subject Index